MEGAPHONE BUREAUCRACY

Megaphone Bureaucracy

Speaking Truth to Power in the Age of the New Normal

Dennis C. Grube

Fountaindale Public Library
Bolingbrook, IL
(630) 759-2102

PRINCETON UNIVERSITY PRESS

PRINCETON AND OXFORD

Copyright © 2019 by Princeton University Press

Published by Princeton University Press
41 William Street, Princeton, New Jersey 08540
6 Oxford Street, Woodstock, Oxfordshire OX20 1TR

press.princeton.edu

All Rights Reserved

Library of Congress Control Number: 2018958698
ISBN 978-0-691-17967-4

British Library Cataloging-in-Publication Data is available

Editorial: Sarah Caro, Hannah Paul, and Charlie Allen
Production Editorial: Mark Bellis
Jacket Design: Lorraine Doneker
Production: Erin Suydam
Publicity: Tayler Lord and Caroline Priday

This book has been composed in Adobe Text Pro and Gotham

Printed on acid-free paper. ∞

Printed in the United States of America

10 9 8 7 6 5 4 3 2 1

CONTENTS

ACKNOWLEDGMENTS

Writing a book is a ridiculous thing to do. It taxes you intellectually, drains you emotionally, and leaves you staring vacantly at your own ceiling for hours on end. Needless to say, none of that would actually result in words on paper without the tremendous support, encouragement, and belief of many wonderful people to whom I owe a debt of gratitude.

Sarah Caro at Princeton University Press deserves a chapter all to herself. As a scholar, you imagine what it must be like to work with an editor who brings out the best in you, challenges you to be better, wraps you in support, and bowls you over with their professionalism—well I know what that feels like, and it's terrific. Thank you so much, Sarah, to you and the PUP team—especially Hannah Paul, Mark Bellis, Charlie Allen, and Stephanie Rojas—for an extraordinary ride. Thanks also to Francis Eaves for immense copy-editing diligence.

I must thank and acknowledge the Australian Research Council as this book flows directly from the research they supported through a three-year DECRA grant awarded in 2013 (DE130101131). My thanks also to the anonymous reviewers of the book whose rich insights were invaluable in revising and re-working the material. Much of the early research took place at Griffith University in Brisbane, Australia, where I must thank my academic and administrative colleagues for establishing an environment that combined thoughtful critique with relentless support in just the right measure. To name you all would mean stretching this book into a second volume, so I simply offer you the most heartfelt collective thanks. I extend that same thanks also to my former colleagues in the Institute for the Study of Social Change at the University of Tasmania—and especially Richard Eccleston—for extraordinary support.

Many of the ideas that now appear in this book were refined and crystallised through the kind of conversations that make academic life so rewarding. In particular, I thank John Kane, Haig Patapan, Pat Weller, Rod Rhodes, Jack Corbett, and Anne Tiernan for always being so interesting to talk to about this topic. I've been fortunate to have some tremendous research assistants support me along the way, so I'd like to acknowledge and thank Stefanie Plage, Glenn Kefford, Isi Unikowski, and Calum White for digging through archives, speech transcripts, and newspaper databases at great length. A book like this would also not be possible without the kind agreement of the many former senior civil servants who gave their time to be interviewed for this project—I am very grateful to you all.

Since joining Cambridge in 2016, I have been inundated with support and encouragement. David Runciman is owed a particular individual thanks, but my public policy colleagues—Finbarr Livesey, Mike Kenny, Laura Diaz Anadon, Diane Coyle, Cristina Penasco, and Matt Barr—have all taught me things about public policy that I am really most grateful for. Colleagues right across the Department of Politics and International Studies have been incredibly supportive and it is a pleasure to spend each day in your collective company.

Many of the arguments that come together in this book have been developed over the past six years through a series of articles examining different aspects of the connection between administrative leaders and the wider world. All have been added to and revised, but my thanks to the journals involved for their permission to reproduce some of that material here, including: 'Rules, Prudence and Public Value: Public Servants and Social Media in Comparative Perspective' *Government and Opposition* 52(1): 75–99; 'Promiscuously Partisan? Public Service Impartiality and Responsiveness in Westminster Systems' *Governance* 29(4): 517–533, with Cosmo Howard; 'Back to the Future: Rediscovering the Lost Arts of the Victorian Mandarin' *Parliamentary Affairs* 69(3): 708–728; 'Responsibility to be Enthusiastic? Public Servants and the Public Face of "Promiscuous Partisanship"' *Governance* 28(3): 305–320; 'An Invidious Position? The Public Dance of the Promiscuous Partisan' *The Political Quarterly* 85(4): 420–427; 'Administrative Learning or Political Blaming? Public Servants, Parliamentary Committees and the Drama of Public Accountability' *Australian Journal of Political Science* 49(2): 221–236; 'Public Voices from Anonymous Corridors: The Public Face of the Public Service in a Westminster System' *Canadian Public Administration* 56(1): 3–25; 'A Very Public Search for Public Value: "Rhetorical Secretaries" in Westminster Jurisdictions' *Public Administration* 90(2): 445–465.

I finish with a personal thank-you to my family and friends. Thanks to Matt Killingsworth, Gavin Daly, and Anthony Page for those morning coffee conversations which literally made my day. A special thanks to Mum and Dad for over four decades of love and understanding. And finally to Kathy—who shackled herself to a madman over twenty years ago—love is a wonderful thing.

Cambridge, January 2019

1

Introduction

FINDING VOICE

Is politics broken? The dramatic events of the past decade have left many commentators convinced that there is something decidedly abnormal going on. A series of shocks—both economic and geopolitical—have combined to generate a 'perfect storm' of popular disquiet with democratically elected leaders around much of the world. First, the global financial crisis of the late noughties stung the world economy. Trailing in its wake has been a gradual but cumulatively dramatic increase in wealth inequality. Works such as Thomas Piketty's *Capital in the Twenty-First Century* have struck an unexpectedly deep popular chord with people convinced that the financial bargain between elites and the rest is no longer holding.

Over the same period, the long civil war in Syria and continued unrest in north Africa has fuelled new waves of refugees desperately striving to find safety in Europe. Their arrival has added to popular disquiet about immigration levels across the continent, triggering intense public debate about their impact on the social and economic life of the EU and its constituent nations. That disquiet has blended with new fears about security to create a more hostile environment towards immigrants than Europe has seen at any time since World War Two. Irregular but not infrequent terrorist attacks have added to the nervousness that perhaps nation states are not able to keep their citizens as safe as they once could, giving further impetus to public calls on the need for better 'border security'.

These events have provided the backdrop to some undeniably seismic political moments. In the USA, Donald Trump was elected president despite breaking almost every established rule in American politics about how to run for the nation's highest office. He openly insulted iconic war heroes, from Senator John McCain to Humayan Khan. He belittled opponents in the Democratic and Republican parties alike with labels like 'crooked Hillary' (for Democratic nominee Hillary Clinton), 'little Marco' (for Republican rival Marco Rubio), and 'Lyin' Ted' (for Republican rival Ted Cruz). He even faced the public release of video and audio footage capturing him boasting about how fame enables men to get away with the sexual assault of women. Any one of these factors alone would have sunk previous candidates. Taken together, they would have sunk the *Titanic*. Yet Trump defied them all. Playing on fears about America's economic decay, and its allegedly porous border with Mexico, he delivered a victory that most scholarly commentators had seen as an electoral impossibility.

In the United Kingdom, the Brexit vote of 2016 delivered its own political earthquake. For decades, the European Union was something countries scrambled to get into rather than out of. So long a symbol of the cosmopolitan benefits of connected globalism, the EU seems to have become something of a victim of its own success by losing touch with some of its more dissatisfied citizens. Nowhere more so than in Britain, where the charismatic figure of Nigel Farage was able to fashion his single-issue United Kingdom Independence Party into a potent force in national debate. In 2016, harnessing a mixed bag of electoral grievances, the 'leave' campaign was successful in galvanising a majority of British voters into choosing to take their country out of the EU. The referendum left the country split almost exactly in half, and at the time of writing it is still in the process of stitching itself back together.

We could add to the list the extraordinary campaign of Emmanuel Macron in France, who—in the space of a year—was able to establish a brand new party strong enough to sweep him to victory in both presidential and parliamentary elections in 2017. At the same time, far-right parties are on the rise in Germany, Poland and Hungary, whilst in Italy a political force founded by a professional comedian topped the poll in the 2018 elections. In short, the western political world is in a state of flux as centrist leaders flounder in the face of a growing number of citizens suddenly sceptical of the benefits of moderation.

Of course, any argument that we live in challenging times must not elide into the assertion that this is necessarily unique. Public leadership has always been difficult. Policy challenges have always been complex. And social, economic and technological change is not a new phenomenon. As the work of Stephen Skowronek (2008), and more recently Wes Widmaier (2016), on the cyclical operation of political time has powerfully argued, disruptive moments occur with regularity when we assess politics across a longer historical horizon. For sure the pace of technological change in the twenty-first century is intense. But the same could have been said during the industrial revolution, and then during the advent of the telephone, motor car and air travel. Equally, the idea of popular discontent with current political settings doesn't look so unusual when compared with the protests and upheavals of 1968 in both Europe and America. In other words, large-scale disruption is a much more common occurrence than contemporary critiques might suggest.

Nevertheless, whenever disruption on such a scale does occur it has impacts in unexpected ways. It places new tensions on established modes of governance. In the twenty-first century, it is testing the constitutional and institutional limits through which power is distributed in democratic societies. We have seen that in the United States, where the Trump administration has clashed repeatedly with the courts over travel bans from some Muslim countries. We see it also in Trump's sacking of James Comey as head of the FBI, and in the probe by Special Counsel Robert Mueller into alleged connections between the Trump campaign and Russia. We have seen it in the United Kingdom, where the House of Lords—an unelected chamber—has pushed back hard on aspects of the May government's Brexit strategy. Here too judges have come under intense media fire when reaching decisions unfavourable to Brexit campaigners.

This sense of disruptive dislocation has also had an impact in some of the usually less visible and less contentious areas of government. One such aspect—which provides the focus of this book—is in the relationship between elected leaders and the bureaucracy. Western democracies have spent centuries establishing norms and conventions for how power should be balanced between elected officials and other arms of the state. Do public servants owe their loyalty to the constitution, the parliament, the people, or to the elected leaders who give them instructions? Such questions, once the stuff of dry constitutional scholarship, have re-entered the realm of contentious political debate.

In particular, this book looks at the increasingly *public* nature of arguments between elected representatives and appointed officials. In response to these 'abnormal times' some non-elected bureaucratic heads are challenging the authority of elected leaders by speaking truth to power through very public interventions. They are making use of their platforms to engage in what I characterise as a form of megaphone bureaucracy. In choosing this label I am of course drawing on the well-known term 'megaphone diplomacy', which describes those moments when states conduct their international relations through public denouncements rather than quiet backroom discussions. In a similar way, bureaucratic leaders are having to make increasing use of public platforms to promote arguments they might once have made to politicians in more private settings. Figures like James Comey are drawing on the independent authority of their positions to push back against elected representatives. They are using their profiles to challenge democratically elected politicians in the arena of public opinion.

At the other end of the spectrum, some administrators are using that same public stage to more openly support the political positions of the government of the day, leading to accusations of partisanship. When to advise in private and when to upbraid or support in public—these are difficult lines of judgement that non-elected officials are having to walk in increasingly public ways. In the pages that follow I argue that it is both theoretically possible and practically desirable for senior administrators to embrace a greater public voice than our governing traditions have previously allowed.[1] In an age of disruption, full of debates about 'fake news', 'echo chambers' and distrust of political processes, the wider distribution of authoritative voices in public debate offers important benefits.

———

Someone didn't get the memo. As President Donald Trump and the First Lady swayed across the dance floor at three inaugural balls, civil servants at one national agency were getting a dressing-down. Late on 20 January 2017, the Department of the Interior was told to shut down all its official Twitter accounts until further notice. The feed from the National Park Service had a few hours earlier re-tweeted a picture from a *New York Times* reporter which suggested that crowds for Trump's inauguration were less than for Obama's eight years before. A second re-tweet had drawn unfavourable attention to the lack of policy content about climate change on the new White House website. Less than twelve hours after the inauguration of a new president, and civil servants had already been reminded of the dangers of publicly wrestling with politics.

Ten days later, the new president signed an executive order closing America's borders to refugees, and to the citizens of seven Muslim-majority countries. Administratively and politically, all hell broke loose. At the nation's airports, officials scurried to play catch-up. In foreign capitals, leaders alternated between hand-wringing, open denunciation, and a considered silence. In Washington, another non-elected official decided to write her own script. Sally Yates was hardly a household name. An Obama appointee, she had simply stayed in place as acting attorney general whilst President Trump's preferred nominee remained embroiled in the contentions of Senate confirmation. Trump took to Twitter to lash the Democrats for holding up his nominee, leaving him stuck with an 'Obama A.G'.

Yates jumped into the national conversation by issuing a statement to her department essentially telling them not to enforce the president's executive order. 'My responsibility', she wrote, 'is to ensure that the position of the Department of Justice is not only legally defensible, but is informed by our best view of what the law is after consideration of all the facts.' She suggested that a law must be assessed on the basis of whether it is 'wise and just'. The White House responded quickly and decisively by relieving Yates of her responsibilities. The language was uncompromising. 'The acting Attorney General, Sally Yates, has betrayed the Department of Justice by refusing to enforce a legal order designed to protect the citizens of the United States.'

On the other side of the Atlantic, the British political establishment had started 2017 by constructing its own piece of theatre. The British ambassador to the EU, Sir Ivan Rogers, had expressed reservations about the British government's approach to striking a Brexit deal, and in early January 2017 he could take it no more. He resigned his commission, but didn't do so quietly. In an email to colleagues which immediately went public, he encouraged them to hold tight in the face of political difficulty. 'I hope you will continue to challenge ill-founded arguments and muddled thinking and that you will never be afraid to speak the truth to those in power. I hope that you will support each other in those difficult moments where you have to deliver messages that are disagreeable to those who need to hear them.' The email caused a media storm of its own and led the news for at least twenty-four hours. And the government returned fire. Former Conservative leader and prominent supporter of Brexit Iain Duncan Smith took Rogers to task for having aired his views in public.

I don't agree that somehow all [Rogers] did was write a little email to various colleagues. He knew very well what he was doing. [He] probably also knew very well what he was doing when the previous email got leaked—it reeked. It gets to a point when a civil servant starts to go public on stuff that you, as ministers, can no longer trust that individual. You must have absolute trust and cooperation and you cannot have this stuff coming out publicly. (*Daily Express* 2017)

Did Rogers, Yates and the National Park Service do the right thing, or did they cross a line? Did they, as one Democratic advisor asserted of Yates, simply 'speak truth to power' (*Guardian* 2017), or did they misjudge their roles as non-elected public officials and wade into partisan political debates that should have been avoided? In the coming pages, this book will ask whether civil servants have a legitimate role to play in public debate, and indeed whether they can avoid publicity in the age of social media when even the president of the United States is not above calling them out on Twitter. And does the alleged responsibility to be discrete only apply to serving officials, or do retired mandarins also retain a higher level of responsibility to exercise their influence privately rather than through public debates?

Civil servants and public executives in modern democracies face extraordinary challenges. Blame games are common (Hood 2010) and fickle political mandates leave them grappling with unclear expectations (Moore 1995; 2013). They face contradictory demands to be innovative and risk-averse at one and the same time. These dilemmas are played out against the background of an unpredictable and unforgiving hyper-partisan political atmosphere. None of these things are necessarily new—civil service leaders have always faced the need to balance politics and policy, and the need to respond to the vagaries of their elected masters. What adds to the degree of difficulty today is that such challenges are wrapped up in an environment of relentless public scrutiny. The defining feature of modern governance in advanced democracies is that it is carried out in the full glare of an unremitting transparency. The traditional private spaces for deliberation and elite interaction that once co-existed with the demands of public debate have been replaced by a type of scrutiny that leaves little room for concealment (Schudson 2015; Vincent 1999). The era of 'governing in public' has arrived.[2]

A key role of civil servants has long been that of 'speaking truth to power'.[3] The phrase itself is most commonly associated with the seminal work of Aaron Wildavsky, who added it to the title of his 1979 book *The Art and Craft of Policy Analysis*. Importantly, for Wildavsky speaking truth to power is not just about presenting facts, but also about 'persuasive performance' (1979, 401) whereby policy analysts have to combine the insights from data with the capacity to persuade decision-makers of its utility. He suggests that 'the truth we speak is partial. There is always more than one version of the truth and we can be most certain that the latest statement isn't it' (1979, 404). So if 'truth' is a site of contestation that cannot be resolved by analysis alone, it follows that we need a wider set of authoritative voices willing to provide their take on the 'truth' to enable a more informed public debate.

In a twenty-four-hour media world, where there are no hiding places from controversy, what does speaking truth to power look like for public leaders today? Is it to publicly push back when they disagree with government and be willing to fight pitched political battles in defence of their own policy integrity? This book draws on examples from a range of advanced democracies to argue that officials are becoming public figures whether they like it or not, and are having to find ways to defend themselves whilst still protecting their non-partisan status. I argue that the very fact that disagreements are becoming more public means that perceptions of politicisation will follow, leaving administrative leaders with little choice but to defend themselves. I present this not as a dichotomous choice, but rather as an extra variable for senior officials to weigh up when considering how best to serve ministers without compromising their own integrity. Whilst this book of necessity focuses most of its attention on sites of conflict, that does not imply that administrative professionals have lost the ability to work successfully with politicians. As decades of research have shown, senior civil servants are frequently very adept at working with elected leaders in ways that prevent either party being manoeuvred into corners (see for example Rhodes 2011; Hood and Lodge 2006; Weller 2001). But the modern governance environment is making that harder.

In the process of creating and protecting their 'public face', leaders are having to grapple with the practical end of three theoretical debates that have been exercising the minds of scholars in the field of public policy and public administration. First, many critics have suggested that civil servants are becoming politicised and are no longer able to stand up to their elected masters successfully (Aucoin 2012; Savoie 2003; 2008; Heintzman 2014). Whilst the pressures are undoubtedly real, this book will argue not only that civil service leaders still retain a high degree of agency, but that the age of social media is providing opportunities to exercise that agency in newly proactive ways.

Second, there continues to be intense debate about the extent to which civil servants should measure their success in terms of the 'public value' they are able to generate (Moore 1995; 2013; Rhodes and Wanna 2009). I will suggest that part of pursuing public value now involves the willingness to 'go public', sometimes without the blessing of politicians, and that this changes the risk matrix facing bureaucratic leaders as they calculate how best to build and protect their public face. Third, the 'discursive turn' in public policy has demonstrated the importance of ideas, narratives and traditions as driving forces (Stone 2012; Fischer 2003). This book will argue that the 'public' nature of the modern governance environment means that modern public executives have become first and foremost communicators of ideas, who must learn to navigate the political minefields that the public communication of those ideas exposes them to. Civil servants and public executives have been pushed out onto the main stage alongside elected politicians—and must perform appropriately.

In facing these challenges, bureaucratic leaders have to work within the confines of the system of government in which they find themselves. For the group of democracies who inherited their political traditions from the United Kingdom—Australia, Canada, New Zealand and many others—the Westminster system presents a different institutional architecture to that facing public officials in the United States. The Westminster system of public administration is based on traditions and conventions; Washington is based on institutional power and legislatively embedded role definitions. Civil servants in both systems start with some advantages—Westminster with strong informal knowledge about how to stay out of trouble and Washington with institutional protection to push back against public criticism. But both also run too easily into difficulty. In Washington, overreach by civil servants leads to highly politicised confrontations, and in Westminster a lack of protective structures leaves mandarins with little solid ground to fall back on when push comes to shove.

Whilst choosing here to focus on arrangements in the USA and 'Westminster countries', it is important to note that dilemmas about how best to structure relations between elected leaders and unelected bureaucracies exist in all governmental systems. Each country, in the context of its own cultural and governmental traditions, has shaped its own version of this relationship. From the nuances of the French semi-presidential system (see Suleiman 1974; see Elgie 2014 for semi-presidential systems more widely), to the complexities of working with consociational multi-party systems in much of northern Europe, to local variations of the Westminster inheritance in parts of Asia (see Patapan et al. 2005), senior officials are always iteratively evolving their role in sync with their political executives. Montgomery Van Wart's (2013) review article on the state of administrative leadership theory provides an insight into the collective breadth of this work. The full body of research on related aspects of executive government around the globe is too vast to cover here, but it does highlight that there is a need for further comparative work on the changing public face of bureaucracy beyond the jurisdictions covered in this book.[4]

Unlike the UK, the American system of government has long understood that non-elected administrative executives are no less publicly accountable figures than elected politicians. Their role is different, but the style of scrutiny applied to them frequently is not. The leaders of government organisations are expected to publicly advance the interests of their agencies, and advocate on behalf of them, whilst regularly and publicly answering for all aspects of finance and administration. In an era of hyper-partisanship, this kind of public profile has taken on a more sharply visible political edge, leaving administrators exposed to highly politicised public judgements on their performance. Through often extraordinarily combative appearances before congressional committee hearings, and robust interactions with the news media, public executives are finding themselves drawn into political controversies that inhibit their capacity to perform as non-partisan administrators.

In countries that operate under the Westminster system of government, the institutions, traditions and conventions that underpin the power of civil servants are fundamentally different. The architecture of the Westminster system of public administration reflects the circumstances in which it was conceived in the mid-nineteenth century. For much of the last 150 years, communications between ministers and civil servants were conducted through internal documents and memos, or direct private conversations, without public scrutiny of the processes involved (see Hennessy 1989; Lowe 2011). They were 'privileged' conversations in every sense of the term. Parliamentary scrutiny of the executive occurred on the floor of the House of Commons rather than through the questioning of officials by parliamentary committees. Newspaper coverage could be harsh, and satire abounded, but it was focused on the visible manifestations of policy rather than investigating and prying into the processes which made government tick.

In the twenty-first century, this private world has given way to a new paradigm—'governing in public'. The relentless emphasis on transparency and accountability means that all government actors must be ready to be 'public' actors whenever the situation demands. As Rod Rhodes has recently asserted, based on an ethnographic study, 'nowadays senior civil servants speak in public almost as often as ministers' (2011, 9). Civil servants are finding that their increased public profile is leading to accusations that they are becoming politicised partisans rather than the objective instruments of good government (see Savoie 2003; 2008). This can extend even to the traditionally most secretive arms of the state. For example, in the UK the head of the Joint Intelligence Committee before the Iraq war, John Scarlett, found himself pulled into the public eye by the Hutton inquiry in 2003. The inquiry focused on the case of Dr David Kelly, a government scientist found dead at his home after having been publicly outed as the source for BBC news stories. The stories had questioned the veracity of the intelligence dossier on Iraq's weapons of mass destruction that had been used to justify the UK's decision to go to war—a dossier which Scarlett had been heavily involved in producing. Scarlett's appearance at the inquiry drew intense media interest and made him a public figure. Alastair Campbell noted in his diaries of the time how hard this must have been for Scarlett: 'It must be dreadful for someone whose entire life has been about secrets, and dependent on staying low profile, now to be so out there in the public domain' (Campbell 2007, 746).

In the United States, institutional structures and governance traditions mean the challenges of public leadership are shaped differently. To begin with, thousands of leadership positions change with each new administration. The practice recognises that bureaucracies have a central role to play in implementing the policies and furthering the interests of the elected president (see Lewis 2008). Once appointed, the Hatch Act ensures that pursuit of the president's policy programme does not morph into openly partisan advocacy of a political agenda. Leaders are appointed to roles in which their responsibilities are frequently defined by statute, providing them in theory with protections against accusations of overstepping their boundaries. They also take on a high degree of personal responsibility for the organisation that they come to lead, and are able to adopt a style of leadership that unashamedly promotes and defends specific policy decisions. If mistakes are made, those administrative leaders are expected to take responsibility alongside their political masters. This juxtaposes starkly against Westminster tradition, where the doctrine of ministerial responsibility to parliament means that ministers are the public face of their departments, and it is they who are expected to take the blame for any blunders that emerge on their watch (Kitson Clark 1959).

The challenge for US administrators is that in assuming such a public style of responsibility for how they exercise their leadership, they are finding themselves drawn into the midst of an increasingly polarised and politicised governance environment. Without the protection of Westminster traditions of anonymity, or of permanency of tenure at the upper levels, US administrators are left with little choice but to fight bitter public battles in defence of their decision-making. Their ostensibly administrative role can all too easily become a highly politicised flashpoint for public political disagreements. So how did it come to this? I turn now to briefly outline the transition from governing in private to governing in public in both the UK and the USA.

Emerging from Anonymity

> I consciously tried not to take a public place . . . I believe in the faceless bureaucrat; I believe in it deeply. (Former Canadian permanent secretary, author interview, 2015)

Throughout the nineteenth and early twentieth centuries, private spaces formed one of the central underpinnings of the governance environment on both sides of the Atlantic. Political and administrative actors alike were not inclined to take the public into their confidence about the more intricate aspects of governing. As the academic Jeffrey Tulis asserts of US presidents, '[p]rior to this century, presidents preferred written communications between the branches of government to oral addresses to "the people"' (Tulis 1987, 5). A wide series of changes over the last forty years has transformed this world of governing in private to one of governing in public. Elements such as freedom of information, scrutiny by oversight committees, social media, network governance and 24/7 news media have not only re-defined modern government, but importantly have turned administrative leaders into public actors in new ways.

THE WESTMINSTER STORY

Democracy was seen as a very dangerous idea in mid-Victorian Britain. The thought that the processes of government were things to be debated in public—so that people could exercise their preferences at the ballot box— was one that caused intense disquiet amongst much of the governing class. Benjamin Disraeli wrote in his 1870 novel *Lothair* that 'the world is weary of statesmen whom democracy has degraded into politicians'. The future Lord Salisbury lamented in an 1860 piece for the *Quarterly Review* that 'wherever democracy has prevailed, the power of the State has been used in some form or other to plunder the well-to-do classes for the benefit of the poor'. The Whig prime minister Lord Palmerston asserted that

The Truth is that a vote is not a *Right* but a *Trust*. All the Nation cannot by Possibility be brought together to vote and therefore a Selected few are appointed by Law to perform this Function for the Rest and the Publicity attached to the Performance of this Trust is a Security that it will be responsibly performed. (1864 letter to Charles Barrington, cited in Ridley 1970, 565.)

The world of nineteenth-century British government was a world of elites. Even whilst powerful external forces—from Chartism to Irish separatism to organised labour—periodically pushed their way into the political consciousness of the nation, their proximity to the levers of power remained very much at arm's length. Whig aristocrats, Tory landed gentry, philosophical liberals and even some emerging radicals all shared a similar trajectory to the halls of power. Theirs was an ascendancy forged in the drawing rooms of great houses, the public schools of Eton, Harrow and Winchester, the colleges of Oxford and Cambridge and the secluded corners of London's gentlemen's clubs. It was in this environment that the conventions, traditions and institutions of the Westminster system of government were given their modern shape.

The Northcote-Trevelyan report of 1854 is still widely hailed as the birth certificate of the modern civil service in the United Kingdom, and by extension also of the civil service in its former dominions in Australia, Canada and New Zealand. The report itself was a surprisingly short and didactic piece of political advocacy masquerading as objective analysis, but its influence remains substantial. In its nineteen pages of flowing prose, it set out the foundations of a merit-based employment system, and suggested a division of labour between the monotony of clerical work and the more cerebral activities of policymaking. Importantly for modern arguments about politicisation, what it most certainly did not advocate was an 'apolitical' civil service that should operate in the shadows. Sir Stafford Northcote, Sir Charles Trevelyan and their contemporaries were in many ways policy entrepreneurs, men with strong political opinions who frequently sought to shape the administrative and policy worlds in very public ways. Over time, that aspect of their history has given way to the embrace of public anonymity as a cornerstone of civil service identity.

For more than a century, Trevelyan's successors at the head of the UK civil service matched his level of engagement in the work of government, but were more circumspect in choosing the moments when they would expose themselves to public scrutiny. Permanent secretaries such as Edward

Bridges, Warren Fisher, Percival Waterfield, Evelyn Sharp, Otto Clarke, Norman Brook and Burke Trend were towering figures who wielded great power, but were careful to do so only at the edges of the public consciousness. An excellent composite biographical study of many of these figures by Theakston (1999) confirms that the natural discretion of mandarins often belied what was in reality a wide engagement with the world beyond Whitehall.

Across this era, there were of course some notable exceptions to the prevailing tendency towards anonymity. John Maynard Keynes was able to combine the role of government adviser with that of public intellectual, and his *Economic Consequences of the Peace* was an extraordinarily influential bestseller in the immediate aftermath of World War One. During World War Two, Robert Vansittart—having recently retired as permanent under-secretary of foreign affairs—penned a book entitled *Black Record: Germans Past and Present*, strongly supporting the government's war efforts. Outside of the extraordinary exigencies of war time, perhaps the most notable transition figure between anonymity and the embrace of a more public face was William Armstrong, head of the home civil service in the pivotal years of the early 1970s. The British National Archives hold a fascinating set of files containing transcripts and speeches associated with Armstrong's many TV appearances and interviews in this period.[5]

Following the exhortation of the 1968 Fulton report for the civil service to be more open and outward-facing, Armstrong personified exactly this new style of leadership. In a public lecture of 1970, he explicitly addressed the need for civil servants to be seen as less remote from the people they serve.

> One way of picturing the remoteness people feel about Government—especially if they are coming to believe that the aspect of Government which affects them most is in the hands of civil servants—is to call them 'mandarins', to picture them as isolated beings ruling as it were an alien population—to demand their appearance in public, their submission to public scrutiny, their public accountability: there is also a demand that they should not be in any way different—they should be 'of us'—a sort of cross-section of the community as a whole, suffering at all points as we do.[6]

Such was Armstrong's influence in the Heath government that he was known colloquially as the 'deputy prime minister'. The strains of office also led him to suffer a quite spectacular nervous breakdown, the details of which were revealed by former Labour adviser and minister Bernard Donoughue in volume two of his *Downing Street Diary*.

In facing the pressures of administrative leadership, most twentieth-century mandarins had two key advantages not easily available to contemporary civil service leaders today. First, they worked more closely in concert with ministers, who were more willing to see their civil servants as executive partners rather than road-blocks to be manoeuvred out of the way. Second, their behaviour was not subjected to the same intensity of public scrutiny that modern mandarins face. Cabinet secretaries like Norman Brook and Burke Trend were certainly not wilting violets who chose to be largely anonymous out of a lack of self-confidence. They were every bit as frank and fearless in their advice as Charles Trevelyan was in his, but they largely offered their analysis in the privacy behind closed doors. They flourished at a time of a 'consensual conservative approach to bureaucracy' (Greenaway 1992), in which an elite mandarinate was seen as being of a piece with the political class it served. Coinciding with a long period of majority governments from 1924 to 1974, there was a general stability around the roles expected of senior civil servants.

By maintaining a low public profile, mandarins insulated themselves from the public assessments of those who might have wished to critique their advice as evidence of some kind of politicisation. In keeping with conceptions of the traditional public sector bargain (see Hood and Lodge 2006), this also guaranteed that public accountability remained with ministers rather than officials. Civil service leaders are meant to have strong views, and the confidence to take them up with their minister. The successful working of the Westminster system relies upon it. But now, mandarins are also having to engage far more widely with the world beyond government departments. In a governing environment characterised increasingly by hybrid forms of collaboration between government and non-government actors, civil servants have had to reach out to try and persuade people over whom they have no direct hierarchical authority. Instead of simply pulling levers in Whitehall (not that it was ever that simple), they need to engage in public outreach to guide, cajole and motivate others. And they need to do all of this transparently, with government departments recalibrated to look outwards and be more 'open' to the people they serve. This forced relinquishment of anonymity has drawn civil service leaders into the public domain, and created room for allegations of politicisation to emerge from critics willing to frame their words as a political defence of government policy.

This link between anonymity and perceived breaches of impartiality creates a difficult balancing act for current senior civil servants who are exhorted to be more open and engaged with the community, only to then be excoriated for alleged 'politicisation' if their remarks are seen as too close to ministers. Should they go the other way and openly criticise the decisions of ministers, political displeasure quickly follows. It's a conundrum that was recognised but not resolved in the 1960s by the Fulton report, which argued that the risks in reducing anonymity were outweighed by the benefits:

> The argument of the preceding paragraphs has important implications for the traditional anonymity of civil servants. It is already being eroded by Parliament and to a more limited extent by the pressures of the press, radio and television; the process will continue and we see no reason to seek to reverse it . . . We do not under-estimate the risks involved in such a change. It is often difficult to explain without also appearing to argue; however impartially one presents the facts, there will always be those who think that the presentation is biased . . . We believe that this will have to be faced and that Ministers and M.P.s should take a tolerant view of the civil servant who inadvertently steps out of line. (Fulton 1968, paras. 283–4)

As discussed in subsequent chapters, contemporary evidence suggests that ministers and MPs are not necessarily predisposed to taking a 'tolerant view of the civil servant who inadvertently steps out of line'.

THE VIEW FROM WASHINGTON

> A nation that rests on the will of the people must also depend on individuals to support its institutions in whatever ways are appropriate if it is to flourish. Persons qualified for public office should feel some obligation to make that contribution. (Thomas Jefferson)

Thomas Jefferson was a great believer in civic duty. The talents of men who had talent to share should be placed at the feet of their fellow citizens. This did not mean that he embraced modern ideals of a meritocratic civil service. Administrative traditions in the USA may not have emerged from the gentrified corridors of Whitehall, but were in many ways no less patrician and no more openly democratic. Nineteenth-century America faced the same issues of excessive patronage, individual empire building and capacity gaps that had led to the Northcote-Trevelyan report in the UK. In what Carpenter (2001) describes as the 'clerical state', US bureaucracy was seen as an unimaginative keeper of official records rather than a positive force for change.

Just as civil service reform in the UK relied on the driving energy of Charles Trevelyan, so too did US reform rely on the consistent advocacy of George W. Curtis. A writer, editor of *Harper's Weekly*, staunch Republican, and president of the National Civil Service Reform Association, Curtis was appointed by President Grant to chair his 1871 Civil Service Commission. Despite Grant's initial backing, the move for reform was undermined by a group of Republicans who favoured maintaining a form of the spoils system as a way of rewarding followers. It took the assassination of President Garfield by an unsuccessful civil service jobseeker to create the political will necessary to allow the passage of the 1883 Pendleton Act. The Act laid the groundwork for meritocratic appointments based on a civil service exam, established the Civil Service Commission on a more permanent footing, and contained measures to protect the tenure of employees from political interference.

In the UK, it took many decades for the ideas outlined in the Northcote-Trevelyan report to find their way into both law and practice. Similarly in the USA, the Pendleton Act may have laid the groundwork to reform segments of the federal bureaucracy but it took many further decades for those reforms to spread across all agencies, and further afield into State civil services. What the Act did not do was institute any greater degree of transparency into government decision-making. Civil servants may have slowly grown more secure in their employment, but that security was never intended to translate into a more democratic form of public engagement.

There is, however, a long tradition in American public administration of leaders willing to act as administrative entrepreneurs, building their own profile in tandem with the profile of the agency that they lead. What has grown over the last century is the tendency to take that profile to a much more public stage. Scholars such as Eugene Lewis, Erwin C. Hargrove and Philip Selznick have all helped enormously in expanding our understanding of how agency leadership has changed in the US over that time. Collectively, their research has restored some sense of purposive agency to the role of administrative leaders, even amidst institutional and structural constraints. For instance, Lewis's 1980 study highlights the examples of Hyman Rickover in the US navy, J. Edgar Hoover at the FBI and Robert Moses in New York to show that determined administrative leadership by public entrepreneurs inevitably leads to a high public profile and towards the exercise of a form of political power from unelected office. Such men were able to 'weaponise' what Lewis terms their 'apolitical shield' by making a virtue of resisting political pressure at the same time as engaging in heavily political acts themselves.

The USA's shift towards governing in public in many ways mirrors that of the United Kingdom in temporal terms, despite starting from quite different institutional traditions. As described by Michael Schudson (2015), the embrace from the 1950s onwards of an open government agenda reflected the idea that citizens in a democracy have a fundamental right to know what their government is up to. Landmark moments such as the passage of the Freedom of Information Act in 1966 interacted with forces outside of government itself as a more educated and curious populace began to demand more knowledge about just what their representatives were doing on their behalf. This included not just their political representatives, but also those administrators charged with implementing everything from racial integration to environmental protection. The result was a more outward-facing governance style, which has continued to expand up to the present day. Concomitantly, in an environment characterised by hyper-partisanship, this means that public executives can find their roles overtaken by political contention, with a commensurate impact on their ability to exercise their office independently and objectively.

The Public Face of the Modern Mandarin

The behaviour and leadership approach of Victorian civil service leaders like Charles Trevelyan serves as a reminder that the Westminster system has always been fluid. Conventions and traditions have evolved over time. The emergence of mandarins as increasingly public figures in the twenty-first century may represent a break with recent tradition, but that does not mean that the Westminster system is suddenly broken. Evolution involves change, but it is always change built on what was there before. Those modern mandarins who speak out in public debates have not suddenly abandoned their commitment to Westminster traditions of impartiality. Their willing emergence from anonymity has not translated into a willing embrace of partisanship. But the public nature of their modern role means that *perceptions* of partisanship are now perhaps harder to control than they were previously.

In the United States, as the departments of state grew larger from the turn of the twentieth century onwards, so too did the power and authority wielded by both their political masters and their non-elected leaders. This is not necessarily a bad thing, as the scholarship of John Rohr (1986; 1995; 2002) in particular has demonstrated. Strong public leadership by administrators is not *ipso facto* an example of over-reach that undermines democracy. On the contrary, Rohr has argued that public administrators in the US draw their legitimacy directly from the constitution itself, and that their first allegiance is to faithfully follow the dictates of the constitution rather than blindly following the orders of politicians. He suggests that '[a]dministration is political; but like the judiciary, it has its own style of politics and its distinctive functions within the constitutional order' (1986, 184). For Rohr, public administrators have a responsibility to maintain a sense of their own independent authority, which must then be exercised cautiously in the face of political realities. At the same time, he acknowledges the pressures that have been placed on the Senior Executive Service in the US to be more politically responsive since the passage of the Civil Service Reform Act of 1978 (1995, 257).

As Selznick observed as long ago as 1957, the US system of government to some extent *relies* on non-elected public figures taking a prominent place in national leadership. He suggested that 'they have become increasingly *public* in nature, attached to such interests and dealing with such problems as affect the welfare of the entire community' (1957, 1–2). So American public executives of today are certainly building on a long legacy. Unlike their Westminster-system counterparts, their emergence onto the public stage has been less dramatic, because traditions of anonymity in American public administration have never run as deep.

Much of the recent scholarly work on administrative leadership has emphasised that it needs to be studied as part of the wider world of public leadership as a whole, rather than as something separate from the political domain (see Ospina 2016; 't Hart 2014). All public leaders—elected or not—face the same challenge of asserting authority within the complex world of transparent, fast-paced decision-making under the unforgiving gaze of voters. As Rhodes (2014, 112–13) explains, 'administrative leadership is about the constitutional and political role of public administration in the polity; it is not just about better management'. In other words, senior bureaucrats are not simply functionaries in a Weberian machine, but agents contributing their part to the wider task of public leadership and the search for some form of public value (see Crosby and Bryson 2005; 2017).

What is making that task more difficult for today's cohort of officials is the combined magnifying effect of a hyper-vigilant uncivil media looking for mistakes (see Mutz 2015), and the lack of private spaces to engage in any kind of reflective decision-making. The speed of government makes reflection difficult. Modern bureaucratic leaders have to walk a precarious public path between serving the government of the day and protecting their reputation as non-partisan administrators. Through their speeches, their social media outreach and their public appearances, they are engaging in acts of public persuasion—both about what they and their departments are doing, and about what the policy challenges are that governments will have to address in the short, medium and longer term. They have become public rhetoricians who once only whispered to their political masters behind the scenes and must now join them out on the front stage. And where necessary, they are quite prepared to defend themselves from political attack in the process.

The twenty-first century thrives on communication. Information is ubiquitous, as are the opinions of anyone able to master a computer sufficiently to engage on Twitter, Facebook or YouTube (to name just a few). In this world, the powerful are those who are best able to harness communications technology to persuade the public. The discursive turn in public policy captures the extent to which the business of public administration in the twenty-first century is less about the trading of influence based on interests, and more about the trading of ideas in a communications marketplace. The successful policy entrepreneurs are the ones who can persuade successfully using the full Aristotelian rhetorical toolset.

The transparency and accountability requirements of modern government have seen senior public executives held more rigorously and more publicly to account through forums like congressional or parliamentary committee hearings. These appearances in turn have received coverage through the voracious appetite of the 24/7 news media, boosting the profile of the public servants involved. Secondly, the complexities of network governance have seen these leaders engage with a wider range of groups in a wider range of forums than was traditionally the case. Speeches at these engagement events are often—through the advances of social media—made publicly available for critics and commentators to reflect upon.

American public executives are perhaps more used to carrying a higher degree of individual responsibility for mistakes than their Westminster counterparts, who in theory at least enjoy the protection provided by the ministerial responsibility doctrine. When the BP oil spill disaster hit in the Gulf of Mexico, it was Elizabeth Birnbaum—the head of the US Minerals Management Service (MMS)—who took public responsibility for regulation failures by resigning. President Obama and his cabinet appointees expressed displeasure at a range of failings by BP and by federal agencies, but no cabinet-level executive had to accept responsibility and resign, and Minister of the Interior Ken Salazar continued in post.

The public nature of contemporary civil service leadership becomes most apparent when it involves politically contentious policy questions. The line between appropriate 'responsiveness' and inappropriate 'politicisation' is a deeply contested one (see Mulgan 2008). When it comes to the public behaviour of civil servants, what can be termed 'functional politicisation' (Hustedt and Salomonsen 2014) can be measured by the degree to which loyalty to the government of the day spills over into a more enthusiastic advocacy for its inherently partisan policy positions.

Where the former stops and the latter starts is inevitably a question of perception. For example, in the UK in 2013 Cabinet Secretary Jeremy Heywood and Head of the Civil Service Bob Kerslake were accused of partisanship for writing a newspaper opinion piece on the occasion of Margaret Thatcher's death which some Labour MP's saw as too supportive of the former prime minister. When FBI director James Comey stated that he was re-opening his investigation into Hillary Clinton's emails in October 2016, Democrat politicians suggested that he'd violated the Hatch Act's prohibition on officials influencing elections. In Australia in mid-2014, Treasury Secretary Martin Parkinson was perceived as having criticised the Labor opposition with his remarks in a speech critiquing those who relied on 'vague notions of fairness' in attacking the government's budget (Parkinson 2014; Bourke 2014). There is little to suggest that any of these figures were being deliberately partisan, but there can be little doubt that all three made profoundly 'political' interventions.

Such incidents have fed the concerns of scholarly critics (e.g., Aucoin 2012; Savoie 2008) who argue that civil services have become increasingly politicised in partisan ways, and that this is reflected in the roles that senior civil servants are prepared to play in public. One of the strongest critiques is from the late Peter Aucoin, who asserted that traditional boundaries in Westminster-system countries like Canada were breaking down.

> The anonymity of public servants, as invisible to parliament or the public, disappeared some time ago. In the environment of N[ew] P[olitical] G[overnance], moreover, ministers, sometimes explicitly, usually implicitly, expect those public servants who are seen and heard in countless public forums to support government policy, that is, to go beyond mere description and explanation . . . The expectation is not that they engage in the partisan political process, for example, at elections or political rallies. Rather, it is that they be promiscuously or serially partisan, that is, to be the agents of the government of the day in relation to stakeholders, organized interests, citizens, media, and parliamentarians as they engage in consultations, service delivery, media communications, reporting to parliament, and appearing before parliamentary committees. (Aucoin 2012, 189)

In other words, according to Aucoin, the politicisation of civil servants is reflected in their willingness to toe uncritically a government line in public forums with business, interest groups and the like.[7] The counter-argument of course is that it has always been the role of civil servants to serve the executive government of the day. The difference, arguably, is that translating that type of service from a private to a public forum results in increased *perceptions* of politicisation, even if in reality civil servants are only loyally supporting the government of the day as they have always done. Equally, when civil servants dare to provide something less than immediate and full-throated support for government policies, they can very quickly find themselves under fire from the government that they serve. The very nature of public engagement means that it is hard for individual actors to control the way their interventions might be perceived. As former Australian mandarin Peter Shergold notes, publicly explaining policy decisions 'could, of course, easily be perceived to be spruiking [promoting] their virtue' (Shergold 2014, 86).

So what's the answer? In the following chapter I propose and develop a 'Washminster' model for the conscious construction of leaders' 'public faces' in ways that allow them to speak truth to power effectively. The term 'Washminster' was originally coined in Australia to describe its hybrid political institutions. With an elected senate based on the US model, a lower house based on the British House of Commons and a written constitution, Australia's political make-up reflected the influence of both British and American structures. Elaine Thompson initiated the term in her influential 1980 article 'The "Washminster" Mutation'. It has also recently been used by Felicity Matthews and Matthew Flinders (2015) to capture the growing importance of parliamentary committees in British government. I use it here to develop a new and broader conceptualisation of the ways in which administrative leaders on both sides of the Atlantic and beyond are balancing the competing demands of building a public profile without themselves becoming politicised.

By marrying the nuances of Westminster conventions with the institutionalised boldness of Washington practice, a Washminster model acknowledges that the work of public executives will always involve 'political' aspects. As many theorists across the social sciences have now shown, the line between public and private has become blurred to the point of non-existence in many aspects of community life. Politics and public policy are no different. The successful forging of a resilient public face capable of standing up to political power relies on leaders being willing essentially to ignore the distinction between private and public. Speaking truth to power and speaking truth to the wider public need to be viewed as one and the same activity. Where once it was possible to run dual messages—one for the political ear and one for wider consumption—this is now no longer consistent with the demands of 'governing in public'.

Drawing on the New Zealand case, I argue here for an approach that recognises the heads of public agencies as exercising an independent public voice in political debate, based on the expertise that resides in the organisations that they lead. Public leadership should be exercised in a determinedly non-partisan way, but without any unrealistic expectation that this will in and of itself allow bureaucratic leaders to stay out of political contention. In an atmosphere of hyper-partisanship, politics is not a variable capable of being modelled out of the way, and must instead be built into the heart of structures of public leadership. As expressed by one former New Zealand departmental permanent secretary, 'I think you have a role as a chief executive not only to represent your department but also to help inform that debate and help—again in a non-political way—but maybe correct information that's out there that may be strongly misleading' (author interview, New Zealand, 2016).

But this does not mean the embrace of some kind of political free-for-all in which every bureaucrat conceives it their job to simply fight their corner against all comers. It relies rather on a nuanced appreciation of the many varieties of public face now required of agency heads. Some forays into the public domain are of necessity politically edgy, whereas many are simply routine. In Figure 1, I characterise public interaction as either proactive or

Degree of political contention →

Levels of Media Coverage

Type of Public Face		Low	High
Pro-active		Quadrant 1 Communication aimed at an audience of other Civil Servants.	Quadrant 3 Voluntarily expressing views on issues that are the subject of political debate.
Reactive		Quadrant 2 Unavoidable but uncontroversial. • Routine appearances in front of congressional or parliamentary committees. • Profile pieces.	Quadrant 4 • Drawn into a public role in a political controversy. • Responding to allegations of largescale administrative mismanagement.

FIGURE 1. Proactive and reactive public leadership

reactive, and then set those categories against the degree of media coverage likely to result. The degree of political tension rises with the degree of media coverage. Each quadrant requires its own strategy for public executives and civil servants as they manage their public face. Figure 1 is intended to capture and conceptualise current practice, rather than providing a prescription. An examination of the ways in which these practices might be encapsulated into a more normatively desirable 'Washminster' approach is set out in chapter two.

QUADRANT 1

The kinds of public communication that fall within quadrant 1 are those which are intended primarily for internal audiences. In all democratic countries, senior civil servants engage widely with their peers to learn from each other's mistakes and to emulate each other's successes. The kinds of interaction can range from traditional—in the form of a speech to a small group of colleagues in a closed session with the transcript later becoming available—through to innovative uses of modern technology. An example of the latter was Bob Kerslake's willingness as head of the UK civil service to answer questions in real time through live web chats. Whilst this attracted some media coverage, it was undoubtedly low-level and overwhelmingly positive—with some of the coverage coming from the pen of Kerslake himself (e.g., Kerslake 2012). It self-evidently did not involve high-level risks of political contention.

QUADRANT 2

Quadrant 2 embraces the public appearances and communications that agency heads may not necessarily make of their own volition, but that are nevertheless required of them as part of their formal role. For example, as accounting officers responsible for the financial management of their departments, departmental permanent secretaries in the UK are regularly required to appear in front of the Public Accounts Committee of the House of Commons. Similarly in the Australian context, secretaries often find themselves appearing in front of Senate Estimates Committees. The majority of such appearances could be considered 'routine' in terms of their wider interest to the public and any controversy that might ensue.

The exceptions occur when there is an area of activity that has become the subject of either a political row or allegations of gross administrative mismanagement. On such occasions, cases move from the routine nature of quadrant 2 to the contested and confrontational nature of quadrant 4. Other examples of quadrant 2 publicity include the kind of profile pieces that often accompany the arrival of a new leader in a key role. For example, when Scott Pruitt's appointment as the incoming head of the EPA was confirmed by the Trump administration, journalists naturally sought to do profile pieces on where he might take the EPA under his leadership. Writing in *The Wall Street Journal*, Kimberley Strassel (2017) positioned Pruitt as someone determined to keep the EPA focused on its core business. She quotes Pruitt as saying, 'Agencies exist to administer the law. Congress passes statutes, and those statutes are very clear on the job EPA has to do. We're going to do that job.' The interview presented an opportunity for Pruitt to frame his priorities for leadership, whilst being careful to avoid weighing into controversies about President Trump's first weeks in office. Many bureaucratic leaders only wearily accept this new kind of media intrusion. As one UK former secretary noted, 'Of course the media now like personalities. They will talk about civil servants when the cabinet secretary comes to be renewed and Jeremy Heywood eventually retires, there will be 'runners and riders' stories and all that kind of fluff. You know, it's really trivial and it's very tiresome for the people concerned but you can't really stop it' (author interview, United Kingdom, 2014).

QUADRANT 3

The third quadrant focuses on those occasions in which public executives and senior civil servants proactively enter the public domain, but do so in an area or on an issue that is the subject of contemporary political debate. The political saliency of the issues being covered lead to greater media interest and coverage of any remarks, with commentators keenly looking for evidence of a leader either being at odds with government policy, or of making comments that could be interpreted through a political lens. For example, in 2010 President Obama sacked General Stanley McChrystal, the US commander in Afghanistan, because of comments he'd made to a journalist which formed the basis for a cover story in *Rolling Stone* magazine (Hastings 2010). McChrystal had aired criticisms of the President's national security team, of Vice President Joe Biden, and by extension of the way that President Obama was conducting policy in Afghanistan.

In a way, this is the type of political controversy most easily avoided by bureaucratic leaders simply by exercising their discretion in such a way as not to get involved. Leaders make choices, and this includes choices about which policy battles they want to get involved in. But increasingly that sense of choice is an illusory one. Any policy issue in which an agency has a stake becomes one on which the media will come asking for a viewpoint. Sometimes refusing to offer a public view itself becomes the story, interpreted as being for or against the government policy in question. And secondly, as the line between private and public advice becomes blurred in an age of transparency, the privately expressed views of leaders are frequently leaked anyway.

Current views amongst former permanent secretaries in the UK and Australia are split between support for proactive engagement, and for trying to avoid public comment altogether. Said one UK mandarin, 'I think what you need is a proactive role which is how you manage the response to the 24/7 media and what information, how you put a context in it' (UK former secretary, author interview, 2014). This contrasted to one Australian's view: 'I never felt that I should be the one commenting. I wasn't the elected official . . . I mean, they're elected and they have the responsibility in my view to make the public comment' (author interview, Australia, 2015).

QUADRANT 4

Quadrant 4 is perhaps the most difficult terrain for public executives and civil servants to traverse. It encompasses aspects of their role that they cannot choose to avoid or downplay, because it covers scenarios that are inherently reactive rather than proactive in nature. This is where crises and blunders are played out in the public spotlight, with administrative decision-making being examined in areas of high public interest. This can involve reacting to decisions made by politicians, or to a disaster that suddenly drags an agency into the spotlight. For example, in 2005 Hurricane Katrina wreaked havoc in New Orleans, immediately putting the Federal Emergency Management Authority (FEMA) in the eye of its own media storm. FEMA head Michael Brown became the focus for intense criticism during the immediate response operation, and then in subsequent combative appearances in front of committees of inquiry in the aftermath of the disaster.

Equally, agency heads can find themselves drawn into controversy because of the political nature of the things they are asked to do. For example, UK Cabinet Secretary Jeremy Heywood was heavily criticised by a House of Commons select committee in 2013 for his handling of an investigation into allegations that the then government chief whip, Andrew Mitchell, had called policemen 'plebs' at the gates of 10 Downing Street. The committee's report received wide publicity with its criticisms reported in all sections of the British press. It suggested that Heywood should have been more diligent in questioning the veracity of the allegation itself and investigating whether Mitchell may have been unfairly targeted. *The Sun* ran a story under the headline 'Pleb botcher: Cabinet Secretary rapped over duff probe' (Newton Dunn 2013), with further unflattering coverage in *The Guardian* (e.g., Watt 2013; see also Wintour 2012) and *The Daily Telegraph* (e.g., Mason 2013a).

Modern public executives and senior civil servants have a complicated relationship with the public gaze. They recognise that in an age of transparency and accountability, with a 24/7 news cycle, the level of anonymity that their profession once enjoyed cannot reasonably endure. But as professionals of long experience in public administration, they are rightly wary of being drawn into becoming figureheads for governments in ways that politicise them. They are fully aware of the ways that their image can potentially be manipulated by politicians. As one UK former secretary noted, 'what they wanted to do is to use me as a figure of propriety in their support' (author interview, United Kingdom, 2014). The same secretary reflected on what can happen to civil servants who find themselves in the media limelight—'I think you don't become politicised, but you become damaged.'

Media scrutiny offers powerful opportunities for public executives and senior civil servants to define the boundaries of their role simply by being willing to stick their head above the parapet. By being willing to give public speeches, mandarins are asserting by their actions that a system doesn't have to be opaque in order to be impartial. Equally, the way that they respond in front of congressional and parliamentary committees draws the public lines for what these leaders perceive as being their duty and those things that are seen as beyond the pale. Through these public acts, mandarins are continuously writing and re-writing the institutional boundaries and traditions that define what it means to exercise leadership in twenty-first century government.

The careers of nineteenth-century luminaries like Charles Trevelyan in the UK and George Curtis in the US demonstrate how one could be noisy, risky, even controversial, and still be a widely respected public figure. That is no mean feat, although if anything the task has become even more difficult for contemporary mandarins who may wish to adopt a similar approach. It is arguable that the twenty-first century governance environment, with its focus on transparency, accountability and delivery—all under the watchful eye of the 24/7 media—is not likely to be as forgiving of public service leaders who pursue goals with a single-minded indifference to the views of critics. Allegations of partisanship are easier to make than they are to refute.

But in embracing opportunities for 'public' leadership, today's public executives and senior civil servants are demonstrating the kind of skills necessary to operate in a governance environment in which public persuasion is a growing part of their role. It's bureaucracy, but not as we know it. It's 'bureaucracy with a megaphone', allowing the voices of officials to reach far beyond the ears of ministers to a wider audience of citizens themselves. This is different from embracing technocracy—I am not suggesting that non-elected officials know best. Democratically elected leaders must continue to be the final decision-makers if citizens are to maintain confidence in the democratic system, and institutions are to avoid falling prey to a 'democratic deficit' argument (see Flinders 2011). What a full embrace of 'governing in public' does mean is that non-elected officials are able to add an authoritative voice to public debates, to help citizens make up their own minds in differentiating between fake news, 'facts' and rhetorical hyperbole.

In the next chapter, I set out how a 'Washminster' approach to public leadership might help bureaucratic heads conceptualise what it is they are now having to do as outward-facing leaders. I also lay out the ways in which such an approach might naturally emerge from existing political science theories about institutions, rhetoric and public value. Subsequent chapters then chart a course through the many forms of public engagement that leaders are now confronted with. From communicating in writing with new audiences, to appearing in front of oversight committees, and to wrestling with social media, I examine current practice and potential ways forward. I conclude by outlining a spectrum of public actions available to adventurous modern mandarins as they continue to walk the fine line between public service and political catastrophe.

2

Governing in Public

Civil servants are political actors. Period. Claims to the contrary are constitutional fictions invented for convenience. Actors who are surrounded by politics, work with and for politicians and implement decisions taken for political reasons cannot—by definition—be apolitical. What they can be— and are—is non-partisan, but this is not the same as drawing a comfortable line between politics and bureaucracy. For centuries theorists, governments and civil servants themselves have sought ways out of this quandary. Silk walls and bamboo curtains have been erected between political decision-making on one-hand and administrative decision-making on the other; as if two people sitting around a kitchen table together are somehow not eating the same meal. In reality, politics, policy and administration are an intertwined whole not capable of being parsed and separated out. There nevertheless remains an important debate over the extent to which individual issues can be 'depoliticised' and whether such attempts to de-couple politics from technocracy actually leads to popular dissatisfaction with politics and bureaucracy alike (see Flinders and Wood 2014; Fawcett and Marsh 2014).[1]

In all systems of government, rulers need people to get things done. They need people capable of advising, suggesting and implementing decisions. These are all processes suffused with politics. That's why such people need powerful political antennae. Increasingly, politicians also need people to take the blame when things go wrong. Public executives fulfil that role as much now as they did in the days of Charles Trevelyan and George Curtis—or for that matter Henry VIII. The leaders atop the bureaucratic pyramid today are no more immune from politics than Cardinal Wolsey and Thomas Cromwell were in carrying out the agenda of the Tudor king. What has changed is that today's leaders are governing in public. And the public gaze is an unforgiving one.

I advocate here a reconceptualisation of public bureaucratic leadership to meet the realities of modern governance. Before the days of the 24/7 news cycle; before the rise of social media; before the age of transparency, freedom of information and ubiquitous accountability—it was still possible to maintain the false distinction between capital-P political actors and administrative functionaries. When governing in private, it was possible for bureaucratic leaders to play their part in guiding, advising, shaping and administering policy in collaboration with ministers—and then have ministers take the public responsibility. There was a backroom in which bureaucrats could operate and pretend to be faceless functionaries. In the era of governing in public, that backroom simply no longer exists. All public officials—political and administrative—now dance on the same stage, and so we need to evolve new conventions for how we expect them to function.

In proposing a new framework, I draw on empirical evidence to make both a theoretical point and a normative argument. I term this new model the 'Washminster' approach to public leadership. A hybrid of Westminster conventions and Washington practice, the Washminster framework analyses how contemporary public executives can survive in a hyper-partisan political world. From the Westminster system, it draws on principles of ministerial responsibility, traditions of anonymity and conventions on where the line should be drawn between the political and the administrative. From the American system, it draws on institutionalised expectations of robust leadership, incorporating a right to self-defence, a proactive style of advocacy on behalf of one's organization and the pursuit of 'public value' as something that exists independently of the political wishes of the government of the day. Subsequent chapters show how these characteristics of a 'Washminster' model of public leadership can operate in practice through the different types of public interaction expected of modern administrative leaders.

Such an approach takes as its starting point that all bureaucratic leaders are today 'governing in public'. It suggests that the roles senior public executives previously fulfilled behind closed doors are now largely undertaken in the spotlight of the public gaze. I do not argue that bureaucratic leaders are suddenly more *partisan* as a result, but simply that they are more *public*, exposing them to greater levels of critique from the media, political

Westminster Tradition		'Washminster' Hybrid Approach		Washington Practice
Doctrine of ministerial responsibility (civil servants have no constitutional identity separate from that of their minister).	⇨	Accept responsibility as the public face of agency/department, but emphasize that ministers set the direction and parameters under which public executives are able to act.	⇦	Higher levels of direct individual responsibility.
Civil Servants generally do not comment publicly in response to criticism from ministers.	⇨	A robust right to non-partisan self-defence when criticised by politicians or the media.	⇦	A right to self-defence during 'blame games', especially in front of Congressional Committees.
Responsiveness to the Government rather than independent agendas.	⇨	Exercise an independent identity able to contribute directly to policy debates in non-partisan ways, through the public provision of data and evidence.	⇦	Pursue 'public value' through greater exercise of individual agency.
Traditions of anonymity.	⇨	Build a public leadership profile through proactive engagement with stakeholders and the press.	⇦	Stronger independent identity amongst agency leaders.

FIGURE 2. Building a 'Washminster' approach to governing in public

commentators and 'ordinary' citizens on social media. It politicises them in the sense that they become the focus of attention in their own right—forced to take public responsibility for both political and administrative errors, and not only those of their own making. To deal with the complexity of 'governing in public', a 'Washminster' approach suggests re-calibrating the leadership posture of public officials by marrying the nuance of Westminster conventions with the more combative instincts of the American system. Bureaucratic leaders must consciously embrace a public face, or else unwittingly have one thrust upon them. Some elements of what this Washminster hybrid might look like are captured in Figure 2. In the next section, I examine each of these proposed elements in turn.

In constructing the traditions from which to draw such a hybrid approach, it is important to note the pre-existing legal differences that are reflected in the manner of appointment and the power to fire. In the United States, there are over nine thousand positions in all that are subject to what is termed 'noncompetitive appointment', meaning they are essentially political appointments. These positions are set out every four years in what is known as the 'Plum Book', published by the Senate Committee on Homeland Security and Governmental Affairs or its counterpart the House Committee on Oversight and Government Reform. As the Foreword to the most recent (2016) manifestation of the Plum Book notes, 'The duties of many such positions may involve advocacy of Administration policies and programs and the incumbents usually have a close and confidential working relationship with the agency head or other key officials' (US Government 2016, iii). So there is an expectation that leaders will be vocal.[2] In both the USA and Westminster-system democracies, there are also numerous independent agencies whose leaders enjoy statutory protection from being fired by the executive alone (for the USA, see Breger and Edles 2015; for the UK, see Flinders 2008), allowing them to engage in open critique of government in the policy areas the agency is responsible for.

Separate Identity, Clear Responsibilities

Under Westminster convention, civil servants have no separate existence from the ministers they serve. As established by the Haldane report in the UK in 1918, the political and bureaucratic arms of the executive are indivisible. Civil servants are accountable to ministers, and ministers are accountable to parliament. As confirmed in the Armstrong Letter in 1985 (a statement issued by the then head of the UK civil service), 'The Civil Service as such has no constitutional personality or responsibility separate from the duly constituted Government of the day' (Armstrong 1985).

This indivisibility has been slowly eroded in recent decades. Academics Dave Richards and Martin Smith argue that New Public Management and constant cycles of civil service reform in the UK have essentially hollowed out the convention (Richards and Smith 2016). The change has been perhaps even more apparent in other Westminster jurisdictions, like Australia and New Zealand, where the permanency of tenure for senior civil servants has been replaced by contracts and outcomes-based assessment of performance. I argue that what has now rendered the convention theoretically problematic and practically ineffective is that new modes of transparency and accountability have left bureaucrats exposed to the full glare of the public spotlight.

Ironically, at the very moment of revolution when technology and accountability have made governing in public the new normal, elected politicians have never been more paranoid in attempting to control all government communication. The futility of that enterprise is on daily display. The breadth and complexity of information running through the veins of modern government—and the multiple channels through which it can find its way out—means that presidents and prime ministers simply do not have enough hands to cover all the holes in the information colander. Threats over leaks, new and more stringent rules on social media engagement, centralisation of messaging and other moves have only served to highlight the absurdity.

The way forward is not to damn the wind for blowing the ship of state off course, but to build sails better able to harness new realities. Ministers under the Westminster system, and presidents and members of Congress in the US, remain the final decision-makers. Equally, bureaucrats have always played an enormous part in contributing to the making of the decisions. The fact that they are now doing so in the full light of day rather than in the backroom does not mean the system is broken, just that it needs to adapt. If all governmental actors are now public, there are opportunities to be harnessed. There is room for senior public executives to actively enter public debate if governments allow policy advice to be publicly released as a matter of course. These bureaucratic leaders would need to accept full responsibility for the content of their public advice—for its accuracy, its rigour and the judgements that underlie it. They would face even more searching questioning from oversight committees and the media than they do now, but could do so on their own terms.

Non-government organisations, third sector organisations and others can then contest that advice in the public marketplace of ideas. The important change is that ministers will have to explain which pieces of advice they are taking, and why, and where necessary justify their decision to depart from departmental advice. Democratic control of decision-making can and must remain with elected representatives. They can and must continue to work closely with the bureaucracy on implementing their policy decisions. The difference is simply that both ministers *and* bureaucrats have to take public responsibility for their public stances.

Empirically, this is simply an extension of current practice, rather than a radical departure. It very much reflects the levels of leadership responsibility currently expected of US public executives. It would be coupled with a Westminster level of cautious awareness in treading the lines between the political and the partisan. The New Zealand Treasury provides an interesting example of how this can work in practice. During his period as its head, John Whitehead operated as a fearless public policy advocate, explicitly expressing a 'Treasury view' on matters in ways that did not simply endorse the view of the government of the day.

When one examines a snapshot of Whitehead's speeches over the period 2009–10, a picture emerges of a Treasury department capable of operating as a 'critical friend', stretching the thinking of government in non-partisan ways. In none of his speeches did he purport to speak on behalf of the government, or to defend the government from external critics. Instead, he was prepared to act as a critic himself. For example, in a 2009 speech he criticised the government for strangling innovation.

> The sure way to kill innovation, investment and change is to have rules or laws that discourage or prevent it. We've seen nearly 30,000 new pages of primary legislation over the last decade and a slip in our competitiveness as this slide shows. (Whitehead 2009a)

And later in the same speech he gave a pointed warning about stimulus policies. 'All that means that while some fiscal stimulus has been warranted and is sensible, we're deluding ourselves if we think we can simply spend our way out of our troubles . . . Don't pass on a huge debt burden to the next generation' (Whitehead 2009a). He was equally critical of the tax system. 'Our tax system should be encouraging investment to keep coming here and skilled people to keep staying here. Unfortunately that doesn't appear to be the case at the moment' (Whitehead 2009b).

He was consistently prepared to explicitly criticise current policy settings—by implication laying the blame for New Zealand's economic difficulties at the feet of the elected government that had supported those policy settings. 'While some people may believe that the government accounts are under control, the tough spending decisions have not yet been made. There are also tough decisions to make about how tax reform and structural policy reform can best improve incentives to raise growth and reduce vulnerabilities' (Whitehead 2009c).

The Treasury's 'Long Term Fiscal Statement' in 2009 was presented like a discussion paper from an external lobby group—providing publicly released, explicit advice to government.

> This document is to create discussion about which policy decisions by government might best make a difference to the future fiscal situation and to show the possible impact of different choices, actions, or inaction . . . This is Treasury's document. Governments make policy decisions and what is set out here is not government policy. Nor is it policy advice. It sets out options and the consequences of various decisions; because dealing with fiscal issues is all about making choices. (Whitehead 2009d)

This type of robust independent expression was not seen as out of step with the requirements of Westminster governance. This is for at least two reasons. Firstly, New Zealand has an exceptionally transparent right-to-information regime in place. It is normal for briefings to government from departments to be regularly placed in the public domain. This forces politicians to explain their reasons for departing from official advice, and protects bureaucrats from being 'verballed' for advice they did not give. But equally, it means bureaucrats become publicly accountable for what they do say, and for the quality of the advice they give.

As one former senior public servant in New Zealand reflected,

> [T]his is interesting in the New Zealand context. I think public servants have a kind of a role as the stewards of the public interest if you like or the system, precisely what that means probably a lot of people haven't thought about particularly deeply . . . Another key aspect I think would be the extent to which you can help inform debate in a non-political, non-partisan sort of way. And in New Zealand we've formalised some of that and then there's informal dimensions as well. (Author interview, 2015)

Of course New Zealand has all the advantages of being a small jurisdiction in the distant south Pacific, where the proximity of senior bureaucrats to the government they serve creates closer personal ties than might be easily established in Washington or London. But what their example demonstrates is that allowing senior administrators to express strong views doesn't break the system of democratic control. Just because government departments publicly give advice to politicians doesn't mean they have to take it.

As discussed in chapter one, we are living through a period of complex political change and popular disillusionment with mainstream political leaders. Disruptors like Trump and Macron have been catapulted into office precisely because citizens expect them to operate differently from the norm. This has occurred in the wider context of concerns over 'fake news' and 'echo chambers' meaning that many citizens are not gaining access to the breadth of well-informed debate by authoritative voices that was previously taken as a given. To the extent that Trump has had his power and authority as president challenged, that challenge has come from non-elected officials willing to argue with him in public on policy matters. It has come from people like Sally Yates and James Comey, who have exercised their own independent judgement. The final authority rests with the president—as it should—and he sacked both people for their stance. But that has generated the kind of fierce public debate that is surely the hallmark of a healthy democracy in action. Allowing senior officials a voice doesn't guarantee smooth government, but it's certainly more likely to offer good government in the long run.

A Right to Self-Defence

Until recently there has been a peculiar requirement associated with Westminster-system civil servants. Like Benedictine monks, they effectively take a vow of silence. They are not the public face of government, so it is not their place to speak. They are silent witnesses to the absurdities of political life. This is part of the traditional public service bargain—the trading away of the right to a public opinion in return for security of tenure and the joys of working at the heart of government (see Hood and Lodge 2006). But part of that bargain was that ministers would take public responsibility for them—to be their sword and shield in leading the department in which they work. This is proving ever more illusory. Increasingly in Westminster jurisdictions over the past three decades, ministers are not simply failing to defend the civil service, but are in fact joining the vanguard of its attackers. By publicly passing blame and judgement onto civil servants for mistakes made, ministers are breaking the bargain. A succession of governments have seen their civil servants as recalcitrant when faced with reform, causing politicians to publicly vent their frustrations. Most famously, Tony Blair gave a speech to the British Venture Capitalists Association in 1999 citing the 'scars on my back' that came from trying to push the UK civil service to embrace new approaches.

This places civil servants in a harrowing quandary. Either they must sit quietly by whilst their public reputations are traduced by their political partners, or they must buck tradition and speak out in their own defence. The benefits of the Washington system, by comparison, is that presidential appointees are expected to publicly take responsibility and blame, and where necessary fight their corner in return. When FBI director James Comey fronted a congressional committee he expected to get vigorously and aggressively questioned. And in return, his political interrogators expected him to defend himself with equal levels of vigour and passion. It is a public debate—accountability between equals rather than the disciplining of a voiceless public servant.

The drawback is that it's very hard to maintain levels of trust between bureaucrats and politicians when they are tangling with each other across the airwaves. When a president and an agency head are at public loggerheads, government becomes something of a spectacle. It's open government—but also open war. For example, in August 2017 Trump advisor Corey Lewandowski called on the head of the Consumer Financial Protection Bureau (an Obama-era appointee) to be sacked because of his alleged but undeclared ambitions to run for political office himself. Lewandowski suggested that the CFPB head, Richard Cordray, was 'an unelected bureaucrat sitting in an office' and called on White House Chief of Staff John Kelly to move him on. As noted by *LA Times* columnist David Lazarus, 'Lewandowski wants Kelly, an unelected bureaucrat, to fire Cordray for being an unelected bureaucrat, which is nothing short of bizarre. All Cabinet members and agency heads are unelected bureaucrats' (Lazarus 2017).

A Washminster approach builds in a right to self-defence, but frames it around reactive boundaries. It is not, and should not, be the role of public executives to launch pre-emptive political strikes against elected politicians. That's what opposition political parties are for. But equally, if senior bureaucrats are to be able to govern in public effectively, they need to be able to defend themselves from public attack.

A recent UK situation over a prolonged flood crisis in 2013 illustrates the possibilities. Flood defence in the UK falls largely within the remit of the Environment Agency (EA). The EA is set up as an arm's-length agency, technically known as a 'non-departmental public body' (NPDB) in the formal lingo of UK government. The EA's mission includes protecting the British environment from threats such as flooding and pollution. The governance of the EA falls between a CEO and a chair, and from 2008 to 2014 the chair and public face of the agency was Chris Smith (Lord Smith of Finsbury), who was himself no stranger to politics. He had previously been a cabinet minister in the first Blair government, and had been very active with a number of charities and other bodies in between.

In late 2013 and early 2014, the United Kingdom experienced extraordinarily high levels of rainfall. Flooding resulted in many parts of the country. Amongst the hardest hit areas was Somerset in England's southwest. The impact on the people who lived there was severe, as homes went under water, and farmland was inundated in the area known as the Somerset Levels. The EA came under fierce criticism for not have carried out river dredging prior to the flooding onslaught, with strong local perceptions that this would have alleviated the resulting damage. Lord Smith, as chair of the Agency, became very much the public face of perceived bureaucratic incompetence. Importantly, he faced attack not just from local residents who were livid about the damage to their homes and property, but also from the government's own elected representatives.

For example, the MP for Bridgwater and Somerset, Ian Liddell-Grainger, was vociferous in his criticism in February 2014 as Lord Smith visited the flood zone. Whilst calling for Lord Smith's resignation, he didn't spare any blushes in expressing his feelings.

They won't tell me where he's going, but I'm going to get him. I've got my farmers, I've got all my landowners, waiting for this guy. . . . If I just have to stick his head down the loo and flush, I will, because he is going to get this message. He is going to get this message. I don't care how long it takes, and I don't care how nasty and brutal we all are about it. They are going to learn . . . I hope he falls in the river. I don't mean that cruelly, but I do hope he drops in the river so he can see what we are living with. This man has done an awful lot of damage. (Quoted in Jivanda 2014)

Perhaps even more significantly, at cabinet level the Communities Secretary Eric Pickles did not weigh in to defend the agency, but instead joined the chorus of those questioning its professionalism. He apologised on behalf of the government for not having dredged in Somerset, but blamed that decision on the EA, saying, 'We thought we were dealing with experts' (Wintour 2014). He also pointedly gave his views on Lord Smith's leadership in particular. 'I don't see myself becoming the advocate of the "Save Chris Smith" campaign or printing "Save The Environment Agency One" T-shirts' (quoted in Walters 2014).

Such a robust exchange would certainly be nothing new in American government. When crisis hits, the agencies expected to deal with things are not infrequently put on notice by their own government. As I discuss in chapter six, President Obama was very clear in his criticisms over the response to the BP oil spill in the Gulf of Mexico. In Westminster systems, that kind of criticism is traditionally less common. Ministers accept responsibility and agree to work with officials to fix things. Civil servants are protected from public expressions of wrath. It is of course important to note that the target for ministerial criticism in this case was an arm's-length agency, which is expected to operate with a heightened degree of accountability. What happened next was a departure from the tradition of bureaucrats refusing to publicly respond to political criticism. Lord Smith, rather than quietly ignoring the barrage, mounted a very public defence of himself and his agency.

Smith wrote an op-ed in *The Guardian* newspaper, defending the agency and criticising the government for funding cuts. He sought to place the damage in the wider context of the EA's work. 'During the past 10 weeks, about 5,000 houses have been flooded, in many different parts of the country. At the same time, it's important to realise that some 1.3 million homes—that would otherwise have flooded—have been protected by Environment Agency defences and the dedicated work of EA staff' (Smith 2014). He then explained that the EA had been willing and ready to contribute towards dredging in Somerset, but that Treasury rules had held back the level of funds that could be dedicated to the task. 'So when politicians start saying it's Environment Agency advice or decisions that are to blame, they need to realise that it's in fact government rules—laid down by successive governments, Labour and Tory—that are at the heart of the problem' (Smith 2014). Smith criticised the use of the EA as a 'political football for a good media story'.

The day the article came out, Smith also undertook some forty media interviews in support of his arguments. He has subsequently emphasised that he had two goals in pursuing this media blitz. The first was to defend the hardworking people of the EA who had been labouring for months on addressing all aspects of the flood. He wanted to emphasise that their expertise should not be called into question. The second was to make sure people understood that the government, not the EA, actually sets the parameters for policy and available funding. Smith essentially re-framed the problem, from one of EA inaction to one of the EA being hamstrung by politicians. 'I'm not having government ministers criticising us for doing the things that the government lay down for us; with the limits the government impose on us; with the finances the government give us, and carrying out their instructions to the letter' (author interview, 2017).

Smith recognises that he was pushing past the 'normal' restraints of practice, but argues that he had little choice. 'Now what I did, technically it's not what the chair of an NDPB is supposed to do. Was it the right thing to do? Absolutely it was the right thing to do'. Smith agrees that a more forthright capacity for public leadership is part and parcel of this kind of role. 'Not every chair, let alone chief executive of an NDPB, is going to be able to do that happily. But I think increasingly it will have to become part of the suite of skills that someone in that sort of position has. They have to be prepared to become more public' (author interview, 2017).

If modern government is to function well in the era of governing in public, then this kind of robust exchange is going to become ever-more commonplace. Frank and fearless exchanges are going to occur not just behind closed doors but also in public. There is an argument to be made that all players in the governance environment need to be allowed a voice, leaving the public to make up their own minds. The exchange over the Somerset flooding demonstrates the benefits and the drawbacks. Eric Pickles was surely within his rights to criticise what he saw as the leadership failings at the EA. The government could not feasibly just sit out the flooding without being seen to respond to community frustrations. Just as surely, Chris Smith did the right thing by placing the EA's side of that story on the public record. If bureaucratic leaders are to be held accountable they must also have the right to speak in their own defence. Equally, if their actions are considered inadequate—in other words if they lose the public debate and with it the public's trust—ministers would be within their rights to call for their resignation. It's messy, but more accurately reflects the balance of responsibilities in a transparent style of governing in public.

Proactive Public Profile

The quintessential Westminster mandarins of the past operated in an anonymous world. Shunning the limelight, their power was great precisely because it was exercised away from the public glare. Lord Salter, in his 1961 *Memoirs of a Public Servant*, reflected that 'the civil servant . . . works in a cloistered secrecy and rarely writes about himself or what he does' (Salter 1961, 11). This was not just Salter's view, but the embedded understanding held in common by civil servants across the Westminster world. Sir Edward Bridges presented a lecture entitled 'Portrait of a Profession' in 1950 (Bridges 1953), at the height of his power as head of the home civil service. The lecture depicts civil servants as cautious and risk-averse, steeped in what Bridges describes as the 'Civil Service tradition' of impartial administration coupled with a professional detachment from the daily passions of politics.

> Our most obvious defects spring from the constitutional position of Civil Servants. They are at all times answerable to some Minister who will get the praise and blame for what they do, and this determines many of their actions and reactions . . . It is the same absence of direct responsibility which makes the average Civil Servant uncomfortable and infelicitous in his relations with the Press . . . The same absence of direct responsibility is perhaps also responsible for the Civil Servant's highly developed sense of caution. (Bridges 1953, 29)

As I've already suggested, the realities underpinning this worldview have changed. Firstly, civil servants are now more likely to carry direct responsibility, and to receive public blame from politicians and oversight committees when things go wrong. Secondly, the pace of government is now such that there is no longer the same amount of time to exercise the 'caution' that Bridges speaks of. And thirdly, the environment has shifted decisively towards governing in public. In the age of social media, 24/7 news, right-to-information, aggressive oversight committees, network governance with external stakeholders to be engaged with, and more, transparency is the new normal, and bureaucratic leaders find themselves standing on the front stage.

Many of the leaders interviewed for this book—recognising the changing environment—have shown themselves willing to proactively embrace the opportunities for shaping a more public profile for themselves and their organisation. Others remain staunchly defiant in holding to Westminster traditions of what constitutes public decorum.

One Canadian interviewee was quite explicitly at the latter end of the spectrum. 'I'm like the traditionals. I think the faceless bureaucrat is an objective I want to aspire to. Ministers are the ones who should get the attention and have a profile in a public place' (author interview, 2015, Canada). Those at the 'enthusiastic explainer' end of the spectrum saw it as a major part of their job to be a conduit for the government, but expressly in a non-partisan way. '[I]s your job to communicate what the government's trying to achieve in a non-partisan way? I think that's actually part of the job . . . that deputy ministers have a big job to go out and be reaching out . . . both communicating out to Canadians and also to listen to bring back in' (author interview, 2015, Canada).

American public executives have less of a tradition of anonymity. They may not be household names—simply because there may not be much public interest in who is in charge of particular services at any given point in time—but that is not the same as a convention of anonymity. When things go wrong, they will be required to step up and answer for it. And equally, when things go right, senior officials are likely to gain public recognition to some degree. So proactively building a public profile makes as much sense for public executives as it does for the new head of a major private company who wants to show shareholders that s/he is in control and has a clear idea of the direction of travel they will pursue. It is the norm for new appointments in the US to be followed by media profile pieces, in which agency heads and senior public executives introduce themselves and their agenda.

This kind of media engagement is by no means new. For example, Robert Moses—the man who shaped much of the physical landscape of New York City from the 1920s to the 1960s—was able to sustain an apolitical reputation by in fact being very political in using the media to cultivate a particular persona. 'He carefully orchestrated public opinion by fooling the press into viewing him and his many operations as being in opposition to elected politicians. The myth which he sold (and which nearly everybody bought) was that Robert Moses and his loyal troops wanted to build public facilities without political patronage and without gain of any sort' (Lewis 1980, 19).

So the media have always been important, and new administrations are often happy for their appointees to announce their arrival, especially if it happens to reflect in politically useful ways on the government. It's something of an emerging trend in Westminster-system countries, where the choice of senior civil servants is seen as a signpost for the government's thinking in particular areas. For example, when John Lloyd was appointed Australian public service commissioner in December 2014, his arrival was accompanied by a flurry of media pieces. Lloyd brought significant policy experience in workplace relations, which saw him lauded as a reformer by his supporters and derided as anti-union by his critics. Lloyd defended himself in press interviews, rather than quietly relying on ministers to justify his appointment. He continued in the same vein, maintaining a strong public profile on issues touching on the work, competency or shape of the Australian public service until he stepped down in August 2018. He frequently gave speeches at key events across the country and when asked his opinion, he gave it.[3]

In an edited collection published in 1987, Doig and Hargrove delineated two classes of non-elected public executive in the United States, the 'rhetorical leaders' and the 'administrative entrepreneurs'. The former category embraces those leaders able to mobilise 'evocative symbols and language as political resources' (Doig and Hargrove 1987, 15). This approach inevitably translates into the building of a higher public profile, as 'these leaders may become independent political figures to whom elected politicians turn for help in their own work' (1987, 15).

At the top of the list of such figures in the US is David Lilienthal, whose leadership of the Tennessee Valley Authority (TVA) in the 1930s has become the stuff of legend in US public administration. As analysed more fully in Hargrove's single-author monograph, *Prisoners of Myth* (1994), Lilienthal's stint as director and later chairman of the TVA was so successfully framed by the man himself that subsequent leaders of the organisation found themselves locked into perceptions of their own inadequacy when juxtaposed against such past greatness. There were of course very 'real' successes attached to the TVA, not least its extraordinary ability to translate the generation of electricity into an act of economic and social transformation. Those successes have been well documented (see Selznick 1966), but Hargrove's study demonstrates how a non-elected leader can seize the possibilities of rhetorical leadership to become an influential public figure by how they choose to frame their own activities.

Theory and Methods

In fleshing out the opportunities for leaders that accompany the shift towards 'governing in public', I draw on a number of streams of existing theory in order to build the case for something new. As I explain below, I build on insights from discursive institutionalism, public value theory and rhetorical studies to argue three things. First, that our theoretical understandings regarding the work of senior bureaucratic leaders are no longer sufficiently grounded in empirical reality. Second, that there are strong normative grounds for shifting our view. And third, that theory which empowers prudent judgement in public executives, rather than the hierarchical imposition of unworkable rules, stands a greater chance of being not only right, but useful.

The past two decades have seen the emergence of a very welcome scholarly debate on one of the core foci of political science—namely the relationship between institutions and individual agency in the begetting of change. The so-called 'new institutionalisms' have been competing for supremacy in how best to account for both continuity and change. Whether it's through the calculation of interests envisaged in rational choice institutionalism; the constricting influence of past decisions envisaged in historical institutionalism; or the irresistible shaping influence of culture envisaged by sociological institutionalism—the new institutionalisms have provided important new theoretical frameworks for scholars of public administration to consider (see Hall and Taylor 1996). The most recent addition, that has turned this trio of explanations into a quartet, is discursive institutionalism (DI).

Schmidt (2010, 2) argues that DI provides a theoretical umbrella broad enough to embrace the wide range of approaches advocated by scholars who view ideas and discourse as being the core factors that explain how institutions are maintained or re-shaped. Institutions, in Schmidt's conception of DI, are

> simultaneously constraining structures and enabling constructs of meaning, which are internal to 'sentient' (thinking and speaking) agents whose 'background ideational abilities' explain how they create and maintain institutions at the same time that their 'foreground discursive abilities' enable them to communicate critically about those institutions, to change (or maintain) them (Schmidt 2010, 4).

The interaction of ideas and the way that actors communicate them is central to explaining the power of bureaucratic leaders to shape the institutions that they lead. As the work of constructivist institutionalists like Mark Blyth (2002; 2013) and Colin Hay argues, how leaders perceive their interests is 'irredeemably ideational' (Hay 2010), leading them, I would argue, to try to rhetorically shape their organisations in their own image. As they interpret their roles through the prism of ideas of what public service means, they then seek to express and embody those ideas through their own public communicative behaviour. The power and reach of those communicative actions is determined in large part by how they are interpreted and framed by the media. It is the attention of the media that can turn an appearance by a mandarin in front of a select committee into a national event.

But self-evidently, not every public action by a mandarin is considered newsworthy or likely to generate extensive media coverage. Many speech acts (Austin 1962) by public servants are fairly dry affairs aimed largely at an internal audience, as discussed in chapter one. They may help to shape institutional boundaries internally, but are unlikely to have much wider impact on public perceptions of the institutions concerned. And not all acts of public communication are ones that bureaucratic leaders would necessarily choose to make of their own volition, if they could avoid doing so. Thus it is important to distinguish between acts that can be categorised as proactive (launched largely voluntarily), and those that are reactive (launched in response to a crisis or investigation into mismanagement). Both can generate intense media scrutiny, although reactive forms of public outreach often occur in contexts that are already self-evidently heated in nature. So if public discourse matters, how can bureaucratic leaders help to shape it?

In 1987, Jeffery Tulis set out a theoretical framework for what he termed 'the rhetorical presidency'. At its core, the rhetorical presidency recognises that in a true separation-of-powers regime like the US, presidents are heavily restricted in the levers they can pull to actually make things happen. As has become all too apparent to a frustrated President Trump, when Congress and the court system don't line up behind the president's wishes, a governing agenda can quickly become stalled. The president can't single-handedly pass a budget, repeal a law or overrule a court. Executive orders have increasingly been used under both the Obama and Trump administrations to circumvent intransigence, but they can only go so far.

So what then are American presidents to do when faced with institutions that won't let them implement their agenda? The rhetorical presidency suggests that one answer to that question lies in the power of presidential communication. The rhetorical presidency is essentially a pulpit: a stage from which presidents can reach out directly to the public to make their case for change. The theory is that this allows them to enlist the public as their supporters not just at election time, but also to shame or scare Congress or the judiciary into supporting the president's policies. Samuel Kernell (2006) frames it as 'going public'—as presidents choosing to place an issue in the court of public opinion. With the emergence of new technology, the power of the rhetorical presidency to reach out past the traditional institutions of government has never been greater. President Trump's use of Twitter has turbo-charged the rhetorical presidency for the information age.

The emergence of social media will undoubtedly now drive a further generation of analysis of the rhetorical presidency, building on two decades of extensive scholarship that has sought to extend and apply Tulis's concept (for a flavour, see Friedman and Friedman 2012; Medhurst 2006; Stuckey 2010). Although starting later, a body of work by scholars of Westminster-system countries has also begun applying insights about rhetorical leadership to the study of government in parliamentary systems (Atkins et al. 2014; Bennister 2013; Grube 2013; Kane and Patapan 2010; Martin 2015; Rolfe 2008; Uhr and Walter 2014; 2015; Young 2007). This includes important historical insights into how rhetorical leadership has changed over time as power has shifted away from parliament in favour of political executives (see Toye 2011; 2014).

The key that unlocks the power of the rhetorical presidency is rhetoric itself. Rhetoric, in its Aristotelian conception, is all about persuasion. By definition, the study of rhetoric is the study of the means of persuasion. It's about identifying what it is that makes us hang on every word of John F. Kennedy's inaugural, whilst drifting into intellectual unconsciousness during a senate filibuster. Aristotle identified three components to the persuasion puzzle: logos, pathos and ethos. Logos refers to the content of the argument itself—whether it's logically constructed and convincing. Pathos is about the emotional impact of the argument—whether it has a resonance capable of connecting with listeners, swaying them not just with rational thoughts but through the power of ideas and the emotions they stimulate. The odd one out of the three is ethos. Unlike its siblings, it is not something generated during the speech act itself. It is carried not by the words that are spoken, but by the reputation and authority of the person who speaks them. Ethos encompasses both the formal position of the orator—such as prime minister or president—but, crucially, also what is known about their lives and world view. Ethos is what makes us listen to Nelson Mandela differently, because in hearing him speak we are also remembering his life experience, his imprisonment and his commitment to building a peaceful post-apartheid South

Africa. At its core, ethos is about trust and authenticity. Do we think the speaker is saying what they truly believe, or just what they think we want to hear? Authenticity is of course not an objective fact but a perception. In the context of modern democratic politics, leaders who are seen as speaking their minds—like President Trump—can be seen as authentic just for breaking the prevailing modes of political speech, even if what they are saying is not always factually accurate or consistent.

Politics is a persuasion business. In no system of government can a ruler long survive through hierarchy alone. Even autocrats have to persuade some of the people some of the time if they are to sustain their power. In a democracy the challenge is even more central. Persuasion is what every MP is engaged in on the hustings, every presidential candidate is striving for and every elected leader needs every day. Persuasion has been the core tool of politics for millennia. What has changed in modern democracies is that persuasion has to be carried out on a mass public scale. Politicians who once had to convince only the elites of which they were a part now have to reach for ways to pull the multitudes towards their camp.

If the arguments of this book are correct and bureaucrats are now taking their place on a more public stage alongside their elected colleagues, then they too need to adopt the tools of that trade. And thus emerges the rhetorical bureaucrat. Professionals who once exercised persuasive techniques in smoke-filled backrooms have to recalibrate those skills for a much more public audience. Public accountability and responsibility is never just a rational reckoning process. As the work of oversight committees demonstrates only too well, there are deeply political agendas at play. Blame is a question of perception as much as a question of fact. Speakers need to be able to marshal their arguments persuasively, to exercise agency in open debate. The rhetorical presidency emerged when presidents—confronted by difficulties with the other two branches of government—realised that they had the power to speak out and over them. No new power was awarded to presidents; they simply began to utilise one that they hadn't realised they possessed. Rhetorical bureaucrats are in the same position. They have a stage, and the power to make use of it. What restrains them is tradition and convention, both of which are in the process of changing.

Rhetorical bureaucrats start with some advantages. Generally speaking, levels of public trust in non-partisan officials is higher than it is for politicians. They have a sense of ethos emanating from their position and the public service institutions they represent. They also have professional experience in dealing with data and evidence. They have the capacity to harness facts to their arguments—logos—in convincing ways. What they have often lacked until now is a wider skillset in communication, an ability to reach out and sway people. Their non-partisan status has traditionally been interpreted as meaning they also have to speak in mundane ways so as not to expose themselves to the opprobrium of their political masters.

I am suggesting that a Washminster compromise is already happening in practice and that theory now needs to catch up. Westminster bureaucrats are exercising a more visible and robust role in public debate, although still a long way short of the dramatics associated with an FBI director's evidence to a congressional committee. A Washminster approach couples the willingness of US leaders to speak up with Westminster reticence in terms of how and when that is appropriate. Bureaucratic leaders should not come out all guns blazing as a first resort, but they clearly now have the power to do so when reacting to the politics of a situation.

So why now? Why is this empirical change emerging, and what's wrong with existing theory? Of course any self-respecting theoretical discussion in public administration always starts with Weber. Our contemporary understanding of what bureaucracy is and how it functions owes a tremendous amount to Weberian conceptions. When people complain about a mindless bureaucracy, bereft of either innovation or inspiration, they are really complaining about the Weberian picture of what bureaucracy is. It is a conception grounded in the belief in legal-rational authority. It believes in hierarchy. It provides the foundation for the principal/agent analyses of the bureaucratic world that continue to be the subject of such contentious scholarly debate. Bureaucracy, in the Weberian conception, offers all the alleged benefits of the consistent application of rational behaviour in response to a chaotic world. To quote Weber,

> The fully developed bureaucratic apparatus compares with other organisations exactly as does the machine with non-mechanical modes of production. Precision, speed, unambiguity, knowledge of the files, continuity, discretion, unity, strict subordination, reduction of friction and of material and personal costs—these are raised to the optimum point in the strictly bureaucratic administration . . . . (Weber 1968, 973)

The issue of course is that what Weber has drawn here is an ideal type—a theoretical statue not grounded in contemporary reality (although the Germany in which he wrote perhaps came closer). Modern bureaucracy is neither precise, nor speedy—and just as importantly, the complexity with which it has to deal means that it cannot be so. It's a messy business.

The classic Weberian conception has been undermined or reinforced (depending on your point of view) over the last three decades through the arrival of New Public Management. Following the perception across Westminster-system countries that the bureaucracy had become too unresponsive to the political will of elected politicians, it was brought to heel. The change was to be enforced through the management mechanisms more traditionally associated with private enterprise. Policy competition was introduced through private consultants, outputs and outcomes were quantified and measured, new delivery agencies were established, and in Australia and New Zealand senior civil servants were stripped of tenure and instead placed on three- to five-year contracts.

The literature on the impact of New Public Management is now voluminous, with critics and fans in equal measure characterising it either as the beginning of the end of sane government, or the process that shook the civil service out of its lethargy. A recent assessment by Christopher Hood and Ruth Dixon has concluded that NPM in the UK context delivered 'a striking increase in running or administration costs in real terms, while levels of complaint and legal challenge also soared' (Hood and Dixon 2015, 1). Just as important as questions about its utility have been the debates over what it has done to the quality of those who occupy the top bureaucratic leadership positions. Have the powerful 'frank and fearless' giants of the twentieth-century civil service given way to a twenty-first century variety that no longer has the courage or institutional protections needed to 'speak truth to power'?

The answer, not surprisingly, depends on who you ask. Canadian scholars such as Donald Savoie and the late Peter Aucoin have argued strongly that the independence of civil servants has been hollowed out. Aucoin suggested that under the conditions of what he termed 'New Political Governance' (NPG), civil servants had become a partisan voice for government.

> NPG is characterized by four main features: the integration of executive governance and the continuous campaign, partisan-political staff as a third force in governance and public administration, a personal politicization of appointments to the senior public service, and an assumption that public service loyalty to, and support for, the government means being promiscuously partisan for the government of the day. (Aucoin 2012, 179)

I've argued elsewhere that both Aucoin and Savoie correctly identify the problems associated with the hollowing out of Westminster traditions of impartiality (see Grube and Howard 2016). What I think is less clear is that mandarins have responded to those changes by ceding their impartiality to put on partisan clothes. I argue that the character of bureaucratic leadership has proven more resilient than these changes might suggest, and that leaders continue to measure themselves against ideals of appropriate behaviour as defined by tradition.

In Washington, judgements on the performance of public executives have been more disaggregated. Of necessity, the main distinction lies between those who are presidential appointments, and those who are permanent members of the senior executive service. For the purposes of comparison, the focus here is on those leaders who are presidential appointments at a sub-cabinet level. These heads and deputy heads of government agencies play the same leadership roles as the top civil servants in Westminster systems.

One of the most influential strains of thought on how American public executives should characterise their role is public value theory, originating in the work of Mark Moore (1995; 2013). Public value includes the adoption of many of the aspects of New Public Management, including performance measurement systems, pay for performance and viewing citizens as 'customers' of government services (Moore 2013, 1). Perhaps most importantly though, as the name might suggest, is its conception of the work of public managers as being about the generation of 'public value'.

Just as a private sector manager seeks private value for a company's shareholders, so too—according to Moore—should public managers seek to add value on behalf of the citizenry. 'As a starting point, let me propose a simple idea: the aim of managerial work in the public sector is to create *public* value just as the aim of managerial work in the private sector is to create *private* value' (Moore 1995, 28). In order for this to be possible, the 'customer' needs to be imagined as a collective rather than an individual.

> Social outcomes are a measure of aggregate social conditions—not of the subjective satisfactions of individuals who transact with government. . . . This suggests that in the public sector, the relevant "customer" is a collective public (local, regional, or national) acting through the imperfect processes of representative democracy rather than an individual consumer making choices about what to buy for personal benefit. (Moore 2013, 3)

The reason the concept of public value has galvanised so much interest from both scholars and practitioners is that it gives a sense of individual agency to the work of public executives. Whilst keeping within the constraints of the 'authorising environment' executives can and should lead change under their own authority. This carries risks when translated into a Westminster environment, where strong hierarchical traditions position ministers, not public servants, as the ones who are accountable, because it is ministers who call the shots. In a strict constitutional sense, civil service leaders have no identity independent of the ministers they serve. Is it then appropriate for them to actively pursue public value as though they have an obligation directly to the wider public—separate from their constitutional responsibility to serve the government of the day? Some scholars such as Rod Rhodes and John Wanna are doubtful, whereas others like John Alford back civil servants to be able to balance the line between public value creation and political overreach (see Grube 2012; Alford 2008; Rhodes and Wanna 2007; 2009).

A Washminster hybrid would address problematic aspects of this balance between Westminster tradition and political reality. Civil servants are no longer adequately protected by ministerial accountability. Nor are they shielded from public debate and critique. A Washminster approach frees them to overtly search for public value, and to face the equally public criticism if they overreach and politicise themselves in partisan ways. Alford and Rhodes are both right. Alford is right that public executives are capable of weighing up political risk, and Rhodes and Wanna are right to be wary of any usurpation of the power of democratically elected ministers. The way to square this circle is to maintain the distinction between advice and decision-making. The latter is the prerogative of politicians. Public executives can join the marketplace of ideas, but can and will be called out by their political masters if they seek to overrule the democratically elected government of the day.

So to summarise, the theoretical pathway underlying my perspective weaves its way through discursive institutionalism, the rhetorical presidency and public value theory. The destination is a theory of rhetorical bureaucracy under a Washminster framework. This encompasses an activist role for public executives in publically driving and defending themselves and their organisations, with the trade-off that they will be publicly accountable themselves when it all goes wrong. It allows for the kind of robust public debates currently occurring in an age of disruption, without undermining the central tenet of democratic control.

The model can of course be challenged on a number of grounds. For example, will activist public executives drive a wedge of distrust between themselves and ministers, meaning politicians will no longer trust the civil service to do their bidding? This is a very valid concern, and reflects the traditional indivisibility of the civil service and the executive under the Westminster model. My argument is that the distrust is already an empirical reality, and that civil service leaders are left exposed as a result. They are having to fight public battles without the protections they once enjoyed from public criticism. Recognising their rhetorical power is about embracing their voice and accepting their place on the public stage. Going back to a pre-transparency age is a lost cause. If we are going to ask bureaucratic leaders to govern in public, we have to provide them with the tools to do so.

Methods

Untangling the bureaucratic world is no easy task. It is a literature littered with various interpretations of what institutions and agents actually are, and how we can expect them to behave, underpinned by predictably visceral ontological controversies about what there is to find out anyway. As ever, there is no one single answer and perspective able to hold the field against all comers. Different approaches invariably push forward different aspects of our understanding even whilst they excite epistemological debate. For example, rational choice scholars have imported the language of economics to cast the issue of bureaucratic control and behaviour as a principal–agent problem. They argue that bureaucratic leaders will behave rationally and seek to maximise their own self-interest and that of their organisation in following the incentives put in place by their democratically elected principals.

While I may not agree with that perspective, it has been undeniably influential in drawing out the way that interests and hierarchy continue to assert themselves in shaping some aspects of bureaucratic behaviour. Very few administrative leaders see themselves as irrational and emotional operators, and rational choice almost certainly helps to explain part of what they do. Equally though, they are not automatons who are robotically running each decision through a statistical model predicting their success or failure. All of us allow both rational and irrational thoughts in our decision-making (see Kahneman 2011). This is particularly so when actors are faced with what interpretivists call dilemmas: those moments where established traditions of behaviour run into an uncomfortable reality that forces those who follow them to look for a new way out.

What I'm presenting here is an agent-centred view of an institutional problem. In Westminster systems, senior civil servants are seeking to conform to a set of traditions and conventions that define what Westminster governance is and how a civil servant should conduct herself within it. This includes adopting anonymity, impartiality and ministerial responsibility, amongst others, as the defining attributes of the system they serve. Those traditions—often characterised in shorthand as the 'Whitehall model' in the UK (see Page 2010)—sit within a wider group of traditions. Some scholars, like Dave Richards and Martin Smith (2015), argue there is a unique 'British Political Tradition' centred around responsible government. Others, like Mark Bevir and Rod Rhodes (2001), argue for a plurality of traditions that can work together at any one time to shape how individual actors interpret their world.

Whether or not we see institutions as structured patterns of thought, or simply as collections of beliefs ossified into traditions, what is important for my argument here is that individual actors have the power to shape and re-shape these structures. Douglass North frames this sense of agency as a form of entrepreneurial behaviour.

> Institutions change, usually incrementally, as political and economic entrepreneurs perceive new opportunities or react to new threats affecting their well-being. Institutional change can result from change in the formal rules, the informal norms, or the enforcement of either of these. (North 2005, 6)

Similarly, Stephen Bell's conception of an agent-centred historical institutionalism (2011) suggests that even though institutions are sticky and hard to move because of their path-dependent characteristics, they will still react over time to the cumulative choices of the actors who inhabit them. And what are these institutions? North conceptualises them as the sum of the beliefs and cultural norms that build 'both a positive model of the way the system works and the normative model of how it should work' (North 2005, 2).

If institutions are shaped through changes in the beliefs of individuals, which can then translate into re-shaped traditions and conventions, then the study of individual actors has to be right at the centre of our investigations. Agents make reality. This means of course that bureaucratic leaders have the ability to shape the norms, conventions and traditions that govern their public behaviour. The extraordinary debut of the Trump administration in January 2017 illustrates the point extraordinarily well. Presidents don't 'usually' communicate policy through Twitter. Press secretaries do not 'normally' aggressively attack the journalists on whom their job depends. 'Normal' behaviour has been shown to be exactly what it is—a construct that can be re-made at will.

Methodologically, my task is to examine the power of individuals to re-shape the nature of executive leadership in the age of 'governing in public'. I therefore do two things to analyse their interpretations of their beliefs, and the extent to which those interpretations are reflected in their actions. First, I observe their behaviour. And second, I ask them what they think they are doing. For triangulation, I then check both of these against the public record, archives and press coverage.

The visible manifestation of rhetorical bureaucracy is the speech act it-self. A communication is made with the intention of putting a position. It might be a written letter to the editor of a newspaper, or a briefing note intended for release. It might be a spoken keynote address, or participation in public stakeholder meetings. It might be a media interview with a single journalist, or a wide-ranging press conference. All are opportunities in which senior officials get the chance to publicly communicate. They get the chance to make a case—to persuade or to defend. And importantly, each type of interaction leaves a public record—a transcript of what happened.

So I observe the behaviour of bureaucrats by looking at what they say. Utilising techniques of rhetorical political analysis (RPA) as laid out by Alan Finlayson and his co-authors (Atkins and Finlayson 2013; Finlayson 2007; Finlayson and Martin 2008), I examine the rhetorical choices bureaucrats make. At the core of RPA is the argument that there is more to rhetori-cal communication than the words that are spoken, because the rhetoric is at one and the same time constitutive and formative of the ideas that are expressed through those words. And, importantly, ideas can only be accessed by studying the arguments made for or against them by political actors employing political rhetoric. So in studying rhetoric, we are in real-ity studying the creation, shaping and re-shaping of political ideas, through the arguments that are being made for or against those ideas. The study of rhetoric becomes, instead of the close study of linguistics, a study of politics itself. To quote Finlayson,

> If we begin with a clear and distinct concept of politics as the 'arena' within which we see expressed the irreducible and contested plurality of public life, the ineradicable contestation of differing world-views, then it is clear that what is distinct in politics is not the presence of beliefs but the presence of beliefs in contradiction with each other, not decisions about courses of action but of dispute over decisions and courses of ac-tion. It then follows that ideational and interpretive analyses have tended to examine the wrong object, which ought to be not ideas but arguments:

their formation, effects and fate in the activity known as persuading. The study of such argument and persuasion necessitates the development of Rhetorical Political Analysis. (Finlayson 2007, 552)

So by looking at what bureaucratic leaders say, I'm studying how they are able to contribute to the political arena. From what they say, we're able to build up a picture of how senior officials are positioning themselves in the public domain—what sort of public face they are creating. The next step is to see whether the creation of this public face represents the conscious exercise of prudent judgement by senior actors. To investigate this, I undertook semi-structured interviews in Canada, Australia, New Zealand and the United Kingdom (N=45). I focused on retired mandarins as a methodological choice. It meant that all had equal freedom to speak their minds, as no longer beholden to the government of the day. It also enabled me to interview a range of leaders, from the recently serving to the long retired, to capture a sense of the change in perceptions of appropriate leadership behaviours over the past two decades. All had been heads either of departments or of arm's-length government agencies, and all were interviewed on the promise of anonymity. In order to live up to that promise, I avoid denoting the exact position of interviewees unless I've received their express permission to do so.

Seeking to understand public officials by reading their public statements and interviewing them provides access to what they say, and what they think. But the crux of the matter is also how both are perceived by the wider world. I therefore examine the public impact of bureaucratic leaders through studying the way their behaviour is reported in the media. Coverage of mandarins in Australia, Canada, the UK and New Zealand shares much in common with the coverage of their US cousins, but significant differences remain. Studies of media portrayals across all five countries reveal the extent to which public executives have had varying success in framing public debates, and defending themselves from criticism. They also reveal the extent to which the self-perception of these bureaucratic leaders actually matches the way they are perceived outside. In the chapters that follow, I examine the public interventions of senior officials by categorising different types of outreach and the different settings in which they occur. We begin with the power of the written word.

3

Writing in Public

In previous congressional testimony, I referred to the fact that the
Federal Bureau of Investigation (FBI) had completed its investigation
of former Secretary Clinton's personal email server. Due to recent
developments, I am writing to supplement my previous testimony.
(Letter to Congress from FBI director James Comey, 28 October, 2016)

The written word is the backbone of political power. There are of course
the foundational documents—like the American Constitution, or the Magna
Carta—that seek to give shape to political values. But equally important in
day-to-day reality are the millions of briefing notes, memos, minutes, files,
letters and emails that pump through the veins of government worldwide.
Individually insignificant, collectively these documents shape our lives. The
overwhelming majority are seen by only a few eyes, not because they are
secret but because of their essential banality. Even in the age of transparency,
where freedom of information regimes are ubiquitous, most of the everyday
processes of government remain dull. And their size and scale is overwhelming. Even documents that are both secretive and potentially incendiary are
easily lost in the wider sea of information. When Wikileaks dumps hundreds
of thousands of documents into the public domain, it still represents a hay-
stack in which the needles are buried and hard to find.

Practitioners of government are well aware of the difference between the mundane majority and the combustible few in the communications that flow through their world. Written words offer great benefits to public executives. They allow for considered responses under pressure. Rather than the muddled messages that emerge in the face of oral questioning, this is a chance to frame things as they want them to be framed. Verbal hand grenades can sometimes explode in the hands of their would-be launchers, but written missives can be more carefully aimed. In Westminster systems, such moments are rarely public ones, as civil servants adhere to traditions of reticence around publicity. It flies against every instinct of the traditional mandarin, who would rather discreetly warn in private than issue a public missive. For the American public executive, they are a more accepted part of the armoury which the skilled practitioner calls upon when needed. Self-evidently, the challenge in all cases is to make the right judgement call about when and what to write and what the political consequences might be.

James Comey knows the power of the written word, and how to deploy it. But is the case of the former FBI director a cautionary tale, or an example of how a robust system of government is supposed to work? The 2016 presidential campaign in the United States was an extraordinary event. In a country that is no stranger to spirited and confrontational political campaigns, 2016 still marks a new high—or low, depending on one's point of view. Facing the starter's gun was a Republican field big enough to constitute a sporting team in most scenarios. An array of governors and senators, side by side with the traditional range of mavericks and left-of-field candidates. And from this ruck emerged the most unlikely presidential nominee in the history of the Grand Old Party. Donald Trump strode into political history leaving a slew of more promising campaigns lying broken in his wake.

On the Democrat side, things ran rather more to script. The establishment candidate and presumptive nominee Hillary Clinton had been waiting decades for this moment. The 2016 election represented an opportunity to bury the demons of her failed 2008 campaign, to make history as the first woman president and to 'save' the country from a Trump presidency. She had seen off a determined challenge from Bernie Sanders, and polls suggested throughout most of 2016 that there was simply no way that she could lose to Trump. Commentators and pundits spoke at length about how the 'math' of the electoral college would allow only one plausible outcome. Up until a month from polling day, that logic seemed to hold true. It was close, but victory was certain.

That version of events hadn't reckoned on a further intervention by James Comey. The FBI director had been appointed by President Obama in 2013. He was an experienced public executive with a distinguished career behind him, having served as deputy attorney general in the administration of George W. Bush. Under his leadership in mid-2015 the FBI opened an official investigation into Hillary Clinton's use of a private email server during her time as secretary of state in the first Obama administration. Almost exactly a year later, in July 2016, he announced that he would not be recommending any charges be laid against Clinton, despite criticising her behaviour in strong terms. The Clinton campaign welcomed the announcement as a kind of vindication which would now allow her to focus her energies (and the minds of voters) more clearly on the campaign.

All that changed again a few months later. On 28 October, with less than a fortnight to go before the presidential election, Comey wrote a letter to congressional committee chairs. It was a letter that contained no openly incendiary phrases. There was no hyperbole or violent language. Yet it dropped like a bomb into the midst of the tight election campaign, as Comey surely knew that it would. In the letter, Comey announced that the FBI was re-opening its investigation into the Clinton emails on the basis of new information. The new information related to emails found on the computer of former New York congressman Anthony Weiner, who was himself under investigation for other matters and was at the time married to high-level Clinton aide Huma Abedin. Comey wrote,

> [T]he FBI has learned of the existence of emails that appear to be pertinent to the investigation . . . I agreed that the FBI should take appropriate investigative steps designed to allow investigators to review these emails to determine whether they contain classified information, as well as to assess their importance to our investigation. Although the FBI cannot yet assess whether or not this material may be significant, and I cannot predict how long it will take us to complete this additional work, I believe it is important to update your Committee about our efforts in light of my previous testimony. (Comey 2016)

Unsurprisingly, all hell broke loose. Democrats accused Comey of having inappropriately interfered in an election. The Trump campaign and Republicans in general dusted off their narratives about how Clinton couldn't be trusted. Clinton has since claimed that Comey's intervention was in and of itself the decisive factor that cost her the election. But Comey wasn't finished. After little more than a week, and within days of the election, he released a further statement clarifying that the new evidence had not led him to change his earlier conclusion that a prosecution of Clinton was not warranted by the facts. Even in a country which is used to strong public executives having an influence, the story of Comey, Clinton and Congress is a standout tale.

Comey was forced to defend himself in an extraordinary public debate about his activities as head of the FBI. It exposed the challenges facing non-partisan figures when they are confronted with the realities of political complexity. In deciding to send his letter about the re-opening of the Clinton investigation, Comey was damned if he did and damned if he didn't—and he knew it. Testifying before the Senate Judiciary Committee in May 2017, he said that it made him feel 'mildly nauseous' that his actions may have impacted on the election result, but he stood by his decisions. He has been roundly criticised by both Democrats and Republicans, and his actions have since been somewhat overshadowed by the manner of his dismissal by President Trump. The question of course remains—what should he have done? Was there a pathway here that would have resulted in bipartisan applause rather than bipartisan condemnation?

It's hard to imagine any set of actions that would have brought about such an outcome. Comey was experienced enough to see that. So he relied on his own internal decision-making matrix to pursue what seemed to him to be the most morally and ethically defensible course of action. He claims to have followed the dictates of his conscience in the belief that it would have been indefensible to have said nothing if it later transpired that Clinton had committed a serious breach. The answer as to whether that was prudent perhaps centres largely on the public nature of his actions. Whether or not the FBI was investigating Clinton was only an issue when it became a *public* issue. And it was Comey's choice to make his case in the public domain.

As indicated in the introduction, the greatest danger of overreach by public executives lies in proactive entry into political questions of high salience. Comey took that chance, and he lost. In the absence of Westminster conventions about what can and can't be done during election campaigns—known as 'caretaker' or 'purdah' in Westminster-system countries—Comey walked into a political firestorm by choosing to write in public rather than advising in private. It was an approach that would have been foreign to his Westminster-system counterparts. To draw out this distinction, the remainder of this chapter is split into three parts. The first dives deeper into history to examine the civil service career of Charles Trevelyan in Victorian Britain, to see how the chief author of the Northcote-Trevelyan report of 1854 shaped

Westminster traditions about the public profile of mandarins; the second presents a series of four short case studies to see how more contemporary leaders have dealt with taking a public stance on controversial questions; and the third presents an analysis of whether it is in fact possible for modern officials to be both public and apolitical at the same time.

Westminster Traditions

Under the traditional conventions of Westminster government, the ability to provide private advice was seen as the cornerstone needed to maintain the trust between ministers and civil servants, upon which good governance depended. As several senior civil servants discussed in semi-structured interviews for the present project, they would never allow themselves to be publicly drawn into an election campaign—or onto politically contested terrain at other times. Whilst freedom of information regimes and a default setting of transparency now apply, administrative leaders retain significant discretion in choosing what to write, and an awareness of how their words might be deployed by critics in the blame games of modern government.

The sense from mandarins who have operated in the Westminster system is that proactively reaching out into a public political issue is tantamount to looking for trouble. This sentiment was equally apparent amongst those who saw themselves as Westminster traditionalists and those who supported a more openly communicative posture.

As one former Canadian permanent secretary noted,

> We've had, over the history of Canada over my term in public service, a series of examples of where public servants have been demonised and/ or encouraged to take a public place, even by ministers, and then gotten into trouble when they did. And other examples where public servants have resigned because they can't defend themselves and be political actors. (Author interview, Canada, 2015)

In Westminster systems there is a strong tradition of sorting things out in private when issues arise that might cause disagreement. As a former Australian permanent secretary reflected,

> Usually I would say to a minister . . . , 'Minister, you know, that wasn't quite right' . . . or 'What your adviser said, that isn't actually what happened, let me explain'. But I'd prefer to do it privately. (Author interview, Australia, 2015)

To understand where this predisposition towards private debate comes from, we need to reach back to the mid-Victorian era when civil service traditions were originally shaped.

Sir James Stephen was a distinguished under-secretary of state at the British Colonial Office from 1836 to 1847. In 1854 he was asked for his views on the idea expressed in the Northcote-Trevelyan report that civil servants should be selected on merit through competitive examination, rather than through the system of patronage that then prevailed. He was against the plan, not because of its lack of logical appeal, but because he could see no prospect of people actually being drawn towards a career in the civil service.

> The money to be earned is the solitary attraction. A clerk in a Public Office may not even dream of fame to be acquired in that capacity. He labours in an obscurity as profound as it is unavoidable. His official character is absorbed in that of his superior. He must devote all his talents, and all his learning, to measures, some of which he will assuredly disapprove, without having the slightest power to prevent them; and to some of which he will most essentially contribute, without having any share whatever in the credit of them.[1]

It is this view that civil servants operate in a kind of obscurity that underpins much of how the system functions to this day.

If (by some miracle!) people of real ability did happen to decide it was worth taking the test to become a civil servant, Stephen was sure that they would 'not usually be the kind of man wanted'. The brightest people would simply be too self-reliant and resourceful.

> Excellent gifts for a combatant in the open fields of professional competition, but gifts ill suited, and even inconvenient, to one who is to be entombed for life as a clerk in a Public Office in Downing Street. Why invite an athlete into a theatre, where no combat, and no applause, and no reward, awaits him?[2]

Of course, despite such objections, the Northcote-Trevelyan report's commitment to meritocracy enforced by examination was ultimately embraced, and the report is still hailed today as forming the foundation stone for ideas of what a Westminster civil service should embody. But the obscurity or anonymity of which Stephen wrote has played a central role in the life of Westminster-system civil servants ever since. And this anonymity included even those at the very top of the civil service hierarchy. Throughout the twentieth century, the all-powerful mandarins who wielded immense influence at the centre of government were largely unknown to the wider public. To quote Peter Hennessy from the 2011 BBC documentary *The Secret World of Whitehall*, 'they were scarcely household names in their own household'. With, as Stephen put it, 'no combat, and no applause, and no reward'—other than a quietly bestowed knighthood—such mandarins diligently went about their work behind the scenes.

Of course, the Westminster system of government is not some objective standard that is held in place by rigid institutional boundaries, but rather a collection of traditions, beliefs and conventions that give the 'idea' of Westminster meaning in the minds and behaviours of individual actors (see Rhodes et al. 2009). The convention that mandarins should remain largely anonymous or faceless became part of Westminster practice over time. The idea was not explicitly mentioned in the Northcote-Trevelyan report of 1854, and yet was seen as a necessary corollary of the principle of ministerial responsibility, as Stephen's comments about civil servants labouring in obscurity demonstrate. But the power to 'go public' was never formally expunged either.

In fact, Stephen's contemporaries—including Charles Trevelyan himself—were not above wading into public debate through their writings, irrespective of the political sensitivities involved. Trevelyan, despite being a civil servant, was perfectly happy to publish things under his own name or under a pseudonym if he thought it warranted. His 1848 monograph *The Irish Crisis* was not destined to remain a reflective work intended only for the eyes of his colleagues.[3] As the historian Jenifer Hart noted,

> He sent it to everyone he could think of from the pope, the king of Prussia, and Guizot, to minor officials in the commissariat; and he was always quite certain the recipients would read it with interest, especially as it was 'prepared with so much labour and attention to accuracy', and since he was, in his view, in a better position than anyone else to write it. (Hart 1960, 102)

He also maintained a prodigious output of letters to the press throughout his civil service career and into retirement—and they often drew controversy. For example, in the early 1840s he wrote a two-part letter to *The Morning Chronicle* under the pseudonym 'Philalethes' about the state of Ireland after the arrest of the popular leader Daniel O'Connell. Trevelyan was of course assistant secretary to the Treasury at the time, and had given a private briefing to the prime minister and Home Secretary on the state of Ireland—a briefing his political masters had thought would remain private.

When the letters appeared in *The Morning Chronicle*, the indignant prime minister—Robert Peel—wrote to the Home Secretary, Sir James Graham, asking how Trevelyan 'could think it consistent with common decency to reveal to the Editor of the *Morning Chronicle* and to the world—all he told us . . . He must be a consummate fool' (cited in Kitson Clark 1959, 31).

Whether or not Trevelyan was a fool was a matter of contemporary debate, but he certainly displayed remarkable political skills—and what might today be called 'networking' abilities—to publicly pursue his policy ends. He used the press at a time when it was the only available vehicle for reaching a mass audience in order to influence public debate. In addition to his several pseudonyms, whilst still assistant secretary at the Treasury he wrote under his own name to *The Times* about diverse topics including emigration policy for the Scottish Highlands in the 1850s, in 1847 about the nature of 'Distress in Ireland', in 1855 about military supplies in the Crimean war, and in 1858 on the 'Western Bank of Scotland' and a second letter debating the need for teaching Sanskrit to civil servants posted to India.

Trevelyan was an unapologetic political player, but not in an overtly partisan manner. He in fact believed fervently in non-partisanship. Trevelyan's views were that a mandarin should be above party—insisting in fact on not voting himself in elections (Hart 1960, 109)—but his own actions attest that this did not mean that civil service leaders should remain above politics broadly construed. All policy decisions were full of politics, and Trevelyan did not shy away from placing his own views on the public record, and publicly defending the actions he undertook as Treasury assistant secretary. For example, in his book on Ireland he was willing to attack by name a leading Conservative critic, Lord George Bentinck, over his proposal for a large public works rail scheme (Trevelyan 1848, 180).

Trevelyan instinctively understood that public policy does not operate in some kind of 'apolitical' parallel universe. He didn't just quietly advise on public policy; he pursued it publicly and relentlessly through all avenues open to him. In doing so, he was following the methods of pioneering and reforming civil servants like Edwin Chadwick and Kay Shuttleworth (see Kitson Clark 1959; Gowan 1987). As Kitson Clark writes of Chadwick's social reforms, 'the schemes in question were his schemes and known to be so, warmly praised or bitterly attacked as the work of his hands. Neutrality would have been meaningless for him, anonymity was impossible' (1959, 32). The same could easily be said for Trevelyan and many others among his mandarin contemporaries. The collected views of mandarins on the changes proposed by the Northcote-Trevelyan report, published in 1855 as *Papers*

Relating to the Re-Organisation of the Civil Service, show just how fiercely engaged senior civil servants were on the topic. This ranged from those, like James Stephen, who felt that the 'obscurity' of civil service work would not attract the best and the brightest (75), through to Rowland Hill, who lauded attempts 'to purify and elevate the Public Service' (243).

Trevelyan and his contemporaries were politically aware entrepreneurs of reform, with some willing to take part as active participants in public debate, whilst still jealously guarding their non-partisan status. Trevelyan's success at maintaining that balance can be attested to by the fact that he remained in post for nearly twenty years, serving numerous successive governments who inevitably defended his performance. This in itself suggests that if bureaucratic leaders today also adopted a more public posture it would not necessarily 'break' the Westminster system. It has adapted before, and can do so again.

It was in the twentieth century that the principle of anonymity became an embedded part of Westminster convention, as bureaucracies expanded to become vast administrative machines controlled by the kind of anonymous 'establishment' men in bowler hats beloved of caricaturists. This perception of permanent secretaries as being too far removed from the community led the Fulton committee in 1968 to recommend that conventions of anonymity be softened, as we have already seen.

Traditionally, anonymity is not only part of the mystique of powerful mandarins, but has also been seen as fundamental to the workings of notions of ministerial responsibility. It is ministers—not mandarins—who are theoretically to be called to account for governance failings. As Dillman has expressed it, 'If a minister cannot defend the actions of his civil servants to the satisfaction of Parliament he or she is obliged to resign, preserving the anonymity of the civil servant' (Dillman 2007, 884). The strength of the anonymity convention was tested in Canada in 1978 when Jean-Pierre Goyer—then a minister—criticised one of his officials by name inside and outside the parliament. The official sued for libel, and in finding for the plaintiff (later overturned in the Court of Appeal), Justice Lieff reiterated that

> It is a long-standing convention of parliamentary democracy and the doctrine of ministerial responsibility which it encompasses that civil servants are *to remain faceless to the public*. Civil servants are responsible to their Ministers. Ministers, as elected officials, are responsible to the public.[4]

This kind of 'facelessness' that was perhaps still possible in the 1970s now seems to have been superseded by the challenges of twenty-first-century governance.

The next section explores four case studies in which contemporary mandarins have faced allegations of politicisation through being publicly seen as too close to the agenda of the government of the day. In all four cases, the difficulties for civil servants arose not simply from the content of their policy advice, but from its public nature. The media, opposition parties and external commentators were all able to offer their assessments on the performance of civil servants because their comments became part of the public debate.

Australia: Prime Minister Rudd and the Treasury Figures[5]

The 2013 Australian election was a feisty affair, held against the backdrop of years of Labor infighting that had seen Kevin Rudd spectacularly lose and then regain the prime ministership in the space of a little over three years. On 29 August, with barely a week to go until election day, Rudd, Treasurer Chris Bowen and Finance Minister Penny Wong held a joint press conference in Melbourne. Their goal was to highlight the alleged shortcomings of the policy costings thus far released by the Tony Abbott-led opposition. In time-honoured pre-election tradition, Rudd claimed to have identified a fiscal black hole, declaring that it was 'quite clear that there is now a massive $10 billion hole in the $30 billion that they are claiming' (Rudd et al. 2013).

Importantly for what was to follow, Treasurer Chris Bowen went on to assert that it was the public service who had discovered the error. 'There is an error of $10 billion . . . This is based on advice from the departments of Treasury and Finance and the Parliamentary Budget Office (PBO) which we are releasing today'. Bowen acknowledged that it was not normal practice to place public service advice so directly into the public domain, suggesting by implication that the importance of the discovery left him with no choice on this occasion. 'As I said before, releasing advice to Ministers is not something we do lightly. It's something we do after consideration' (Rudd et al. 2013). Finance Minister Wong followed suit, releasing information from the Parliamentary Budget Office questioning the level of savings that the opposition were asserting could be made through a round of public service job cuts.

At the core of the arguments being made by Rudd, Bowen and Wong was the idea that they were relying on independent non-partisan advice from the public service—seeking to inject a sense of evidence-based authority to buttress their political arguments. At first, the tactic looked like it might be successful, with early news reports picking up on the fact that the costings hole had been discovered by Treasury public servants. One ABC radio news bulletin noted, 'We've got copies of Treasury minutes and minutes from the Parliamentary Budget Office which have costed various measures that were announced yesterday by the Opposition' (ABC 2013). But the direction of the coverage turned very quickly when senior public servants themselves entered the fray.

Within hours of the prime minister's press conference, the head of the Treasury Department, Martin Parkinson, and the head of the Finance Department, David Tune, issued a media release contradicting their elected leaders.

> There have been a series of reports today regarding costings undertaken by the Department of the Treasury and the Department of Finance and Deregulation. . . . These costings were not prepared under the elections costings commitments' process outlined in the *Charter of Budget Honesty Act 1998*. At no stage prior to the Caretaker period has either Department costed Opposition policies. Different costing assumptions, such as the start date of a policy, take up assumptions, indexation and the coverage that applies, will inevitably generate different financial outcomes. (Parkinson and Tune 2013)

They were soon joined by the parliamentary budget officer, Phil Bowen, also putting out a media release directly criticising the government for misrepresenting PBO advice.

> When an individual parliamentarian or a political party chooses to publicly release a PBO costing that has been prepared on a confidential basis for them, it is inappropriate to claim that the PBO has costed the policy of any other parliamentarian or political party. Unless all of the policy specifications were identical, the financial implications of the policy could vary markedly. (Bowen 2013)

These interventions were pivotal in changing the media narrative around the story from focusing on the costings to instead focusing on the rebuke delivered to Rudd and his ministers. A selection of the newspaper headlines from the next day shows how the authority of the public servants had caused Rudd's attack to misfire: 'Treasury pans Rudd claim on $10b flaw' (Kenny 2013); 'Treasury backlash against $10b hole' (Wright and Probyn 2013); and 'Treasury torpedoes budget attack' (Greber and Coorey 2013). What had been intended as a political attack on the opposition had instead turned into an interrogation of the ethical acceptability of using the non-partisan authority of the public service in such a way.

By intervening publically, Parkinson, Tune and Bowen had entered a political argument in order to protect the non-partisan status of their organisations. To quote Australian journalist and professorial fellow Michelle Grattan, 'The departments and PBO heads are not trying to be political. Their intention is the opposite—they want to show they're apolitical'. Grattan concluded that Parkinson had been very clear in his intent: 'He and his public servant colleagues understand how the system should work—they have stood up for their own reputations and those of the organisations for which they work' (Grattan 2013). The actions of Parkinson, Tune and Bowen demonstrate the realities of an environment in which 'governing in public' is the new normal. Their advice was being used in a political way in the public domain, leaving them with the difficult choice of vacating the field through silence or protesting their independence through a public missive of their own.

The difficulty of that decision was apparent in my interviews for this project with recently retired Australian mandarins, although none were critical of the choice that Parkinson, Tune and Bowen had made. Said one, 'I think that what they did in that very difficult environment was correct because they needed to correct what was the advice they had given, and hadn't given. . . . Very unusual but I think in that instance it was really crucial because of the way in which in my view the advice that was given was clearly being abused for party political processes within an election campaign' (author interview, Australia, 2015).

It is certainly possible to argue that Parkinson and Tune, knowing from the polls that Rudd was about to lose, made the strategic decision that their self-interest lay in publicly rebuking the prime minister in order to better position themselves to serve the incoming government. But whilst strategic self-interest might have formed part of their decision-making matrix, it simply cannot explain all of Parkinson and Tune's actions. Parkinson was told by the incoming government that he would be sacked within the year, hardly a result suggesting that he was pursuing a savvy agenda of career self-interest. The case shows that when pushed, public executives have the power to engage publicly on controversial issues. Their preference is to act privately, working in partnership with the minister to avoid public disputes. But where that is not possible, they are willing to stand their ground publicly.

Canada: Wayne Wouters and Kevin Page

Kevin Page was Canada's parliamentary budget officer (PBO) between 2008 and 2013. His was an independent statutory role tasked, inter alia, with estimating the financial costs of various government policies and programmes. Page became something of a controversial figure for his willingness to consistently contradict government ministers and official papers in their estimates of policy costs. As an independent statutory officer, his public disagreements with government policy are less surprising than those of traditionally anonymous public servants taking on a more public role. The very nature of the position of parliamentary budget officer makes it a public role in which independent analysis is likely to sometimes produce results that might be disputed by the political arm of government. The interest here is how the traditional head of the Canadian public service, Clerk of the Privy Council Wayne Wouters, got drawn into disputes between Page and the government.

The Canadian budget of 2012 was focused by the Harper government on tackling Canada's budget deficit, with billions of dollars in projected savings. Page, in his role as parliamentary budget officer, sought specific details from the government and deputy ministers (the equivalent of UK permanent secretaries) about how departments planned to reach their fiscal targets under the budget. As clerk of the Privy Council, Wayne Wouters was portrayed in the media as being in a battle with Kevin Page to withhold information and was later accused of having politicised his role in seeking to protect the government from Page's requests for fiscal detail.

In a 2014 report by think tank Canada 2020, Wouters was portrayed as having taken on the role of publicly defending the Harper government in a partisan manner. The allegations of partisanship centred around a letter that Wouters sent to Page in September 2012, in which he refused to pass on some information and defended the government's need to provide 'credible' deficit reduction measures. The Canada 2020 report, authored by Prof. Ralph Heintzman at the University of Ottawa, argued that

> [t]he Clerk of the Privy Council not only took on the highly political role of spokesperson for blocking parliamentary oversight of public finance—a political role that should *never* be assumed by a professional public service in a *parliamentary* democracy. He did so in what can only be described as a forthrightly partisan manner. (Heintzman 2014, 9)

The Heintzman paper received considerable media publicity, and the Privy Council Office defended Wouters's actions, with a spokesman reported as saying that Wouters had communicated not 'on behalf of government, but rather as head of the public service' (quoted in May 2014).

Was Wouters acting in a partisan manner, or was he merely doing his job? Under the terms of the legislation governing the work of the Parliamentary

Budget Office, deputy ministers are tasked with providing information to the PBO upon request (Parliament of Canada Act, section 79.4(1)). In other words, the legislation envisages the passing of information as taking place between administrative leaders rather than the political leaders of the government. There were arguments about whether Wouters had the power to respond collectively on behalf of deputy ministers, but the fact that the PBO was not happy with Wouters's stance does not automatically make him partisan. What led to the *perceptions* of partisanship was the public nature of the debate between Page and Wouters, including public comment on the correspondence between the two men. As administrative historians can testify, civil service files across the Westminster world are full of disputatious correspondence between departments. The difference, of course, is that in the past such correspondence seldom saw the light of day, and therefore seldom drew bureaucrats into the kinds of public spat that can lead to perceptions of partisanship.

United Kingdom: Nicholas Macpherson on a Scottish Currency

The lead-up to the Scottish independence referendum in 2014 saw a wide-ranging debate over what the impact of a 'yes' vote would be on things that Scotland and the rest of the UK hold in common. High up on that list was the currency—the British pound—and whether it would be feasible or desirable for Scotland and the rest of the UK to maintain a currency union even if the political union was dissolved. The British Labour party, the Conservative party and the Liberal Democrats all campaigned against a 'yes' vote, and the coalition government sought and received policy advice from the civil service on what some of the implications of a 'yes' vote might be.

In February 2014, Chancellor of the Exchequer George Osborne gave a speech in Edinburgh outlining some of the potential challenges and pitfalls should Scotland choose to vote for independence. What made the speech controversial was not so much what the Chancellor said, but the use he made of advice he had received from the permanent secretary to the Treasury, Sir Nicholas Macpherson. In his speech, Osborne announced, 'Alongside this analysis I am also taking the exceptional step of publishing the internal advice I have received from the permanent secretary to the Treasury, Sir Nicholas Macpherson' (Osborne 2014). Macpherson's advice was both clear and clearly worded, leading to wide coverage in all sections of the British media.

Currency unions between sovereign states are fraught with difficulty. They require extraordinary commitment, and a genuine desire to see closer union between the people involved . . . I would advise strongly against a currency union as currently advocated, if Scotland were to vote for independence. (Macpherson 2014)[7]

The advice went on to reflect critically on fiscal policy in Scotland.

Finally, Treasury analysis suggests that fiscal policy in Scotland and the rest of UK would become increasingly misaligned in the medium term. Of course, if the Scottish Government had demonstrated a strong commitment to a rigorous fiscal policy in recent months, it might be possible to discount this. But recent spending and tax commitments by the Scottish Government point in the opposite direction, as do their persistently optimistic projections of North Sea revenues, which are at odds not just with the Treasury but with the Office of Budget Responsibility and other credible independent forecasters. (Macpherson 2014)

In response, Scottish First Minister Alex Salmond suggested in a TV interview that UK civil servants were merely following the political line of their ministers.

Treasury civil servants do what they are told by George Osborne . . . Sir Nicholas Macpherson, in making the unprecedented publication of this advice, I think he might come to regret that step because he will be asked for his advice on other things like the consequences of withdrawal from the EU, for example . . . I'm afraid we are in a situation where the UK government departments and civil servants do what they are told by their political masters. (Quoted in *The Scotsman* [*Scotsman* 2014])

Macpherson himself, appearing before a hearing of the Public Administration Committee of the House of Commons in April 2014, insisted that he had not been politicised and that it had been his decision to allow publication of his advice. He asserted that civil servants had a duty to 'serve the national interest' and that 'if publishing advice could strengthen the credibility of the Government's position, it was my duty to do it'.[6] But Macpherson also stressed that he saw this as an exceptional case, and that 'this is not something I would want to make a habit of'.[7]

Macpherson stressed in the hearing that he had served governments of both political persuasions and had always sought to do so impartially. Could his actions on this occasion be construed as partisan, or simply as fulfilling his duty as Treasury secretary? All defenders of the civil service, both practitioners and academics, would support the idea that civil servants should give frank and fearless advice. They should have no hesitation in 'speaking truth to power'. In this case, Macpherson did so, and did so in very clear language. The advice certainly fitted well with the political view of the Chancellor of the Exchequer, but does that immediately make it partisan? The idea that civil servants should disagree with their ministers on every point simply to avoid being seen as partisan is patently absurd. What caused the difficulty in this case was that the advice was made public, and used politically by the Chancellor in his speech in Edinburgh. It immediately dragged the Treasury secretary into the public limelight, where his views were then open to the perceptions of others who saw them as partisan because they had been used for political ends by the Chancellor.

In the UK, mandarins I interviewed for this project were on the whole of the view that Macpherson had skated a little close to the line.

> Now where I think the Nick Macpherson advice was interesting is because that felt quite close to private policy advice being made public. I couldn't easily in my own mind draw a distinction between the kind of advice you would give in the context of Scottish independence frankly to any other kind of advice that you might give privately. (Author interview, UK, 2014)

Another went further.

> He shouldn't have a political view. Of course he will have a view in relation to how the economics of the thing will work as a separate country. IOC quoted him as the permanent secretary in the newspapers in a way that sounded political. Now I know Nick. I know his politics and I know he is also very good . . . but because he was quoted in the newspaper, the public will see the head of the treasury as he was described—[a] civil servant as having a political view as to the future of Scotland. (Author interview, UK, 2014)

Even those who felt that the publication of Macpherson's advice was warranted conceded that it was a tight judgement call to have made.

> [T]his was a very exceptional circumstance where it felt appropriate for the permanent secretary to express his views publicly. The kind of challenge to that, which has something to it, is that you know, in a sense who decides when that advice is public, you know, if it's available for this issue why wouldn't it be available for something else. So I think there is a point on that. (Author interview, UK, 2016)

But concern was not universal. One former colleague saw no problem. 'Nick Macpherson I think was quite right. I mean I don't think that was a policy issue, I think he was making statements of fact and correcting things that had been said elsewhere' (author interview, UK, 2014). When I put the example to permanent secretaries in other places many were equally unconcerned. Said one New Zealander,

> I think he'd have an obligation to say it to the government, and if the government wanted to use it, that's up to them. I wouldn't be afraid by this. You can't stop a dog eating meat. If I felt that the government should have that advice, that I knew in giving that advice that they'd use it politically, that wouldn't stop me doing it either, because my first obligation is to make sure they're well informed. If in the knowledge they were going to use it for political purposes, would that stop me giving them advice? No, it wouldn't. (Author interview, New Zealand, 2016)

United Kingdom: Reflecting on Margaret Thatcher's Legacy

In early April 2013 Margaret Thatcher, one of the towering political figures of twentieth-century Britain, passed away. In death, as in life, Thatcher remained an extraordinarily divisive figure. Her death saw a wave of national reflection on her personality, her leadership skills and her legacy. The ideological battles of the 1980s provided the foundations for the obituary battles of 2013. *The Guardian* published an epitaph by the late Hugo Young under the headline 'Margaret Thatcher left a dark legacy that has still not disappeared' (Young 2013). In contrast, writing in *The Daily Telegraph*, Iain Duncan Smith's piece appeared under the headline 'Margaret Thatcher's legacy is a better country and a safer world for my girls' (Duncan Smith 2013).

In this febrile environment of intense reflection, the UK's two highest-ranked civil servants thought they could make a contribution by reflecting on how Thatcher had interacted with the civil service when she was prime minister. The cabinet secretary Jeremy Heywood and the head of the civil service Bob Kerslake co-authored a newspaper article in *The Daily Telegraph*, giving an intimate view of the relationship between Thatcher and her officials. The headline undoubtedly contributed to the controversy that followed: 'Margaret Thatcher: our kindly boss, by Britain's top civil servants' (Heywood and Kerslake 2013). The text of the piece was uncritical in its tone, with the intention of conveying an almost ethnographic picture of personal insight.

Her infamous working hours allowed the prime minister to consume vast quantities of briefings and from her No 10 flat she would nourish her civil servants with home-cooked shepherd's pie whenever they were working late. . . . She was kindly and unswervingly loyal to her team and, once she had decided what she thought, provided clear and consistent direction. To the country she was an Iron Lady, to those who worked with her she was a kind and considerate boss. (Heywood and Kerslake 2013)

Whilst not containing any overt support for particular Thatcherite policies, the article was heavily criticised by MPs from the opposition Labour party for its general lack of acknowledgement of any criticism of Thatcher and her policies. The two civil servants were accused by Labour MP Paul Flynn of having 'prostituted your high office and deserted your political neutrality' (Syal 2013). The piece generated its own news cycle focused on the prudence of their decision to write the article. Heywood insisted that people crying foul on political grounds were missing the point. 'We didn't think it was a political article at all . . . It didn't make a comment one way or the other about her politics. The article was about the civil service's relationship with Margaret Thatcher as a person, as a human being' (quoted in Mason 2013b).

Opinions were divided amongst the former UK permanent secretaries interviewed for this project on whether it had been a good and defensible idea for Heywood and Kerslake to write the piece. Said one, 'She was a big figure, you know, a serious, serious figure in British politics. She died and it was not unreasonable as part of . . . the total story, to capture the views of those who worked with her and communicate it' (author interview, UK, 2015). Another took a less forgiving line. 'I thought it was ill-judged, I just thought it was excruciating' (author interview, UK, 2015). Others were more likely to be sympathetic but concerned about the impression given. 'I thought [it] was ill-advised. Because I think it was likely to be used in the way that it was, as a sign of partisan behaviour . . . Because it's not a question of them supporting or not supporting the party of the day, it's a question about them giving the impression that they are not generally impartial. I think you've got to be very careful about that' (author interview, UK, 2014).

Anonymity, Impartiality and a Washminster Approach

The cases are illustrative of the fact that when senior civil servants communicate publicly their actions are scrutinised through a public lens. Their advice is assessed by a wide variety of commentators who then offer public judgements, which can lead to allegations of partisanship. Policy advice given privately can always be seen as neutral, whereas all public statements will be read through whichever lens external observers wish to place upon them. This places civil servants in the challenging position that although they may simply be offering frank and fearless advice in the best traditions of the Westminster system, they may be perceived as having politicised themselves. It illustrates the vital role that the Westminster convention of civil service anonymity has traditionally played in buttressing the equally important Westminster tradition of civil service non-partisanship.

What has changed is not that civil service leaders have suddenly become partisan, but rather that they have recently become 'public', allowing for *perceptions* of partisanship to emerge. Senior mandarins work at the interface of politics and administration. Their job is self-evidently not removed from the politics which surrounds it. If Westminster systems are moving towards expecting civil servants to play a more public role—and empirically this seems undeniable—then some reconsideration of what the Westminster ideal expects of administrative leaders is required. Westminster tradition and convention needs to catch up with the new realities of practice and evolve some guidelines that allow civil servants to fulfil their public roles without being targeted by allegations of partisanship.

I argue that the demands of modern governance simply will not allow a system of relative anonymity for senior officials to be maintained. In the age of social media and 24/7 news cycles, bureaucratic leaders cannot insulate themselves from forms of communication that have become part of how they interact with the community. It may be that the decline in anonymity is simply part of the next evolution of the ever-malleable Westminster system of government. There is after all no single body of rules that constitutes 'the Westminster system'. As Rhodes, Wanna and Weller have long argued, Westminster is an idea that is continually shaped and re-shaped by the actors who seek to cite it as authoritative support for their approach to governing (see Rhodes et al. 2009). But it is important to assess the extent to which a decline in anonymity will also compromise the commitment to non-partisan impartiality that forms a core feature of permanent bureaucracies across much of the democratic world. Certainly at senior leadership level, civil servants who gain a public profile become a natural magnet for those who wish to examine their public comments for evidence of partisanship or politicisation.

The emergence of mandarins as participants in public debates is a significant change from Westminster tradition but—I suggest—an unavoidable one. The role of various statutory officers shows that it is quite possible to have strongly independent public voices that scrutinise government performance in a non-partisan way. Extending such a robust 'right to comment' to the administrative leaders of government departments would be full of difficulties around lines of accountability and responsibility, but these are not insurmountable. In the absence of new settled conventions, claims of partisanship will continue to be levelled at those civil service leaders who undertake acts of public leadership. Over time this can only serve to draw the civil service as an institution further into the middle of political debates.

In covering the different ways that Westminster senior civil servants write in public, this chapter has sought to demonstrate how quickly interventions can come to be seen as partisan in nature. Without any political intent, the politically salient nature of the topic means that civil servants can become the target of intense public criticism. Even documents that are traditionally private, to be used by ministers in arriving at policy decisions, can find their way into the public domain. This can be through freedom of information requests, but equally—as the Scottish referendum example shows—it can result from a conscious choice to release advice into the public arena. So detailed can be the scrutiny that just one word in the wrong place can spark a firestorm of allegations. The Canadian example of Kevin Page criticising Wayne Wouters for speaking on behalf of the government of the day turned largely on Wouter's choice of words in his otherwise routine letter. His use of the word 'we' when describing the government's stance was construed by critics as inappropriately aligning himself as a civil servant with the political arm of the executive.

The article on Thatcher by Heywood and Kerslake is an example of a qualitatively different piece of writing, but one which led to an equal barrage of criticism. In Canada, Wouters had written as one senior civil servant to another (albeit an independent civil servant, given Page's role as parliamentary budget officer). In the UK, Heywood and Kerslake set out to write a public piece by design. It was by definition an outward-facing piece of communication intended for a wider audience during a time of public reflection following Thatcher's death. It was even, strictly speaking, not part of their job, so the amount of choice exercised was extensive.

These Westminster examples juxtapose interestingly against the James Comey case with which we started this chapter. Comey was certainly writing in the normal course of his job when he composed his letters to Congress, but he was also writing knowing that his words would have a much wider audience. He was ultimately writing for public consumption. He neither sought nor received—as far as we know—any permission for his actions. He didn't need it because he could communicate on his own authority. Undoubtedly the Justice Department, through the attorney general, could have attempted to stop him, but it would have resulted in a very awkward political fight on the most contentious grounds imaginable.

To what extent can each of these cases be classified as acts of 'rhetorical bureaucracy'? The distinguishing point is not whether the words were put in writing, but the extent to which they were designed to 'persuade' others. Comey's short missives were nobody's idea of a literary masterpiece, but they were intended to play a persuasive role. Readers, including the wider public once the letter was amplified through the media, were supposed to see the wisdom in Comey's actions. He foresaw and sought to forestall potential criticisms by explaining that he thought he needed to write 'in light of my previous testimony'. Similarly in the Australian and Canadian cases, the statements were not left to speak for themselves. They contained rhetorical framing: presenting facts in a particular way so as to justify action.

The crux of the issue, of course, is whether all this was appropriate. As I've argued, the world of modern governance is now a public one. Transparency, accountability, consultation—these are the watchwords of the age. This has been coupled with a 24/7 media environment, and the technological wonders of social media, to mean there is no place left to hide. Even the head of MI5 gives public speeches these days.

There is no longer a choice to be made as to whether to be public or to remain anonymous. The choice now is about the extent to which bureaucratic leaders might embrace or eschew the opportunities that this state of affairs provides. By temperament and instinct, American public executives are perhaps more likely to want to get out in front of issues than are civil servants encumbered by the traditions of Westminster discretion. And yet the evidence suggests this too is changing. When it comes to writing in public there are some routine and reliably dull outputs in both the proactive and reactive categories I discussed in chapter one. Newsletters, statements of upcoming events, open consultations on topics of low salience—these are the forms of communication that uncontroversially keep the world turning. They are aimed predominantly at an audience of fellow bureaucrats, albeit the general public can look in as interested outsiders if they have a mind to. Such documents are normally freely available on government websites to anyone who wishes to go looking for them. All that is required is to keep them appropriate to the intended audience. As one former department head from New Zealand put it,

[A] good writer has the audience in mind. If you think your audience is the minister or the cabinet, you have those individuals in mind. You're writing for that audience. Once you know it's going to be available to a wider audience, you've got to have that in your mind. Your primary audience is the one you're addressing, but you'd probably be a bit more careful about not having language in there that could be spun in another way. (Author interview, New Zealand, 2016)

It is of course possible for such things to become viral disasters of epic proportions—but it is unusual.

It's only when levels of political interest are high that things get rather more precarious. Proactively, bureaucratic leaders can be voluntarily expressing views on issues that are the subject of political debate. Reactively, they can be drawn into a public role in a political controversy. Both have been in evidence in the cases discussed in this chapter. The Margaret Thatcher intervention definitely falls into the proactive and politically salient category. This was a controversy that could have been avoided. Comey equally had a choice as to whether to act proactively or reactively. In trying to get out in front, he followed his instincts in pre-emptively defending his corner.

The Australian case and the Scottish referendum case were both extraordinary events. It is true that in both cases the bureaucratic leaders were acting proactively to place their views into the public domain. The Australian secretaries could have chosen to just 'let it go' or quietly and privately demand that the politicians correct the record. But in the new public governing environment, they had to make calculations about how their actions might be perceived by others. They had to protect their own reputations and the authority of the Australian public service. Equally, Nicholas Macpherson could have insisted to ministers that his policy advice was for their eyes only rather than for public consumption. They might have overruled him and published anyway, in which case he could then have condemned that action as violating civil service principles. Clearly he did not do so.

Yet I would argue that none of these interventions was in fact inappropriate. They represent officials making use of the public stage available to them to either defend themselves or make reasonable public comment. In Canada, Wouters was simply writing to one of his peers, and the evidence that this was in actuality a partisan intervention remains thin. In Australia, the two secretaries stepped forward to contest the government's framing of their policy advice as some kind of audit of opposition policies. This they were fully entitled to do. In the UK, Heywood and Kerslake wrote an opinion piece about a political figure with whom they had both worked. Thatcher herself will always be a divisive symbol of her times, but that hardly renders a moment of reflection on her passing an act of partisan insurrection.

None of these interventions challenged the supremacy of democratic decision-makers, nor even advocated particular policy directions. The interventions by Macpherson and Comey were different in character because they impacted so directly on policy and electoral matters. In Macpherson's case, he drew on decades of experience as a civil servant to offer clear policy advice on the potential currency consequences of Scottish independence. It was an authoritative voice in an important national debate, offering a particular point of view. Voters and other commentators could and did criticise it and offer counter-views. That is the nature of political contestation in a democracy. It is not inherently wrong or undesirable. The permanent secretary of the Scottish government at the time, Peter Housden, was equally criticised by the House of Commons Public Administration Committee for having been too carelessly pro-independence in his approach to Scottish government documentation. The criticisms are certainly right in suggesting that such interventions go against Westminster tradition. But equally they show that—in the environment of 'governing in public'—traditions are changing.

Which leaves us with Comey. His actions contributed to the outcome of an election. It is perhaps not possible to quantify exactly how significant that impact was, but in a close race small shifts can make a substantial difference. Comey was the independent holder of a statutory office, appointed by a Democratic president and confirmed in congressional hearings. He had a right to do his job. He was fully entitled to make the calculation that he did about the need to write to Congress about the Clinton investigation. He acted within his authority as director of the FBI. None of this of course means that he necessarily made the 'right' decision. I would argue that he exercised poor political judgement in a situation where the stakes could hardly have been higher. But that is the point of governing in public—leaders have to make choices upon which voters can then make up their own minds. That is how it should be.

Bureaucrats are used to writing. In many ways it represents their comfort zone. What they are not used to is writing for a public audience. But as this chapter has shown, every written document can now potentially be for public release—and the authors should be well aware that this is the case. This changes the risk matrix around the written word, and bureaucratic leaders can quickly find themselves on the defensive. The next chapter turns to ways in which mandarins can stop playing defence and start playing offence, by re-framing their role as public leaders.

4

Leading in Public

We live in a world right now where we will never have a major event that doesn't have public participation. (Thad Allen, speaking at MIT in May 2011 about his experience leading the response to the BP oil spill in 2010)

'I dislike the modern craze for publicity, and personally avoid it as much as possible', wrote British Treasury official W. R. Codling in 1938 (cited in Chapman 1988, 234). Codling would undoubtedly have been unimpressed by the modern governance environment. The nature of leadership in both private and public organisations has shifted irreversibly towards an external orientation. It has increasingly become a part of the role of public sector leaders to act as the public face of their organisation in expressing its values, outlining its mission and defending its mistakes. For Westminster-system civil servants, this public type of leadership is not a natural fit with the quietly anonymous style associated with the height of the mandarin era in the mid-twentieth century. As one former UK cabinet secretary put it, 'We have a strong gene against this' (Wilson 2003). In America, the genetic predisposition of public administrators is somewhat different. The possibilities and limitations of such an approach are well captured in key aspects of the career of Stuart Levey.

Levey is not necessarily a household name outside government circles in the USA. But for a period of five to six years he was very much the public face of US attempts to strangle the flow of funds to world terrorism. Levey was appointed by George W. Bush as the country's under-secretary for terrorism and financial intelligence, located in the US Treasury. He was maintained in that post by the Obama administration until March 2011. Levey was already a very experienced public executive, having served in multiple roles in the Department of Justice, including as principal associate deputy attorney general. But it was in his new role that he made his most lasting mark on the public record.

In October 2008, the *New York Times Magazine* ran a feature story entitled 'Stuart Levey's war'. It described how Levey had come up with a proposal to use the resources of government to convince private sector banks to refuse to work with countries that were seen as supporting terrorism. As the piece's author, Robin Wright, explained, 'Levey decided it was time to mobilize the private sector, starting with the world's banks, to join the effort to sanction Iran. His idea was to prevent a country reliant on global trade—as an ancient empire, a station on the Silk Road across Asia and a modern petroleum powerhouse—from being able to do business outside its borders' (Wright 2008).

Scholars of public policy will of course not be surprised by the idea that significant individuals put forward policy ideas and then drive them through. 'Policy entrepreneurs' have been with us a long time (see Kingdon 1984). What is significant here is that the policy entrepreneur was someone working within government, and that he so readily adopted a public profile in bringing the policy to fruition. It is an example of the distinctive traditions that separate Washington and Westminster. In Westminster-system countries, ministers would have run with the policy as their own, and if there was public credit to be had it would have been theirs for the taking. A figure like Levey would traditionally have remained in the background.

Instead, over a period of years, Levey personally prosecuted the 'war' that the *New York Times* had outlined. And he led the drive as its public face. Both supporters and detractors knew it. The *New York Times* piece quotes Iran's former finance minister, Davoud Danesh Jaffari, as complaining to his staff about Levey's zeal. 'They had assigned one of their Zionist deputies to halt the Iranian economy. This person would personally travel to many countries around the world. He would use incentives and encouragement to request cooperation against Iran, and if he failed to get any results he would use threats to pursue his goal' (Wright 2008).

In 2006, the *Washington Post* portrayed him as 'the money man in the terror fight', describing his assignations across the Middle East, including a crucial meeting with then Libyan leader Moammar Gaddafi 'sitting out in a cabana, under an umbrella' (Linzer 2006). Type Levey's name into any media database over his period in office and you will be rewarded with a multitude of hits. Why? Because Levey was actively making the case for the policy, and describing its outcomes at every opportunity. From testifying before House and Senate committees, to giving press interviews, to giving speeches in the United States and across the globe, Levey did not shrink from the limelight.

In Westminster tradition, this kind of visibility by senior departmental officials is almost unheard-of. No self-respecting civil servant in the twentieth century would have dreamt of building such a wide profile, lest they risk outshining their minister. But under the conditions of modern governance, things are starting to shift. It is hard to govern in public, without actually *being* public. As I have argued elsewhere, mandarins in Westminster systems are increasingly showing levels of comfort in giving public speeches to important stakeholder groups (Grube 2012). Even if these are reported in the press in a negative light on occasion, it simply now goes with the territory that public sector leaders have to reach out and engage with the citizenry every bit as much as private sector CEOs have to reach out to shareholders.

This includes commenting on issues at the intersection of politics and public policy. For example, Westminster bureaucrats have become reasonably comfortable in publicly identifying the medium- to long-term policy challenges that need to be considered. Topics like climate change, demographic change and financial constraints are readily canvassed as leaders talk in non-partisan ways about the challenges that lie ahead for all governments, regardless of their politics (see Grube 2013). These events can and do attract significant media attention, but not normally of the duration or intensity associated with US cases. Westminster leaders—even those who are keen to embrace outward-facing opportunities—are more reticent about how it's done. Even high-profile permanent secretaries might only give a handful of public speeches per year. Those leaders with statutorily defined arm's-length powers tend to be prepared to speak more openly and more often, but still retain a strong sense of caution about being seen to become too 'political'.

In interviews, very few mandarins declared themselves as feeling one hundred per cent comfortable in the public space, although most acknowledge that there is now a greater sense of being in the public eye. For many there was a hesitancy about engaging too deeply.

> I guess in general still the public are pretty much shielded from mandarins, if you like, senior civil servants. I mean, there are distinctions now

> because there are some areas where agency heads and the like, they've
> got a lot more publicity because they're out there—for example, going on
> at the minute, the head of the environment agency with the floods, very
> public. So I think when you're running agencies and the like, you've got
> a little bit more personal responsibility and power, then what should go
> with that, quite rightly, is more transparency, more accountability and
> more media. (Author interview, UK, 2014)

Even those in mainline departments felt a desire from within government for
civil service leaders to be more public, but as advocates of the government's
agenda rather than in their own right.

> But I was very clear from both ministers, when I was permanent secretary
> and from Sir Gus O'Donnell as the cabinet secretary that there was an
> expectation there to be out more . . . see how government policies were
> being translated and crucially . . . advocacy. You had to be there making
> the case for reform and change and improvement in the system. So I
> felt that that was a very important part of my work. (Author interview,
> UK, 2015)

Those leaders who had been involved with more explicitly arm's-length
agencies had fewer problems seeing an independent public leadership role.

> So the theory is that in a sophisticated democracy these arm's-length
> agencies ought to be able to chide government and to bear witness to
> evidence in a way that is in the public interest. That means the public
> have got to trust them and the only way they can trust them is if they
> develop some sort of persona that can command public trust and that
> probably means having some sort of spokesman or figurehead. (Author
> interview, UK, 2015)

The same person, however, also noted the confused position of ministers who were keen to be seen to support transparent and accountable
government, but then ran for the hills if they actually received criticism from
public bodies. '[T]hey set up watch dogs and then the first time the watch
dog bark[s], you think they're going to shoot the bloody thing, which they
do fairly regularly' (author interview, UK, 2015). Another was certain that
things were changing, and not for the better. 'I think senior civil servants
are taking a more public role. Some would say they're being forced into it. I
would say they're being pushed into it . . . The problem with having a public
face is that it then becomes very difficult [to be clearly independent]. You

put your job publicly on the line in front of a TV camera, [which] I think is problematic' (author interview, UK, 2014).

The types of public leadership style that emerge from interviews with Westminster permanent secretaries can be split into four categories (see Figure 1), based on the goals they are trying to achieve when 'going public' and the extent of that public engagement. The distinction lies in part between whether mandarins feel they are speaking in their own right, or as government mouthpieces. In analysing the goals that administrative leaders have in going public, I make use of the well-known distinction between transactional and transformational leadership. Since it was introduced by James Burns and expanded by Bernard Bass, this distinction has become one of the most cited in leadership studies (Burns 1978; Bass 1985). Applied mostly to leadership in private enterprise, the dichotomy has also become much debated within the literature on public sector leadership (see Denhardt and Campbell 2006). At its core, the difference between the two conceptions of leadership is an ontological one. Transactional leadership is about getting things done through reward and punishment in the belief that people will make rational choices about their self-interest. Transformational leadership is built on less tangible things like inspiration, lifting people's eyes to the horizon and motivating them through a combination of charisma and care.

I employ the distinction in Table 1 to capture the difference between leaders who tolerate a degree of publicity in order to transact the business that the government requires them to lead, and those who harness it to transform debates and speak on their own authority.

TABLE 1. Transactional and transformational public engagement

		Extent of public engagement	
		Low	High
GOALS OF PUBLIC ENGAGEMENT	*Transactional*	Selective communications to clarify processes for policy delivery. Low-level media exposure as by-product rather than by design.	Wide media presence and reaching out to stakeholders, but focusing on policy *delivery* rather than policy *choice*.
	Transformational	Define and suggest new policy directions, but always in careful concert with ministers. Public profile is cautious.	Wide-ranging public outreach and media presence, with the goal of shaping public opinion.

Transformative public executives harness the opportunities presented by their public face to advocate for policy change, and transactional leaders limit themselves to the administrative pursuit of the government's goals. The typology also allows for the difference between those who try and maintain as low a profile as possible, and those who are embracing their role as rhetorical bureaucrats. Across the various Westminster countries examined, there are some patterns but few definitive distinctions. On the whole, permanent secretaries in the Antipodes (Australia and New Zealand) are rather more likely to embrace a public persona, and come closer to using it to actually act as advocates for policy change. British and Canadian bureaucratic leaders adhere much more stringently to the tradition that they should not court publicity, and that if they do so, it should be to support or explain existing government policy, rather than floating new ideas of their own. In the words of one senior Canadian bureaucrat, 'Public servants are not in a position to argue policy in public, because ministers and members of parliament and senators are going to legitimately be political actors, and public servants are not political actors' (author interview, Canada, 2015).

Politicians also play a central role in deciding how much leeway they are willing to grant to their public executives to engage in public debate. In Westminster-system countries, civil servants are normally expected to toe the government line, and indeed ministers may try to prevent them from speaking out altogether. Canada provides a fascinating recent example. The Canadian interviews for this project were conducted during the period of the Harper government and many interviewees reflected that doing things in public carried more risk under the Harper administration than it had in previous decades. So just at the time when governing in public is becoming unavoidable, the Harper administration was trying extra hard to prevent it. And it had an effect, with one interviewee describing how they would think twice when receiving an invitation to speak somewhere. '[I]f you're a senior public servant, you think like ooh I'm not going to go to your conference and talk about that issue, because the last time I did I got my face ripped off' (author interview, Canada, 2015). There was a sense of reticence based on the level of political control that ministers were seeking to exert over their public servants. 'I would say there's quite a chill over senior public servants or any public servants for that matter, talking publicly. And that I think is a change. It wouldn't have been a big deal like ten years ago, fifteen years ago' (author interview, Canada, 2015).

Another interviewee shared the same view. 'So, in general I would say the scope for anybody, ministers included, to have an independent public role is very, very slight these days, so then that's one factor. So, in that sense I would say that the role for senior public servants to give a speech or make a presentation—we'll come back to parliamentary committees—has diminished' (author interview, Canada, 2015). So, do public executives need a political 'licence to speak' and if so how can they utilise it? In order to tease out these dynamics, I now examine each quadrant of Table 1 in turn to reveal how different leaders position themselves.

Transactional—with Low Levels of Public Engagement

Transactional bureaucrats are those who engage in public only to the extent that they absolutely have to in order to competently carry out their jobs. Caution and tradition loom large as public executives are acutely aware of the dangers of politicising themselves through their public comments.

> Civil servants in our system are permanent civil servants who have got to be prepared to work for whatever government the public returns at an election. So the civil service . . . are not in a position where they can publicly take sides, which would prejudice their ability to serve whatever government is in power. So from that point of view, even if civil servants appear in public, they shouldn't be expressing political opinions which might be prejudicial to their ability to carry out that duty. (Author interview, UK, 2014)

A recently retired New Zealand senior executive made the same point. '[P]olitical leadership and the contesting of ideas is the political domain, not the public service domain and to the extent that there's discussion from chief executives that would be very technical and explanatory' (author interview, New Zealand, 2016). The danger of course is that under the conditions of 'governing in public', executives may not be able to maintain these traditional distinctions, in which case mandarins may need to speak for themselves more readily to make sure they are not publicly misrepresented.

Interviewees were certainly aware that the challenges they face included the impossibility of being able to control the perceptions of others. One New Zealand interviewee reflected on how he had been subject to public criticism because of how others had read his words.

> [W]hatever public servants do in a public environment, there will be people from, whether it's a party political lens, or a stakeholder lens,

from a stakeholder perspective who will apply their lenses to what is said and not said, and attribute rightly or wrongly, partisan political motives to either the acts of commission or acts of omission, and I think that is a real issue. (Author interview, New Zealand, 2016)

The most obvious test for whether executives had managed to avoid the trap of becoming too contentiously public was whether or not they made the news headlines. As another New Zealander reflected, 'You never want to be seen on the front page' (author interview, New Zealand, 2016).

Executives who focused on transactional policy leadership—administratively implementing the will of the government of the day—minimised their public appearances to just what was necessary to do that job. According to one Canadian, 'I'd probably be speaking publicly ten or twelve times a year' (author interview, Canada, 2015). And if it wasn't necessary, it was avoided almost altogether, as one New Zealander reflected. 'That's not my role, to provide the risk for political discourse around policy matters, for me to stimulate that so it causes questions going to the PM's office . . . I don't think that assists my role at all . . . so I just don't do it' (author interview, New Zealand, 2016).

The number one rule for transactionally focused mandarins seeking a low public profile was to make sure it was always clear that it is ministers who can and should provide the public face of government. The 'elected member of the species' (as one Australian delightfully put it) likes to project an image of being in control of events. It is after all politicians who are held responsible at the ballot box. As a result, they don't welcome what former UK Home Secretary Charles Clarke once dubbed 'celebrity' civil servants stealing the limelight. Politicians are drawn to good news in particular. It is an attraction of magnetic proportions. Whilst frequently happy to handball the blame for mistakes, any available credit is clasped in a ministerial bearhug with unrestrained glee. As one New Zealander noted, 'the public sector leader—there's an unwritten rule—[sh]ould never become bigger than the minister' (author interview, New Zealand, 2016).

Transactional—with High Levels of Public Engagement

The second category covers those senior civil servants who maintain their fidelity to the traditional belief that it is politicians who must set policy, but are much more comfortable with maintaining a high public profile in seeing through the government's initiatives. In other words, they embrace the need to govern in public but do not see themselves as drivers of the policy debate. Whilst they might be participants, it is only as representatives of the ministers that they serve. It is a public voice, but not an independent one, as one former UK mandarin explains.

> I never thought I was some thought leader as permanent secretary . . . I was there essentially to advocate, explain, defend, promote the government of the day's policy. So whilst it was a public role it was not a role . . . where I had an independent voice and I think constitutionally it would have been inappropriate for me to have had an independent voice. (Author interview, UK, 2015)

Under the conditions of modern governance, there is a multitude of external actors that government needs to engage with. This leads bureaucrats to wide public engagement, but only with the transactional goal of administering and delivering the government's agenda. One interviewee described how in Canada, for example, outreach to 'industry, unions, academia [. . . has] grown with the growth in non-governmental organisations having an interest in public policy issues' (author interview, Canada, 2015).

Mandarins have to build their own public profile if they are to be successful in carrying out the government's wishes effectively. One New Zealand interviewee believed that if 'you have incentives to manage reputation, you have incentives to promote yourself . . . therefore chief executives themselves have [a] stronger set of incentives . . . to be political—and I say political in a non-partisan/small-p version of that' (author interview, New Zealand, 2016). As some stress, this is simply about informing the public and stakeholder groups by constantly reaching out to explain the government's policy direction. 'For example when we changed the legislation I'd be happy to go out and speak to people about what we'd done; how it now worked; what it meant for them; what we were looking for. But again these were very much factual presentations. So if I was asked to do that, I was happy to do it.' (Author interview, Canada, 2015)

Depending on the policy area in which different leaders worked, there was sometimes no clear avenue for avoiding the resultant public profile. One Canadian in a particularly high-profile area did not relish public duties, not least because it led to a degree of notoriety. 'I'm a very bad public and private speaker, so I hate speaking. But I've often . . . had to do it. And I would say, particularly in my last job, my speeches have sometimes ended up as the lead item on the national television news or the front page of the national paper' (author interview, Canada, 2015).

Transformational—with Low Levels of Public Engagement

One of the policy catchcries across the Westminster world over the last decade has been 'evidence-based policy', built on the belief that the role of the bureaucracy is to provide the objective data that can allow politicians to make the best possible decisions. Some of the more enthusiastic outward-facing mandarins were happy to support contributions to public debates where that meant putting non-partisan evidence into the public domain.

> I think when I look back on some of the best things we did, and the arguments we won . . . [it] was because we did a very thorough piece of economic analysis and published it. It was up there for anyone to question and criticise, but I think it really helped bolster the case. I think there's a greater tendency nowadays for people to justify their policies in public. (Author interview, UK, 2014)

Another British interviewee was supportive of that kind of participation, but only with the knowledge and support of the minister he served. 'I think in terms of a permanent secretary helping to develop a discussion, a debate, a conversation out there on particular policy issues, explaining particularly around management issues and performance issues on be-half of the department I think . . . they should be less secretive.' (Author interview, UK, 2015)

In Australia and New Zealand in particular, certain departments were seen as having a more independent public persona that entitled them to make contributions to public debates. The goal was not to become a partisan player, but to act in some ways like an independent non-government agency putting ideas out into the public domain.

> I mean primarily I think you have a role as a chief executive to not only represent your department but also to help it form that debate and help again in a non-political way but maybe correct information that's out there that may be strongly misleading or whatever. I mean I think pos-sibly where I, and I'm being very frank now, pushed the barrow a bit was kind of on issues where we thought some attention might be needed over time and this was where you get close to the boundary. (Author interview, New Zealand, 2016)

The Treasury Department in particular was seen in both Australia and New Zealand as having a distinctive responsibility to provide economic evidence for the public to weigh up. As one New Zealander explained,

So that's what I mean about there is some licence, particularly as it re-lates to chief executives, if you like, with professional competence . . . And the Treasury pushes the boundaries of that, and I certainly know from talking to ministers in this government that that licence probably is tolerated by the minister of finance, and he is very positive about it. I don't believe it's that accommodated by many other ministers. (Author interview, New Zealand, 2016)

Such behaviour was not universally seen as positive, with some peers casting a critical eye at how their colleagues go about things. 'I didn't as actively use the media interest as some of my contemporaries would. They would actu-ally formally craft and set it up. Some particularly use . . . public speeches . . . to focus on particular challenges' (author interview, New Zealand, 2016).

Without exception, all interviewees were aware that there was 'a line' governing what they could do and say professionally without compromising their non-partisan status as public servants. It could include advocacy, but only within limits. This applied even in New Zealand.

I think it's got to be advocacy-light if it's advocacy at all, because once you start getting into that heavy advocacy role, I think . . . you start to impinge on that ability to be independent because then you get into lobbying. You're trying to change the climate under which these politi-cians are making decisions. Informing people, explaining your view—to me that's cool. Getting into the advocacy, lobbying is not cool. Wouldn't do it. (Author interview, New Zealand, 2016)

Transformational—with High Levels of Public Engagement

The fourth quadrant in Table 1 is in part a window into the future and in some ways sounds a cautionary note. It covers high levels of ubiquitous media engagement in pursuit of a policy goal with which bureaucratic leaders are independently associated. In many ways this level of personal profile is traditionally foreign to the Westminster system. It captures well the ac-tions described in the Stuart Levey case study in the USA with which we began this chapter, but has few empirical matches in Westminster-system countries. But things are changing. For example, there are two categories of public servant whose members are already exercising a wider licence to build a public case for policy change. The first is the heads of arm's-length agencies—like the UK Environment Agency—who have a unique profile of their own and answer to a board rather than directly through the normal departmental structures. The second is what has become known as the 'fourth sector'—those extra-parliamentary officers tasked with watchdog roles over government. Various ombudsmen, commissioners and budget officers have joined longer established institutions like auditors-general in holding government to account in public ways.

In Canada, a former head of one such independent commission reflected that they had largely been able to ignore the rules that applied to mainline public servants during the Harper years. '[M]y only authority was someone with a public authority. So I chose to be much more public. So I gave many speeches, I mean I was giving speeches all the time. I gave many speeches, I did press interviews, my picture was in the paper, I had things to say and I said it publicly, I tabled my report, I had press conferences' (author interview, Canada, 2015). The same official described how it had been possible to assert personal independence in deciding when and how to communicate.

> Well there is a policy, there's a communications policy that in fact requires you to give your speeches in advance; that requires you to review your appearances before committees; that requires a review of documents that are released, and I just told them I wasn't doing it. And this caused my communications people a great deal of grief, because they did go to the meetings so there were communications meetings on a regular basis in an effort to try and sort of corral all this stuff going on in the public service. And I just said, well I'm not doing it. (Author interview, Canada, 2015)

Some leaders of arm's-length agencies actively saw themselves as being very different to the civil service. They had a different mandate, to serve the public directly. One UK interviewee explained the difference in unflattering terms.

> I was on the *Today* programme . . . so often, they invited me to their 50th [birthday] party. I've been on television endlessly, in the newspapers, in the magazines and generally speaking I think that's the way somebody in that sort of body should behave. Nobody elected us and we have to be aware of what the public wants and our relationship with opinion from the public is largely by direct contact. Then if you go back into the civil service, the traditional view is we don't need to talk to the hoi-polloi because we are intelligent people and we run the country on your behalf and you really don't need to know too much about it. I have to say

that attitude is still quite prevalent in a large number of civil servants and probably in a large number of permanent secretaries too. (Author interview, UK, 2015)

Those mainstream civil servants are of course being careful not to compromise their ability to serve future governments. Even some very public secretaries viewed themselves as an embodiment of the institution they were representing.

I think there's two key issues: one is the office is not a personality, and therefore you don't want to inject too much personality; I think the other thing is that it's an explanation of the advice you've given. The worst thing would be to be seen to be out there lobbying, because once you're into that domain, your ability to serve future governments just goes down the toilet, and as soon as governments start to make decisions that you don't like, why would they share things with you? The risk is that they see you as part of the opposition. (Author interview, New Zealand, 2016)

The problem with that view is not that it's inaccurate, but that there may be little that mandarins can do to influence the perceptions of others. For example, recent Australian history demonstrates that incoming governments are prepared to sack permanent secretaries they view as having too enthusiastically supported the policies of the previous administration. When the Abbott government was elected in 2013, literally one of the first actions of the new administration was to sack four permanent secretaries. As one Australian interviewee noted, 'It was largely those secretaries who did have a fairly high profile in relation to a particular issue, in relation to contentious issues such as climate change and immigration' (author interview, Australia, 2015). Few of the Australian interviewees believed that the secretaries who had been sacked were indeed partisan or that they had behaved improperly. They had simply been doing their job in support of the government of the day. If secretaries now have to 'govern in public', how then can they protect themselves when there is a change of government?

There is also one further category of public executive in Westminster-system countries which is seen as having an independent role to play, and that is the titular heads of the respective civil services.[1] In Australia, New Zealand, the UK and Canada, there was universal agreement amongst former heads of the public service interviewed for the present project that there was a particular responsibility on the leaders of the service to represent its interests. These leaders had each on occasion spoken out on issues to do with the health of the service as a whole, and saw it as their job to protect the institution from the criticisms flowing from contemporary political debates if necessary. As one reflected, '[M]inisters aren't going to go out and defend the public service, that ain't going to happen. So accept that constraint and therefore build on it. So I did take a public position on that stuff.' (Author interview, country omitted, 2015).

Case Study: Ken Henry and the Australian Mining Tax

If public servants are encouraged to appear in the media and elsewhere to explain government policy settings, they can become tightly and closely associated with the policy itself in the public mind. Paradoxically, while acting with integrity and impartiality in carefully keeping within Westminster conventions, they can nevertheless find themselves in the middle of political firestorms. The position of former Australian Treasury Secretary Ken Henry in the mining tax debate in Australia in 2010 provides an interesting case study. Henry had been secretary of Treasury since 2001, appointed under the previous coalition government. When the Rudd Labor government was swept into office in 2007, Henry was retained in his post. Henry had slowly carved out a reputation as a publicly engaged Treasury secretary, and it was a perception that increased the longer he spent in office.

In 2008–09 Australia was confronted by the challenges of the global financial crisis. As Lehman Brothers crumbled, and banks the world over suddenly faced potential meltdown, Henry emerged as a key voice in the Australian government's dramatic response. He is credited with having proffered the advice that if the government wanted to stave off recession then it needed to devise a stimulus package that would 'go early, go hard, and go households'. This included in the first instance cash handouts of $900 to all Australian taxpayers as the quickest way to make sure money was spent directly by consumers. As part of a core team of senior ministers and selected bureaucrats, Henry became closely associated with the stimulus package in the public mind. Whilst remaining a determinedly non-partisan figure, he could do little to control the perceptions of those critics of the government's spending who suggested that he was perhaps doing his job a little too enthusiastically.

But more was to come. Throughout 2008 and 2009, Henry had also been working assiduously on a review of the country's taxation system. Announced in May 2008, *Australia's Future Tax System Review* was intended to provide a thorough root-and-branch reassessment of what a twenty-first-century taxation system should look like. The government commissioned Henry to chair the review, in collaboration with a small panel of four other luminaries. But it was Henry whose name became synonymous with the review. In Australian political parlance it became known as the 'Henry tax review'. It was a deliberately outward-focused exercise, with multiple opportunities for public submissions, focus groups and public meetings. Henry himself gave a series of ten keynote speeches on different aspects of the tax system between November 2008 and October 2009 (e.g., Henry 2009).

But the real public interest in the exercise crystallised when the government released the final report in May 2010. The Treasurer and the prime minister were worried. It was etched on their faces. The likelihood that a rampant opposition led by Tony Abbott would frame the report as a tax grab was obvious to everyone. Despite the government's best efforts, that's exactly how it turned out. The government certainly did all it could to control the narrative by holding a media 'lock-up' for the release, including an embargoed press conference with Treasurer Wayne Swan. They sought to distance themselves from those aspects of the document that might be politically controversial. Whilst endorsing a couple of aspects of the review, the government emphasised that 'other recommendations in the review are not government policy' (Swan and Rudd 2010). So worried was the government that the same press release provided a specific list of twenty policies that it was committed to *not* implementing 'at any stage'.

The final review report contained 138 recommendations, of which the government selected only a handful to immediately pursue. And the center-piece was to be a much-vaunted 'resource super profits tax'. Australia was still in the midst of a resources boom, with sales of commodities to China in particular seen as having been a major contributing factor to the country's not sliding into recession during the global financial crisis. With hints of an emerging agreement by major mining companies that some review of their taxation was warranted, there was a window of opportunity for the government to boost the Treasury's coffers. Recommendation 45 of the final report outlined the proposal for a 'uniform resource rent tax' for the extraction of non-renewable resources.

Politically, Treasurer Wayne Swan and Prime Minister Kevin Rudd seized on what they hoped would be a widely applauded transfer of wealth from large multi-national mining companies to the Australian taxpayer. It didn't work out that way. The resource super profits tax (RSPT) proved to be one of the most controversial pieces of Australian public policy for two decades. Industry felt aggrieved by the shape and form of the new tax and mounted an extraordinarily successful public relations campaign against it. With tele-vision commercials portraying mining companies as the heart and soul of outback Australia, the government quickly lost control of the debate. Their standing in the polls, already in trouble, dropped further and the tax debacle contributed to the decision by the party less than two months later to replace Kevin Rudd as prime minister with his deputy Julia Gillard.

What is fascinating for our purposes here is the extent to which Henry became personally synonymous with the tax proposal in the public mind. The tax review which he'd been commissioned to undertake had provided numerous recommendations. It was hardly his fault that the government had zeroed in on the resource tax alone, and indeed that the final shape of the policy did not stick exactly to the parameters Henry had outlined. Nevertheless, so vociferous was the opposition that Henry's public profile continued to grow as he was forced to defend himself from opprobrium. He faced criticism from opposition MPs suggesting that he had politicised his role by being too supportive of the government's policy.

But the publicity was by no means all bad. Henry attracted not just a high public profile, but something of a popular following in his own right. As an opinion piece in *The Age* newspaper by respected journalist Michelle Grattan put it, 'The man's everywhere, into everything—that rare creature, a public servant with a profile some politicians would kill for, a sort of bureaucratic rock star' (Grattan 2010). Others took a dimmer view, with a different opin-ion piece a month later running under the headline 'Ken Henry should get a new career—as a pollie' (Hartwich 2010).

Having had his name irrevocably attached to the RSPT, Henry was de-termined not to allow attacks on the policy proposal to go unanswered. On 18 May 2010 he gave the Treasury secretary's traditional post-budget speech to a group called 'Australian Business Economists'. In the version of the text published on the Treasury website (Henry 2010), he devoted one section of the speech directly to policy questions about the RSPT. He began by using rhetorical techniques to frame the issue as being about a resource that belongs to all Australians. 'Australia is fortunate to have an abundance of natural resources. These natural resources are assets belonging to all Australians, including Australians not yet born. Where we undercharge for the exploitation of these resources the wealth of current and future Austra-lians is eroded'. The resources tax was defended both in terms of its basis in economic theory and its potential impact in raising much-needed revenue. 'The ACC [allowance for corporate capital] recommended by the panel, and subsequently accepted by the Government in the form of the RSPT, would represent world's best practice in charging for the exploitation of non-renewable natural resources'. He then took aim at criticisms which he labelled as 'incorrect'.

> Some of the reactions to the proposed RSPT have suggested that the government bond rate is too low; that it does not reflect the return required due to the riskiness of resource investments; that it does not represent a threshold against which to measure rents; and even that it is inconsistent with basic financial market theory such as the Capital Asset Pricing Model. All of these statements are incorrect.

All the above quotes are from the published version of the text, but the media also picked up on some of the extra comments he inserted into the spoken version. As the ABC reported in its key *PM* radio programme, Henry had suggested that Australian taxpayers should not allow the mining industry to play them for 'mugs'.

> And I think there's a very sound public policy case for making sure that this tax, however we tax resources, is designed in such a way that it's not the taxpayer who ends up being the mug who finances very large streams of income going to people who are capable of taking advantage of arbitrage opportunities in financial markets. (*PM* 2010)

By the end of the RSPT debate, Henry had cemented an unusually wide public profile. The rock star was on stage. But what did his public service colleagues make of it in interviews for this project? One defended Henry, blaming the government for mishandling the tax and rendering it toxic. 'They really stuffed it up' (author interview, Australia, 2015). Another felt that the high profile Henry had garnered had not been a positive thing for him, but again laid the blame at the door of the Rudd government for having placed him in that position. 'It was him [Rudd] that dubbed it 'the Henry tax review', not Ken Henry. But Ken Henry was pulled into that and also the government's response to the global financial crisis, he was pulled into that through Rudd' (author interview, Australia, 2015). The same interviewee explained at length how this had contributed to a weakening of Treasury's authority under both Henry and his successor Martin Parkinson.

> Ken Henry came under pretty sustained attack from the opposition. They no longer trusted him, and to some extent that carried over to Martin Parkinson. And that's an example, in my view, of what happens when secretaries go out and adopt positions which are either political or on

the border of being political, and it leads to that sort of interpretation. I think that is different from the way that I was attacked because I never went out and did that. But that's for others to observe. But between the two of them, especially Ken Henry, they weakened Treasury, in my view . . . the Treasury started to lose authority and respect, I think that's the best way of putting it. And it was interpreted by the then opposition as being partisan. And to some extent Ken Henry was pushed into that by the Rudd government. (Author interview, Australia, 2015)

Some believed that Henry had pushed further than was in fact appropriate. 'In my view Ken Henry went too far on a number of instances in actually I think being public in a way that . . . was actually being party political in terms of the way he was talking about his advice' (author interview, Australia, 2015).

Leading in Public: The Washminster Way?

The Ken Henry case study demonstrates that it is possible for public service leaders in traditional Westminster-type departments to build a strong personal profile without being seen to 'break the system'. Supporters and critics alike view Henry as a fiercely effective contributor to public policy. But the case also demonstrates that a public profile brings with it the opportunity for others to offer public judgements on and critiques of the leader's performance. An assessment of Henry's career over the decades, in which he served both sides of politics, provides little evidence that he should be seen as a partisan official—far from it. But he was certainly very public, and it is that aspect which led to *perceptions* of politicisation on his part.

My argument is that—much like Comey—Henry was damned if he did and damned if he didn't. As a policy professional and a public servant of long standing it was his responsibility to serve the government of the day. That is one of the core tenets of any Westminster-type bureaucracy. He was asked by the prime minister to undertake a root-and-branch tax review. This was hardly something that he could have done in secret, even had he wanted to. Every public policy handbook in the western world now talks about the importance of consultation, communication and collaboration—of reaching out to co-produce policy. This is simply the reality of governing in public.

So if civil servants are becoming public figures, it makes sense for them to proactively build a public profile, rather than waiting to be defined by the judgements of others. Henry, like Levey in the USA, took the decision to be a policy leader; to help drive change in the national interest, whilst maintaining a steadfastly non-partisan approach. It's a very public role, and as such it attracts robust political criticism, but that need not be the same as a partisan role that renders a bureaucratic leader no better than a politician.

There are, of course, many counter-arguments to be made. It unquestionably overturns aspects of the Westminster system that have been carefully protected for over a century. The tight, indivisible relationship between ministers and civil servants, buttressed by the invisibility of the latter in the public gaze is a cornerstone of the system. This was in many ways a very effective model for the twentieth century. The problem is not that it is undesirable; simply that it has been overtaken by the realities of modern governance. Leaders are governing in public, whether we like it or not. Technological change, 24/7 news media, social media, increased transparency and accountability—all these factors militate against the continuation of business as usual in the Westminster system.

As I outlined in the previous chapter when discussing the example of Charles Trevelyan from the nineteenth century, the Westminster system is actually flexible enough to allow for these changes. It has proven itself endlessly adaptive to the needs of the day in previous generations. Moving towards a model of governing in public is only the latest manifestation of that essential flexibility. 'Washminster' is simply a useful tag for describing what that latest adaptation actually entails.

First, Washminster acknowledges that the traditional anonymity of civil servants in Westminster-system countries is no longer sustainable. It therefore looks to Washington to see how Westminster traditions might be able to adjust to the more vocal and public style of leadership apparent in America. A Washminster approach offers a 'licence to lead'. It acknowledges that if bureaucratic leaders are going to be held to account on a public stage, they should have a greater degree of freedom to define their own leadership in the public marketplace. This includes prudent engagement in a particular style of policy advocacy. Bureaucratic leaders—like Ken Henry in Australia and Stuart Levey in the USA—place ideas into the public domain, argue for them, and defend them in non-partisan and evidence-based ways.

Second, the important corollary to allowing a more public style of leadership is maintaining the twin pillars of non-partisanship and democratic control. Elected politicians remain the final decision-makers, as they must. Rhetorical bureaucrats can frame issues, urge courses of action; but they cannot overrule their political masters. We elect politicians to make decisions, and to take responsibility for them at the ballot box. They must retain the full power to dismiss ideas as they see fit. As the dismissal of James Comey by President Trump shows clearly, even the most independent of public bureaucrats answers to democratic authority. In America, the non-partisanship of public leaders is guaranteed by the Hatch Act, which prevents the making of partisan comments whilst carrying out official duties. In Australia, Canada, New Zealand and the UK the same principle is enshrined for civil servants in various pieces of legislation and codes of conduct.

A Washminster approach to rhetorical bureaucracy allows for a more robust public exchange of ideas. Senior civil servants are in an extraordinarily good position to bring reservoirs of deep policy expertise and knowledge to the surface. They have access to the kind of data and evidence that should be part of every public decision-making process and should be able to legitimately place that information into the public domain to stimulate discussion and debate. They cannot and should not directly argue with ministers in public, or take political positions. That is not their role. Their role is that of a policy entrepreneur acting within the necessary restrictions of democratic control.

What a Washminster approach means for Westminster-system countries is the likelihood of more robust public exchanges and discussions. In this era of disruption, having those extra voices involved in the debate may be no bad thing. The scene described in the opening chapter, in which the UK's former ambassador to the EU released his parting shot and was upbraided by Iain Duncan Smith, didn't break the system. Both men in fact behaved as you would expect them to behave in the public governance environment. Both put their case and defended their corner. And in the end, of course, it is up to ministers to apply whatever decisions they then choose to make. Ken Henry's public association with the mining tax was an important part of what became an enormous public debate about Australia's tax system. He provided important evidence-based arguments, backed by some rhetorical flourishes about resources belonging to future generations of Australians. Ultimately, democratically elected politicians made the decisions about whether to impose the tax, the level at which to set it, and then finally to dismantle it altogether upon a change of government. The test is not whether Henry 'won' the debate, but whether it was richer for his contribution. I would argue that it was.

5

Accounting in Public

Who should answer for the performance of our governments? Who should we blame when public policy goes pear-shaped? As Christopher Hood's work on the blame game demonstrates so comprehensively, culpability for failure is circulated amongst our leaders like a pass-the-parcel at a children's birthday party. Only in this case, when the music stops, nobody wants to be left holding the package. Yet the concept of public accountability sits at the very heart of ideas of democratic government. Somebody has to stand up in public and answer on behalf of those who rule. Over time, we have evolved at least two competing theoretical ideas on how to apportion blame amongst those unwilling to receive it.

On one hand, some modern democracies have fashioned what is theoretically a fairly simple solution to this dilemma. Elected leaders are responsible to the people who elect them for whatever is—or is not—done in their name. The buck stops on the desks of ministers, prime ministers and presidents, rather than in the lap of unelected executives. In this version, bureaucrats are simply administrative functionaries. They are accountable to their ministers for how they do their job, but that's where it ends. This is Weberian in the certainty with which it parcels out responsibility, but distinctly un-Weberian in its belief that democratically elected leaders have a chance of reining in bureaucratic power.

The second version casts the net more widely. It suggests that anybody on the public payroll has a responsibility to the public. They must be transparent and accountable because they have a responsibility to serve not just the needs of their political masters, but also the wider public good. They serve the parliament or Congress, and through it the people. As such, their actions must be as open to scrutiny as those of elected representatives. All have made the choice to accept a role in public service, and that brings with it a wider responsibility. This may include searching for 'public value' on behalf of the taxpayer, or answering publicly for how they have made the decisions that cause consternation amongst the public.

Westminster and Washington represent the two ends of this spectrum of theory and practice. The long-running Westminster convention has been that civil servants are an indivisible part of the executive government of the day. They have no constitutional identity separate from the political masters they serve. The US model has by instinct, design and tradition incorporated a much greater public accountability. With a true separation of powers comes a more consistent desire by Congress to question all parts of a presidential administration with gusto. Increasingly leaders in both systems are adopting a higher public profile, and are finding themselves held to a more public form of accountability, whether they like it or not.

The Traditional Westminster Position

> [I]n our system a political minister must face the music in parliament; that is his duty and his privilege. He must take responsibility for his department and its administration . . . Civil servants ought not to be dragged into parliamentary debate . . . it would be deplorable to have their names and views bandied about in Parliament, thus involving the civil servant much against his will in party political controversy. (Sir Robert Menzies [Menzies 1970, 151–2])

In 1970, the former Australian prime minister Sir Robert Menzies published a series of political essays—*The Measure of the Years*—in which he warned against any moves to draw public servants into a more direct type of parliamentary accountability. His argument that public servants should not be called before parliamentarians and compelled to answer questions re-stated what were considered fundamentals of the Westminster system. Ministers, not public servants, provided the public face of government. The doctrine of ministerial responsibility required ministers to answer to parliament and the public for the administration of their departments. Under the traditional public service bargain, a permanent and non-partisan public service would loyally and anonymously carry out the wishes of the government of the day (see Hondeghem 2011). It was not their job to publicly answer for policy outcomes—good or bad (Mulgan 2002, 47).

Things have changed. In part through their appearances in front of parliamentary committees, contemporary public service leaders have become part of the public face of modern government (see Weller 2001, 150–4; Mulgan 2012). Through processes like the Senate Estimates hearings in Australia, opposition politicians now probe for ways to embarrass ministers by embarrassing the public servants who serve them. Under the pressures of a 24/7 news cycle, media outlets use the testimony of public servants as part of their reporting of government performance. Public servants who were once the anonymous instruments of democratically elected governments have become yet another set of players in the very public blame games that characterise the processes of modern governance. A system geared for governing in private now governs in public—leaving practitioners stuck between old conventions and new realities.

Many appearances before parliamentary committees display elements of drama, involving 'clashes' between public servants and MPs that are then amplified by being reported in the press. In pursuing a form of accountability that is both public and dramatic, legislatures across the Westminster world have created the conditions in which public servants can find themselves drawn into the very 'party political controversies' that Menzies was warning against. The fierceness of the political questions raised by this is well captured in a 2011 exchange between former UK Cabinet Secretary Gus O'Donnell and the elected head of the House of Commons Public Accounts Committee (PAC), Margaret Hodge. Hodge recounts the incident in her 2016 memoir *Called to Account* in which she describes how O'Donnell had written to her criticising the PAC's questioning of Anthony Inglese from HM Revenue and Customs (HMRC) over a tax arrangement HMRC had reached with Goldman Sachs. She quotes from O'Donnell's letter at length, in which he wrote,

> First, when questioning him you set out—in clear terms—a view held by your committee that civil servants are directly accountable to Parliament. I disagree strongly with this as a general principle. I am sure you would agree that, to maintain their impartiality, it is essential that civil servants remain accountable to ministers, who are in turn accountable to parliament (2016, 72).

Hodge goes on to reflect that O'Donnell 'seemed unaware of present-day demands for accountability and transparency that, in my view, must trump age-old conventions on the accountability of civil servants'.

Oversight committees take different forms in different jurisdictions. In the United Kingdom, they are generally called 'select committees' and are comprised of MP's from all major parties, and the chair of each committee is elected by a parliamentary vote. Each committee generally 'shadows' the work of a government department, scrutinising the implementation of education policy, or transport policy, for example. There are also several committees that have a more overarching role, to examine government spending (the Public Accounts Committee), and the way government is run (Public Administration Committee). These UK structures are mirrored in most Westminster-system countries, with local variations. In Australia, where the upper house is an elected chamber, Senate committees gain a high public profile through their hearings into decision-making and spending in individual policy areas.

In all jurisdictions, oversight committees remain an inherently political setting. As one Australian former permanent secretary noted about appearing in front of Senate estimates committees, 'How do you protect yourself? Well, you can't really protect yourself that well because it's a political attack' (author interview, Australia, 2015). Accountability, and the form it should take, is an inherently contested concept that means different things in different contexts (Bovens et al. 2008; 't Hart and Wille 2006). One stream in the literature suggests that public accountability mechanisms should provide the conditions for bureaucratic 'learning', encouraging best practice public administration for the future. Bovens, Schillemans and 't Hart argue that the characteristics of a 'learning' type of accountability have to encourage reflection and debate, but in a 'safe' environment where people can be open without fearing the consequences (2008, 233). Even if this is desirable, there is very little evidence that this is how public accountability mechanisms are currently structured. As one New Zealand leader reminisced, 'I was once there when a member of the opposition was asking a long and really critical question of another chief executive, and one of the other committee members said, "Is this a question, or just an insult?"' (author interview, New Zealand, 2016).

Committees bring a sense of drama to the business of public accountability. There is a strong and still-developing literature on the ways in which policymaking processes can be seen and understood as 'dramaturgy' ('t Hart 1993; Hajer 2005a; 2005b; 2006; Freeman and Peck 2007; Peck et al. 2009). Hajer's series of articles in the area argue that the dramaturgy of policymaking contains all the aspects needed in any meaningful piece of theatre: scripting, staging, setting and performance (2005a, 631). Hajer uses dramaturgy theory to examine the mixture of formal and informal policy processes involved in the making of land use and planning decisions (e.g., Hajer 2005a; 2005b). In particular, public engagement and discussion of planning decisions is presented as part of an elaborate staging of consultation in which actors can feel empowered or marginalised by the part they are allowed to play.

As the earlier work of Austin (1962) and Edelman (1964) demonstrates, elements of symbolism, performance and dramaturgy are present in most political processes, and parliamentary committees are no exception. In theory of course—in both Westminster and Washington—the civil service stands impartially aside from 'political' contests. In practice, the processes of public accountability before oversight committees insert public executives into the middle of hotly contested political disputes. The fact that these debates are very much public in nature can create perceptions of engagement in political debate, even if in reality bureaucratic leaders are trying very hard to avoid becoming engaged. Dramaturgy theory provides a different way of examining the formalised accountability processes of committee hearings, as political contests in which there are winners and losers. It draws out the inherent tension between the democratic authority of elected representatives to question the executive and the overriding duty of administrators to loyally support the government of the day.

By seeing committees as a 'setting' through the lens of dramaturgy theory, the format of this institutionalised process of public accountability becomes more apparent. The setting is inherently adversarial: one in which elected members adopt the role of interrogators of reluctant bureaucrats who are presumed to be withholding vital information from the public about the failures and missteps of the government. It's a performance in which the script is constructed as an opportunity for the people's representatives to discipline the people's servants. Like students summoned to the principal's office, bureaucrats know that they are coming to be scolded by their elected masters. When ministers appear before a committee of their fellow MPs, they appear as equals; as democratically elected representatives themselves they have no need to kowtow. Equally in Washington, cabinet-level appointees are disinclined to be pushed around by members of Congress.

For bureaucratic leaders the power dynamic is different. They are being called before a committee that is trying to either attach blame to them for administrative failures, or recruit them as accomplices to shift blame onto the government that they serve. Neither outcome is one that bureaucratic leaders can easily embrace. As one British interviewee noted when asked if they chose their words carefully in front of oversight committees,

Well, you usually choose your words carefully because otherwise they'll hang you. You know, when you're up against, not so much select committees, they're fully house-trained, but the Public Accounts Committee, which is red in tooth and claw, the risk—you'd be choosing your words carefully because basically, they're an adversarial process. They're out to get you and you're out not to be got. (Author interview, UK, 2015)

One of the limitations of dramaturgy theory is that it can't reveal everything about the institutionalised factors that may be driving the way that actors interpret the part they are to play. A second line of theory—'blame game' theory—provides further insights into what leaders are trying to achieve from their appearances in front of oversight committees. Blame game theory as derived from the work of Christopher Hood (2010; see also Weaver 1986) suggests that looking at the working of bureaucracies through the prism of blame avoidance can help to explain the structure and behaviours of public institutions and the actors within them. Hood identifies three types of blame avoidance strategy. These are 'presentational' strategies that are about the spinning or framing of information to present it in the best possible light; 'agency' strategies that involve organising a public agency in such a way that responsibility doesn't settle in any one place or on any one person; and 'policy' strategies which see decision-makers adhere to strict policy processes that remove their discretion and therefore provide the defence, if something goes wrong, that they were 'just following policy'. Faced with the need to deflect or parry blame attribution attempts, public servants appearing before parliamentary committees embrace various of these strategies.

To examine the workings of oversight committees as theatrical vehicles for the public attribution of blame, I look at two aspects: First, what do people actually say in committee hearings? What lines of questioning are employed by committee members, and are they targeting political or administrative matters? And second, what does the media make of what was said? How are bureaucratic appearances portrayed in the press—as politically-charged theatre, or as part of the normal business of public administration?

To analyse these questions through a comparative lens, I undertake three in-depth case studies examining high-profile administrative failures in three countries—the USA, the United Kingdom and Australia. The first case centres on the revelation in 2015 that agents of the US Drug Enforcement Administration (DEA) had been involved in 'sex parties' in Colombia, financed by drug cartels. The second case is the 2012–13 inquiry by the Public Accounts

Committee (PAC) in the United Kingdom into the failed tender process for the West Coast rail franchise. The third case is the 2010 inquiry by the Australian Senate Standing Committee on the Environment, Communications and the Arts into the Rudd government's Home Insulation Program (HIP).

The cases chosen are illustrative of a spectrum on how much oversight committee investigations are driven by administrative or political questions. They are not intended to be representative in a country-specific sense. In other words, I do not claim that select committees in the United Kingdom always operate in the way that the PAC did in the West Coast rail case, or that Australian Senate committees always operate in the way that they did in the HIP case. Rather, the cases show the different ways in which committees can operate, illustrating the breadth of the spectrum that is available to oversight committees. They are test sites—drill holes into practice—revealing the kind of skills in public accountability that public executives across western democracies now need.

The key challenges in using committees of the legislature to hold public executives to account centre on three aspects. First, does it contribute to the perceived politicisation of administrators, by drawing them into political debates? Second, does it diminish democratic responsibility, by holding officials to account rather than elected politicians? And third, does it actually aid in establishing accountability, or does it simply encourage the blame avoidance behaviours identified by Hood (2010)? All three aspects are discussed with reference to each case, before moving to a more general analysis to finish the chapter.

The Cases

USA: DRUG ENFORCEMENT ADMINISTRATION

In April 2015, the Drug Enforcement Administration (DEA) found itself placed under the congressional microscope. Specifically, agency head Michele Leonhart faced a grilling from members of the House Oversight Committee on the alleged misbehaviour of her agents in Colombia. A report the previous month by Justice Department Inspector-General Michael Horowitz had alleged that multiple DEA agents had over a number of years attended sex parties—with media sources confirming that they'd taken place in Colombia, paid for by drug cartels.

In keeping with US traditions of congressional hearings, the questioning was sharp, direct and very confrontational. It was unapologetically aggressive. The political target for blame was not the president or the attorney general, but rather the head of the DEA herself. She was questioned not as a go-between, but as the responsible decision-maker in her own right. In challenging an answer, Committee Chair Jason Chaffetz said, 'You can sit here and cry a pretty picture about how deplorable it is, but your actions suggest otherwise because there was not the consequence that should have happened' (Committee on Oversight 2015, 9). Michele Leonhart fielded questions as the official representative of her organisation, and by extension as the ranking officer for the administration as a whole. In other words, she was held responsible not as a neutral functionary, but as the appointed representative of the president. As Chaffetz put it in his opening statement, 'Based on the testimony we have read from the DEA Administrator, she says she doesn't have the power to simply fire these people. I don't buy it. The American public doesn't buy it . . . this administration, this DEA Administrator, has got to hold those people accountable and get them out of there' (Committee on Oversight 2015, 3).

Interestingly in comparison with most hearings in Westminster-system settings, members of Congress from the Democratic party were just as forthcoming as Republican members in their criticism of the administrator's leadership. For example, Congresswoman Stacey Plaskett dug aggressively into questions of accountability. 'Well, that's interesting that you say that it's your job to deal with the discipline because you've just stated earlier to the chairman that you don't have any say over the discipline. So which one is it? Do you or don't you have say over the discipline of those individuals?' (Committee on Oversight 2015, 11). In Westminster-system cases, MPs from the governing party are more likely to ask less aggressive questions, leaving opposition MPs to look for ways to use the evidence of civil servants to embarrass ministers in the elected government. Civil servants become a proxy target. In Washington, by contrast, unelected senior bureaucrats are attacked individually and collectively as members of the administration. The doctrine of ministerial responsibility that at least in theory functions in Westminster contexts to shield civil servants has no parallel in the US system, where even sub-cabinet-level members of the administration must answer for their stewardship as part of the administration as a whole.

During the hearing, aspects of all three of Hood's strategies for blame avoidance were in evidence. At a presentational level, Leonhart's opening statement tried to broaden the gaze by placing the example of the alleged misbehaviour of agents in Colombia in the context of the wider work the DEA does around the globe.

DEA personnel located in over 300 offices around the world, including 67 foreign countries, are doing extraordinary work under often difficult and dangerous circumstances. And this includes the investigation and arrest of leaders of the most violent and sophisticated drug cartels in the world. Unfortunately, poor choices made by a few individuals can tarnish the reputation and overshadow the outstanding work being done at the DEA. (Committee on Oversight 2015, 5–6)

At an agency and policy level, members of the committee were clearly frustrated at the apparent contradiction that Leonhart was the head of the DEA, and yet did not have the power to fire people. In other words, the organisation of the agency—as required by the civil service rules—was set up to stop the administrator interfering in disciplinary matters. As Leonhart stressed in her opening witness statement, '[C]onsistent with the protections afforded to employees under civil service laws, I do not have ability to change the imposed penalties' (Committee on Oversight 2015, 6). Committee Chair Chaffetz suggested that disciplining the agents by forcing them to take paid leave 'sounds like a vacation to me' (Committee on Oversight 2015, 3).

Some, like Congressman John Mica, accepted Leonhart's assertion that she didn't have the powers that she needed. 'She doesn't have the right to summarily fire people. She has to go through a process, Merit System Protection, the protections of Title V, a Federal act created by Congress' (Committee on Oversight 2015, 13). Congressman Stephen Lynch was less willing to let the DEA off with a process defence. 'I think the problem now is we're protecting these people. That's what's happening in your agency . . . I think there's a mentality here that needs to be extricated root and branch from the DEA operation' (Committee on Oversight 2015, 14). Administrator Leonhart took 'offense' at that assertion, insisting that 'I am trying to fix the system. I can't fire. I'm trying to fix a system.' (Committee on Oversight 2015, 14)

The media response to both the initial report released by the inspector-general for the Department of Justice, and then to the committee hearing itself, was electric. Here was a story that had all the classic elements for a political storm: sex; drugs; misuse of taxpayer funds; unclear lines of bureaucratic accountability—this was a great set of ingredients to work with. The *Washington Post* reported the contents of the statement released by the committee after its hearings. 'After over a decade of serving in top leadership positions at DEA, Administrator Leonhart has been woefully unable to change or positively influence the pervasive "good old boy" culture that exists throughout the agency' (reported by Hicks 2015).

The focus of the media reporting in accountability terms was squarely on Michele Leonhart, with calls for her to resign or be sacked. There was little attempt to widen the circle of accountability to draw in either the president or his cabinet members. Whilst many reports carried Leonhart's arguments in her own defence that she did not in fact have the powers that she needed, the headlines universally called for her to take the blame. Associated Press reported that '[t]he White House declined to give a vote of confidence' to Leonhart following the hearing (Daly 2015), stressing that the president had 'high expectations' of the DEA leadership. CBS evening news seized on the confrontational nature of the committee, describing it as a 'sometimes-explosive hearing', describing the 'sex parties' and noting the absurdity that Attorney General Holder had felt the need to issue a memo clarifying that employees were not allowed to use departmental funds to procure prostitutes (Pelley and Reid 2015).

In the week following the hearing, the attorney general announced that Leonhart would be retiring as DEA head. The statement made no reference to the committee hearing and the issue of agents allegedly hiring prostitutes (Department of Justice 2015), but the media had no difficulty in asserting a connection. The *New York Times* headline was 'Michele Leonhart, Head of D.E.A., to retire over handling of sex scandal' (Davis 2015), and the UK's *Independent* asserted, 'DEA chief Michele Leonhart expected to resign over "sex parties" scandal' (Guion 2015).

UNITED KINGDOM: WEST COAST RAIL CASE

In the United Kingdom, the West Coast rail franchise bidding process had to be abandoned in 2012 after major administrative mistakes were made, costing taxpayers millions of pounds and leading to direct criticism of the Transport Department. Virgin Rail Group—the existing operator of the West Coast line—lost the tender for the new franchise to the preferred bidder FirstGroup in 2012. Within months, the award of the franchise to FirstGroup was withdrawn after errors were found in how the Transport Department had run the process (see Jupe 2013). The PAC instituted an inquiry and took oral evidence on 13 December 2012, when the permanent secretary of the Department of Transport and the director general (corporate) appeared in front of the committee to answer for the alleged mistakes of their department. The PAC brought down its final report in February 2013.

On several occasions during the oral evidence, questions were asked about how much the failure of the franchising process could be related to the cuts imposed on the civil service by the Chancellor George Osborne. In other words, could some political blame be sheeted home to the government of the day? Labour MP Fiona Mactaggert directed a question on the topic to the permanent secretary, Philip Rutnam.

> Q115 FIONA MACTAGGART: Did you get the basics wrong because you were told that you had to cut spending—that you could not have the right resources to do this? Is that one of the reasons why you got the basics wrong? (House of Commons 2013: Ev 13)

In answer, the secretary would only acknowledge that resourcing issues contributed to a challenging environment, but that the main reasons had concerned effective management and leadership.

The issue was taken up again later during the hearing by Labour MP Austin Mitchell, when discussing what had caused confusion over which senior officer in the department had been responsible for the project during a crucial three-month period. 'Is that anything to do with the heavy turnover of staff, because of the requirement to cut your staff down?' (House of Commons 2013: Ev 16) The committee chair, Labour MP Margaret Hodge, joined the exchange by asking, 'Did you not get financial advisers because of the cuts?' After being pressed, Secretary Rutnam did concede that '[t]he environment in relation to using external advisers after the election was clearly to avoid them if you can'. Satisfied that this supported his point, Austin Mitchell thanked him for his answer and said, 'Another triumph for the Osborne cuts, it seems to me' (House of Commons 2013: Ev 17).

The question of ministerial responsibility for the bureaucratic failings of the department was conspicuous largely by its absence, and at no point in the discussion was it suggested that it was up to ministers to resign or accept ultimate responsibility for the errors that had been made. The committee was focused on pursuing the nature of the administrative mistakes and who might be responsible at a departmental level. There was some discussion of whether the department had in fact appropriately briefed ministers, and of the fact that the mistakes had caused considerable public embarrassment at the political level. Chair Margaret Hodge engaged with the department's director general for corporate matters, Claire Moriarty, about whether ministers had been made aware of all the details they should have.

> CLARE MORIARTY: I am speaking from recollection because I didn't see the submission at the time, but the submission was similar to the papers that came to the Board Investment and Commercial

Committee. From recollection, I think that the information about the relative growth in the bid compared with the achieved growth in recent years wasn't in the submission.

CHAIR: That was in?

CLARE MORIARTY: That wasn't in.

CHAIR: Was not in or was in?

CLARE MORIARTY: Was not, as far as I recall.

Q34 CHAIR: Goodness. (House of Commons 2013: Ev 4)

Conservative MP Stewart Jackson pointed out later in the hearing that ministers had not received the full information they should have because of the departmental secretary's exclusion from the decision-making process. He emphasised that ministers had suffered 'serious reputational damage' by being left 'out of the loop' (House of Commons 2013: Ev 14). The question essentially was about who was responsible for having embarrassed ministers, rather than whether ministers should bear ultimate responsibility for the mistakes made.

Hood's characterisation of the 'blame game' as it relates to 'agency strategies' is focused on the design of an organisation in such a way that it makes it difficult to pin down blame—to provide a 'buck stops here' sign for any particular desk (Hood 2010: 67). The transcript from the West Coast rail hearing shows that some such 'agency strategies' were in evidence. For example, PAC members were intrigued by arrangements that meant that no one Single Responsible Owner (SRO) had carriage or oversight of the project from the outset. This resulted in a period of confusion when it was not clear which of two possible SROs was in charge. The Department's secretary and the committee chair discussed the point in one exchange, with the chair asking Rutnam whether he now acknowledged that the internal divided responsibility had been 'mad'. When pressed, Rutnam conceded that he did not 'intend to carry on with that structure in the future' (House of Commons 2013: Ev 3).

There was also a focus from both Rutnam and Moriarty on collectivising responsibility for errors across the multitude of bodies within the department that had played a part in the project. These included the 'Contract Award Committee' and the 'Board Investment and Commercial Committee' (House of Commons 2013: Ev 1), legal officers and mid-level staff who were 'trying to do the best they could' (House of Commons 2013: Ev 16) but hadn't notified their superior officers in time of the challenges being faced. By spreading the blame, the sense of individual responsibility was dispersed across a wide group of actors, making it harder to hold any one person to account.

Whilst the hearings and proceedings of the parliament are of course a matter of public record, in reality the impact of parliamentary committee hearings on public debate is largely mediated by the level of press attention that they attract. During the course of the oral hearings before the PAC on 13 December 2012, newswire services filed stories on the unfolding evidence of the overall costs to the taxpayer of government failure. For example, the Press Association National Newswire posted a story under the headline 'Franchise fiasco bill "could grow"', quoting the permanent secretary of the Transport Department, Philip Rutnam, as saying that he couldn't guarantee that there wouldn't be further calls on the public purse (Woodman 2012). The story described 'stormy scenes' at the hearing.

The Times also reported the tenor of the exchanges between the witnesses and MPs on the committee as 'angry', and on how the Department's leaders had 'admitted' to financial waste and getting the 'basics wrong' (Sherman 2012). *The Daily Telegraph* noted Rutnam's judgement that the department had in this case been 'penny wise' and 'pound foolish' (Thomas 2012). None of these articles linked the testimony of the civil servants back to the ministerial responsibility of the appropriate minister. Rather, the focus of coverage was on the evidence of the civil servants in their own right as accepting the blame themselves for the maladministration of this particular project. It was a debate about public administration rather than a debate about 'political' responsibility.

The tenor of the coverage remained the same when the PAC published its report into the matter on 26 February 2013. For example, *The Guardian* described the report as saying that 'the aborted west coast franchise award was down to a "complete lack of commonsense" from "blinkered, rushed" senior officials' (Topham 2013). *The Daily Telegraph* also placed civil servants front and centre, writing that the 'PAC report is more critical about the lack of leadership and the failure of civil servants to learn from mistakes in other projects' (Gribben 2013). *The Daily Mirror*, under the headline 'Lack of common sense that cost us £50 million: Fury at West Coast rail farce', focused on the 'blinkered' approach of civil servants, and quoted a union leader as saying, 'They could not be trusted to run a whelk stall let alone multi-billion pound contracts' (Ellis 2013). In Liverpool, the *Echo* bucked the trend by quoting an opposition MP demanding a degree of ministerial responsibility for what had occurred, suggesting that ministers should not 'hide behind civil servants' (Williamson 2013). *The Financial*

Times also suggested that the report 'pointed the finger of blame at ministers' (Odell 2013).

Overall, the majority of the media focus was on the alleged incompetence of civil servants, rather than the lack of appropriate oversight or responsibility from ministers: terms such as 'blinkered' and 'lack of common sense' were directed not at them, but squarely at their departmental officials. In other words, media coverage very much reflected the committee's view of the proceedings, not that of the civil servants. The PAC, through its lines of questioning, provided a framing narrative for what had gone wrong, and the media embraced and amplified that narrative.

AUSTRALIA: HOME INSULATION PROGRAM

In Australia, the HIP was one part of a suite of fiscal stimulus measures adopted by the Rudd government in response to the onset of the global financial crisis. Introduced in 2009, in broad terms the scheme's stated goals were to stimulate the economy by providing large rebates to Australians willing to install roof insulation, and simultaneously to improve energy efficiency in Australian homes. Failures in regulation and the fast-paced implementation of the scheme were widely criticised, as at least four insulation installers lost their lives and poor installation practices led to house fires (see Lewis 2012). In October 2009, the Australian Senate Standing Committee on the Environment, Communications and the Arts set up an inquiry into the 'Energy Efficient Homes Package'. The committee took five days of oral evidence, predominantly in Canberra, and questioned at length the public servants who had been involved with the design and implementation of the scheme, from across a broad range of government departments and agencies.

There was a consistent relationship throughout the committee's hearings between lines of questioning and the political elements of decision-making by ministers. Committee members were willing to push public servants for details and opinions, and public servants were prepared to stand their ground and refuse to answer if they felt a question related to matters 'going to the provision of advice' to ministers. For example, an assistant secretary from the Department of Prime Minister and Cabinet refused to answer a particular question in detail 'given the traditions around cabinet in confidence and material going to cabinet' (Official Committee Hansard 2010c, 75).

On some occasions, witnesses were unsuccessful in their attempts to stand their ground, as the following exchange illustrates

SENATOR BARNETT: When did you first become aware of the
government's plan to put together a $41 million rescue package?

MR GRIEW: I think the question you are asking me goes to the
provision of advice that we give to the government—

SENATOR BARNETT: No, with respect—

SENATOR BIRMINGHAM: It is a fairly direct question.

SENATOR BARNETT: Mr Griew, with respect, that is a direct breach
of Senate standing orders. I am asking you for the date—not the
advice you gave to the government, the cabinet or the minister—
when you first became aware of the government's plans to put
together a $41 million rescue package. Can you answer that
question, please? (Official Committee Hansard 2010b, 43)

The witness was pressed and went on to provide an answer. In a second
instance, Senator Barnett accepted that the witness had a legitimate right
not to answer a question on the policy options that were given to a minister
because of the accepted convention against revealing policy advice (Official
Committee Hansard 2010b, 45).

Whilst seldom explicitly raised, the question of ministerial responsibility
was right at the heart of the committee's concerns. Their sharpest questioning was on what ministers were told and when and how they responded.
The committee was probing to establish whether any conclusions could be
drawn about any possible dereliction of duty—either by relevant ministers
or the prime minister. In a sense they were looking for evidence that could
be used politically against the executive, rather than seeking public service-
based explanations for alleged administrative incompetence.

There were long lines of questioning regarding a risk assessment report
on the programme that had been prepared by external consultants Minter
Ellison, and when and if ministers had been made aware of the contents of
that report (see Official Committee Hansard 2010a, 4–42). These extended
into questions of how often ministers were briefed, and whether ministers
had been proactive in asking for briefings.

SENATOR BIRMINGHAM: I want to know the minister's response to
this now. I know you have continually updated him. I want to know
whether he just sat there like a mute or how he responded. Did he
ask for more information? (Official Committee Hansard 2010a, 35)

The Committee was particularly keen to establish whether there had
been any ministerial level directives to rush programme implementation.

SENATOR BIRMINGHAM: What instructions about deadlines did the Prime Minister or Parliamentary Secretary Arbib give you at the commencement of the program?

MR MRDAK: The Prime Minister publicly made clear at the time the urgency of implementing the fiscal stimulus measures, and ministers have reiterated that through the course of the program. The time frames were set out in the National Partnership Agreement, which was agreed by COAG, as Ms Beauchamp has outlined, and the government was very clear about the time frames for the delivery of the program.

SENATOR BIRMINGHAM: Did the Prime Minister ever tell you that there should be no change to any of the announced time lines?

MR MRDAK: No, not explicitly. We worked through the time frames that were provided by government to implement the program. (Official Committee Hansard 2010b, 10)

The apparent focus of the Senate committee members was less on attributing blame to particular departments—although there were elements of that—than on finding information with which they could sheet home political blame to the government for mistakes made. Nevertheless, in providing information on what ministers had said and done at various times, public servants also exhibited some of the blame avoidance strategies outlined by Hood. For example, there were frequent clarifications provided about the fact that different officers were unable to comment on particular things because they had changed role since the events in question. This fits broadly within the 'agency strategies' identified by Hood that enable the avoidance of blame through consistent position churn (Hood 2010, 19). Senators were certainly acutely aware of the issue, as the following exchange illustrates.

SENATOR BIRMINGHAM: I assume Mr Hoffman and others were involved on a day-to-day basis.

MR HOFFMAN: Not personally. I took up my current role on 21 December.

SENATOR BIRMINGHAM: Okay. That is always convenient.

MR HOFFMAN: It is just a fact.

SENATOR BIRMINGHAM: The moving sands of the Public Service. A couple of times today we have hit this issue of changing faces. (Official Committee Hansard 2010c, 83)

The media coverage of the hearings largely followed the political focus of much of the questioning. The overwhelming focus of pieces—both in newspapers and on television news bulletins—was on Minister Garrett and his handling of matters, including the Minter Ellison report which the Senate committee was portrayed as having 'extracted' from Minister Garrett's department at the hearings. Some of the early pieces filed on the same day as the committee evidence was being heard did focus more heavily on the actual evidence being presented by the departmental secretary, Robyn Kruk. The ABC filed a piece noting the secretary's apology to the families of installers who died during the programme (ABC 2010), and AAP filed a piece under the heading 'Bureaucrats kept damning report from Garrett' (Alexander 2010).

The second day of hearings (26 February) saw a similar range of preemptive and then evaluative media coverage. AAP carried a story under the headline 'Top PM officials to front Senate insulation inquiry', introducing Coordinator-General Glenys Beauchamp as 'the bureaucrat responsible for overseeing the government's economic stimulus rollout' and declaring that she 'heads the list of public servants giving evidence' (AAP 2010a). The following day's newspaper coverage focused on the demotion of the responsible minister—Peter Garret—with a reshuffle of his portfolio responsibilities (Coorey 2010; Breusch 2010). *The Canberra Times* reported on the evidence of one senior bureaucrat—Employment and Workplace Relations Associate Secretary Robert Griew—in relation to whether unions had expressed safety concerns about the programme. But once again, the focus was not so much on Griew as on the political culpability of the Rudd government in having ignored the warnings that unions insisted had been given (Beeby 2010a).

The committee's final report was released on 15 July, and its call for a royal commission inquiry into the insulation scheme immediately dominated headlines. For example, AAP began one piece with 'Environment Protection Minister Peter Garrett has dismissed calls for a royal commission into the government's botched insulation scheme as a political campaign by the opposition' (AAP 2010b) and ABC news carried a story headlined 'Senate urges royal commission into insulation scheme' (Kirk 2010). The following day's newspapers also focused on the political dimension of the call for royal commission, emphasising questions of political, rather than departmental or bureaucratic, responsibility for the failures and shortcomings of the scheme.

The Advertiser quoted Minister Garrett as saying, 'There's nothing new that has come through in this recommendation that hasn't already been comprehensively addressed by the government' (*Advertiser* 2010). In Melbourne, *The Age* ran with the opposition's promise to hold a royal commission if the government did not, and quoted the committee chair's frustrations at departments keeping information secret and ministers not appearing before the committee (Harrison 2010). *The Canberra Times* wrote, 'A Senate inquiry into the bungled $2.5 billion home insulation program has called for a royal commission to grill Prime Minister Julia Gillard, senior ministers and top bureaucrats over the scheme's "gross and systematic failures"' (Beeby 2010b).

In summary, in the Australian case, media attention was strongly focused on the political rather than the administrative lessons and repercussions to flow from the HIP. Blame was sheeted home to ministers rather than bureaucratic leaders. The debates over the report occurred in the realm of political point-scoring, rather than assessing bureaucratic accountability for any of the errors made. As in the British case, this suggests that the media embraced the framing narrative of the majority of committee members, and amplified that story through press headlines. The committee had focused on who should be held politically responsible, and the media followed that focus and framed their stories more around alleged failings of political leadership than administrative error on the part of public servants.

The Dramaturgy of Accountability

The three case studies demonstrate that there is a wide spectrum of current practice in the questioning of officials by oversight committees and in subsequent press coverage. In the Australian case, questioning centred on what ministers knew and when and how they responded to unfolding events. Questioning of public service witnesses—whilst leading to some tense exchanges—focused on identifying which ministers could or should be held politically responsible for mistakes. There was little direct criticism of public service processes as opposed to political outcomes. The Australian media largely reflected that focus in its reporting. Public servants were not directly blamed or held accountable, and their evidence was utilised only in so far as it helped to shed light on questions of ministerial responsibility.

By contrast, in the United Kingdom case the focus of questioning was squarely on administrative structures and processes and how they contributed to the failure of the tender process. Civil servants were publicly upbraided by MPs on the PAC, with little mention of their ministerial masters. Press reporting followed the committee's lead. Criticisms—clear, sharp and personal—were levelled at the Transport Department and its bureau-cratic leadership. There was also some focus on how a further repetition of such mistakes in the future could be avoided. It was—at both the PAC and the media level—an exercise in administrative rather than political accountability.

Similarly in the United States case, in the very different institutional set-ting of a congressional oversight committee, the focus was on the leader-ship skills of the public executives being questioned. Specifically, Michele Leonhart was put under the spotlight of sustained and direct criticism, of the way that she was leading her organisation, and for her alleged failures to appropriately discipline DEA agents. It is hard to imagine a parallel in a Westminster committee where individual civil servants would be held so directly and aggressively accountable—although the West Coast Rail case comes close in some aspects. The true extent of Leonhart's accountability was demonstrated by her subsequent swift retirement—taking personal re-sponsibility for the wider failings of her organisation in a way that a minister would in theory (although seldom in practice) be expected to do under Westminster conventions.

There are of course a number of variables that could be contributing to practice here. In the United Kingdom, the PAC is a committee with a long tradition of fierce and largely non-partisan scrutiny of government depart-ments. It is known for going after bureaucrats and ministers in a piercing fashion. In Australia, the Senate committee hearings into the roof insula-tion scheme were instituted in an election year, against the background of an opposition narrative criticising the government for alleged waste and undue haste in the implementation of its fiscal stimulus measures. It was an environment in which fierce partisan disagreement over the home insulation programme dominated political debate. The cost in terms of lives lost and money allegedly misspent had already been heavily covered in the media before the committee's investigation, setting the context for the committee to seek to attribute political blame for these failures. This context may help to explain the political focus of the questioning as against the administrative focus in the United Kingdom example.

Equally, in the US case, the story about the misbehaviour of DEA agents had broken several weeks before, when the report of the inspector-general for the Department of Justice first landed. This set the stage for a hearing that stood little chance of being about policy or procedural learning and inevitably became rather an exercise in ritual humiliation. Stoked by the opportunity for elected representatives to express bipartisan moral outrage, the reality that Leonhart did not in fact have the power to fire agents was an inconvenient truth that could not assuage the avenging anger of committee members.

In terms of dramaturgy theory, the committee hearings in all three cases can be said to have served their purpose. They were set-piece adversarial plays in which the people's democratically elected representatives could flex their muscle against non-elected public servants. They created clear stories, with well-defined 'heroes and villains and innocent victims' (Stone 2012, 158) for public consumption. There were two 'scripts' (Hajer 2005a) that the committee members promulgated. Script one, most prevalent in the Australian case, positioned ministers as the guilty parties and public servants as proxies being used to shield their political masters. Script two, in evidence in both the UK and US cases, positioned bureaucrats as the guilty party that had to be disciplined—and be publicly seen to be disciplined—by the elected representatives of the people. It was administrators more than democratically elected leaders that were presented as having let the public down. The effect of the committee hearings in questioning senior bureaucrats was to embarrass them—and in a public way. By doing so in a setting of adversarial theatre, committees were facilitating accountability to the wider electorate—through the amplifying effect of the media. When viewed through the lens of dramaturgy theory, what on the surface appears to be an exercise in public leaders being subjected to a form of direct accountability to the legislature becomes instead a public act of penance intended for a much wider audience. As one Canadian interviewee reflected about such hearings, 'I don't have any pleasant memories of my last appearances before [a] parliamentary committee. They were not about information at all, they were theatre by and large by all sides' (author interview, Canada, 2015).

The media played their part in the script by amplifying the idea that bureaucrats were on trial. They took their lead from the way that the committee's politicians were framing events. Terms like 'grilling' and 'fiasco' were dotted liberally through the press coverage in the United Kingdom, and the judgmental words of MPs quoted with approval. The committee reports and statements in all three cases also provided the certainty of a 'judgement'—a finding on who should be 'blamed' for what had occurred. The blame avoidance strategies identified by Hood (2010) were certainly prevalent, and were to some extent successful in dispersing blame as widely as possible. In the United Kingdom case, the blame landed on the collective desks of the civil servants leading the Transport Department—so no one single head had to roll. In the Australian case, it settled on the shoulders of the political executive, but did so via the shoulders of bureaucratic leaders having to bear the brunt of the Senate's anger first. In the US case, of course, Leonhart was unable to make her defence of a lack of procedural power stick. As a blame shield it was simply insufficient to disperse responsibility away from her alone. Further media studies in the future will help to reveal whether media coverage of bureaucrats appearing before oversight committees has changed over time, and whether this has affected public perceptions of the degree to which such bureaucrats should be held accountable.

As the designated 'villains' of the piece, and on the wrong end of a power imbalance in the setting of a committee hearing, bureaucratic leaders reacted by protecting themselves as best they could without compromising the administration they served. Earlier work by Sulitzeanu-Kenan (2010) examining commissions of inquiry after crisis events suggests that such commissions are not actually the most effective vehicles for encouraging 'learning', because of the emphasis on finding out who is to 'blame' (although see Stark 2018). The evidence examined here suggests that the same criticism can be made of the appearance of bureaucrats before oversight committees.

The cases described reveal the underlying strengths and weaknesses of engaging bureaucrats in a public form of direct public accountability as part of the theatre of government. At one level, the approach in the United Kingdom case will arguably lead the Transport Department to redouble its efforts to avoid the embarrassment that would accompany any repetition of past mistakes. But in doing so, the department and its leaders have had to shoulder the bulk of the responsibility for errors that under conventions of ministerial accountability really rest with their democratically elected superiors. Amidst calls for bureaucratic heads to roll after administrative failures it is easy to lose sight of the import of Westminster conventions as regards where responsibility ultimately resides.

In the Australian case, the focus by the Senate and the press on political accountability upholds the traditional conventions of ministerial responsibility. But in doing so through the questioning of public servants rather than of ministers, the process draws public servants into what are largely political rather than administrative debates. The committee expressed frustration in its final report that the people it had really wanted to question were the ministers who had refused to appear. Public servants were essentially acting as proxies to soak up the political blame intended for their democratically elected superiors. What the process shows is not so much the strengths of the parliamentary scrutiny of bureaucrats, as the weaknesses of parliamentary scrutiny of ministers.

In the United States case, the head of the DEA had to play her part as the responsible officer by taking the blame on her own shoulders, despite the complexities of how hiring and firing in the DEA actually works. As a showpiece, the committee hearing highlighted the appalling lapses in behaviour at the DEA and gave Leonhart a platform to draw attention to her lack of powers. Whether that will lead to long-term administrative change in procedure seems doubtful.

Appearances before parliamentary and congressional committees provide a very public platform for unelected members of the executive to speak truth to power. It has long been a central leadership function for sub-cabinet level appointees in American administrations to answer directly to Congress. Hearings are often confrontational, aggressive and designed as a public forum for elected members to be seen to be disciplining the bureaucracy. This practice has a much shorter history in Westminster systems, where it has only been in the last thirty years or so that most parliamentary standing committees have become institutionalised vehicles for oversight of executive government (excluding public accounts committees, which have a longer history).

If this kind of appearance has become as regular now for Westminster-system civil service leaders as for American ones, there is a lack of institutional support provided to allow these civil servants to perform this core function. Is it then time to let our public executives slightly further off the leash? The sections of these three case studies dealing with the media suggest that the dominant framing of issues from committees is that generated by the committees themselves in the lines of questioning they adopt. If the turn towards critical policy studies is right—if discourse shapes the policy world—perhaps senior bureaucrats need to fully embrace the chance to shape public perceptions themselves during these hearings, rather than simply accepting a role as the villain of the piece. Why cannot senior civil servants defend themselves and shape narratives around their stewardship with the same vigour as private-sector CEOs or CFOs would seek to frame and shape the way their stewardship of a company is perceived in the public sphere? A more robust culture of self-defence would match the actual level of responsibility being borne, and would better meet the needs of an age of transparent government, without removing ultimate accountability from elected actors who retain the power to hire and fire officials provided they do so within the rules. It would alter the dramatic script, from being one about disciplining wayward servants towards being a sharper exchange, of a type that might help to buttress a greater sense of trust in government.

6

In the Public Eye

Intelligence agencies should never have allowed this fake news to 'leak' into the public. One last shot at me. Are we living in Nazi Germany? (Tweet from Donald Trump, 11 January 2017)

I do take great umbrage at that, and there is no basis for Mr Trump to point fingers at the intelligence community for leaking information that was already available publicly. (Public comments by CIA director John Brennan, 15 January 2017)

In the age of governing in public, news has become weaponised. The media finds itself labelled as both perpetrator and victim of a sinister plot, wedged by the reality that the modern information consumer takes nothing at face value. It is an era in which public discourse is dominated not by facts, but by beliefs about facts. Complexity becomes inexplicable, because explanation is considered obfuscation. Hard facts, fake news, post-truth; our leaders are facing a twenty-four-hour media pitching machine which throws such perplexing curve balls that they can barely see what they're swinging at.

As Diana Mutz explains in her award-winning 2015 book *In-Your-Face Politics*, leaders are confronted by 24/7 news media that are both intrusive and uncivil. Mutz argues that this in itself is not new—the media have long been invasive and rude. What is new, she argues, is the fact that it is now so publicly 'in your face'. The ubiquity of media images of uncivil political exchanges mean that we can't escape them. They reach out of our multitude of screens to grab our attention. This confronting environment impacts not just on political leaders, but also those public servants who lead our bureaucracies, and in some cases the shape of their organisations as they re-align internal structures to face what Thomas Schillemans (2012) has called the 'mediatization' of the public sector. The intrusions of media in all their forms are forcing bureaucratic leaders in particular to evolve new ways of marrying traditional values with the practical realities of governing in public.

Some have reacted in ways that bring them into direct conflict with the political arm of the government they serve. For example, on 19 July 2017 Joel Clement wrote an opinion piece in the pages of the *Washington Post* (Clement 2017). Clement had until recently been the director of the Office of Policy Analysis in the US Department of the Interior. In June 2017, he was told that he was being re-assigned to an accounting position. As Clement observed wryly in the *Post* piece, 'I am not an accountant'. But more importantly he argued that the reason for the move was that he had become too vocal about the dangers of climate change.

> I believe I was retaliated against for speaking out publicly about the dangers that climate change poses to Alaska Native communities. During the months preceding my reassignment, I raised the issue with White House officials, senior Interior officials and the international community, most recently at a U.N. conference in June. It is clear to me that the administration was so uncomfortable with this work, and my disclosures, that I was reassigned with the intent to coerce me into leaving the federal government. (Clement 2017)

Clement's case raises many issues about what we expect of our bureaucratic leaders, and the level of comfort that politicians and constituents have with them operating in public. The more politically charged an issue becomes, the higher the stakes when administrators are perceived to have crossed a line into public criticism.

Equally, administrators can find themselves in political trouble for being seen to misstep when responding to crises not of their making. The importance of being able to project a public air of controlled competence rises with the degree of political pain being felt by elected representatives. This was powerfully illustrated when the young Obama administration was confronted with a human and environmental disaster in the Gulf of Mexico in 2010.

On 20 April 2010, a BP oil platform known as Deepwater Horizon was rocked by an enormous explosion that killed eleven people and injured many others. The platform itself collapsed and sank within two days. The explosion was caused by the escape of methane gas from an exploratory well. What followed was the most extraordinary oil leak of modern times. Over the course of three months, almost five million barrels of oil poured into the ocean, defying multiple efforts to cap the well. The pristine shores of the southern United States saw waves of oil lapping at their beaches, with now iconic images flashed around the world of seabirds covered in oil and unable to move.

This was a corporate failure leading to the tragic death of eleven people and untold environmental damage. But it was also an issue that the US government had to be seen to get to grips with. As Thad Allen—the man brought in to finally 'fix' the problem—later noted, every catastrophe in the modern era is automatically a public catastrophe. With the magnifying effects of social media and a 24/7 news presence, people all over the country became very angry at the perceived incompetence of the US government in dealing with the crisis.

The Obama administration needed leaders who could not only fix the oil leak but also disperse and mitigate the political damage. The chief bureaucratic player on this occasion was the government agency with the misfortune of being the regulator for off-shore drilling, the Minerals Management Service (MMS). The person most directly under fire was Elizabeth Birnbaum, an Obama appointee who had been the director of the MMS since July 2009. Birnbaum had already been an experienced and respected public executive for organisations including American Rivers, and the Committee on House Administration. She was used to working in situations which required her to testify before Congress and manage a public profile as part of her professional persona.

But Deepwater Horizon changed the playing field. There was simply no bigger issue in the USA in 2010. It dominated news cycles for weeks on end, with each failed attempt to address the oil leak leading to a fresh round of media condemnation. It was a crisis played out squarely in the public eye. Images and videos captured the public imagination. In-depth newspaper pieces looked for who was to blame. The president and various cabinet members were trying desperately to look like they were responding in a reassuring way and getting control of the situation. That began by driving home the blame at every opportunity to BP itself, but this did little to quell the anger of those who thought the government should be doing more. As the oil kept flowing, so did the demands for someone to take responsibility for what had happened and Elizabeth Birnbaum seemed to fit the bill.

As the *Washington Post* rather pithily put it in awarding her the 'worst week in Washington' award in late May 2010,

> It's an unofficial rule of official Washington: When something goes wrong with an arm of the government, someone you have never heard of must be sacrificed to show the press corps that Action Is Being Taken.
>   Meet Elizabeth Birnbaum. (Cillizza 2010)

Birnbaum's position as MMS director was not naturally one that caught the public eye. It did not require Senate confirmation, something later addressed as part of the 'reform package' following the disaster. The responses to the crisis in many ways provide a vivid demonstration of the blame avoidance strategies outlined by Hood (2010). There was widespread finger-pointing alleging that long-held concerns about the MMS and problems with its work that had not been addressed. Whatever the truth of those assertions, Birnbaum resigned within weeks of the spill. But her resignation letter, and Interior Secretary Ken Salazar's comment on it, did not even mention the oil spill. Salazar praised her for her 'strong and effective' leadership. Birnbaum herself spoke of the privilege of serving, and of the ongoing work to 'resolve the flaws in the current system that I inherited' (Department of the Interior 2010).

But just as events can demand the sacrifice of one public executive, they can provide an opportunity for another. Every crisis needs a public face, a lightning rod to attract trouble and bring it safely to earth; someone who can be both proactive and reactive in their embrace of the media. For the oil spill disaster, retired coast guard admiral Thad Allen became the public face of the government response, building a profile that was an important part of the government's strategy for controlling the narrative of the crisis. He did that in close connection with his political masters, but also under his own independent authority. It provides an example of how leaders can be very public in their leadership without necessarily banging heads with elected officials.

On 1 May, the secretary of homeland security, Janet Napolitano, publicly announced Allen's appointment as 'National Incident Commander' in charge of overall coordination of the response to the ongoing oil spill. Allen himself lost no time in getting in front of the media, giving a press briefing that very afternoon to introduce himself and lay out some facts. He made sure firstly that people knew that he was up for the job, and secondly that he would continue to hold BP responsible. As one of the few people to have emerged with his reputation enhanced following the Hurricane Katrina response, Allen had an established reputation as a 'straight shooter'.

> My assignment is just a further evolution in our adaptation to this event to make sure that we can carry out our responsibilities and to ensure that British Petroleum carries out their responsibilities . . . This is a continuation of longstanding relationships that I have had in the Gulf Coast for nearly 10 years, and also reflects the ability to interact with the folks down there as I did during the assignment as the principal federal officer for Hurricane Katrina. (White House 2010).

For the next few months, Allen was everywhere. From talk shows, to numerous newspaper articles and magazine features on the crisis, Allen's reassuring presence reached out to envelop America in a bear-hug of measured competence. When he stepped down at the start of October with the heavy lifting done and the oil well finally capped, stories assessing his performance demonstrated the impact he'd had as the 'public face' of the disaster. As the man out in front, he took credit and blame in equal measure. As a piece in *USA Today* termed it, 'Some liken retired Coast Guard admiral Thad Allen to a no-nonsense combat commander—the Gen. Patton of oil spills . . . To others, Allen, national incident commander for the spill, is the public face of the federal government's early fumbling of the response' (Jervis 2010).

What then are the lessons to be drawn from the fates of Birnbaum and Allen? First, that public executives have to be ready to be public figures. Some warm to it naturally, and some have it thrust upon them. Allen stepped up to the leadership role understanding that it was his job to be the public face; he understood that he couldn't lead effectively without also leading publicly and engaging openly with the media. Birnbaum had unwelcome notoriety drop upon her. Though not unused to dealing with the degree of exposure that comes from being a public executive, she was not able to draw upon the kind of archive of intense media experience that Allen had at his disposal. He had spent years building a particular picture of himself as a fixer, a coordinator, someone ready to run towards danger. Neither picture may be a true reflection of either Birnbaum or Allen, but in public leadership terms what mattered was their capacity to project the kind of media persona that was required.

The second lesson is that there is room within government to portray yourself as an authentic, independent leader and yet still serve the needs of the government of the day. Thad Allen was not seen as a partisan, and indeed served both the George W. Bush and Obama administrations in high-profile roles. Yet he worked closely with both presidents, their cabinet members and numerous officials to lead crisis recovery efforts. He was able to build a picture of himself as a leader independent from those that he served, so that if he'd had to publicly disagree with them he could have done so from a position of strength. This contrasts strongly with the position most comparable leaders in Westminster countries find themselves in, as I now go on to discuss.

Westminster Mandarins and the Media

Engaging publicly in the media is much more foreign to bureaucratic leaders in Westminster-system countries than it is in the United States. As we've seen in previous chapters, the conventional belief is that senior civil servants should remain largely anonymous. But, as I have argued, things are changing. Leaders can certainly still make choices about the degree of public limelight they want to attract, but to opt out altogether is now almost untenable. First, there are simply too many media through which bureaucratic leaders have to engage to allow for their continued anonymity. And second, there is a strong functional argument that leaders who are not publicly steering their organisations are not fulfilling the leadership role required in the twenty-first century.

The emergence of the 24/7 news cycle, combined with the increasing visibility of mandarins in their public accountability roles, has played a leading part in drawing them more into the public eye—with an increased opportunity to garner public praise or blame. The data bear this out. In Australia, the UK, New Zealand and Canada, analysis of the quantity and focus of media stories shows a rise in coverage of individual bureaucratic leaders, and often not in a very flattering light.

In order to gauge the level of publicity that senior civil servants are starting to attract in Westminster-system countries, I undertook a cross-jurisdictional media study. In each of Australia, Canada, New Zealand and the UK, three newspapers were selected for examination. In each case, one of the selected newspapers was perceived as 'liberal' or 'left-wing' in its broad orientation, with a second seen as 'conservative' or 'right-wing'. The third in each instance was a popular tabloid. So for example, in the UK *The Guardian*, *The Daily Telegraph* and *The Sun* were selected. A full list is attached in the Appendix. All sources were consulted via the *Factiva* database, allowing for full searchability, but also meaning that any limitations of search capacity within the database were evenly spread across all cases.

Covering the four calendar years 2010 to 2013, the study focused on comparable positions across the four jurisdictions. The positions covered are broken down by department and listed by country in the Appendix. In essence I was looking at a range of the most senior civil servants, including the leader of an arm's-length environmental agency in each country as a control for difference. Searches were done by the names of the individual holders of the positions *and* the position title. In other words, I was keen to see how often leaders were mentioned specifically by name rather than remaining anonymous behind the facade of the institution they represented. The analysis draws out the extent to which individual leaders are named in their own right, rather than simply blending into the quiet anonymity of 'the department'.

Figure 3 breaks down the press coverage by position across the four Westminster-system countries. The data are revealing. Perhaps the first thing to note is that two positions are well out in front in every jurisdiction. The cabinet secretary in the UK is generally considered to represent the apex of the civil service. Apart from a short period under the Cameron government, the cabinet secretary has also usually been the head of the home civil service. The counterpart position in Australia and New Zealand is the head of the Department of Prime Minister and Cabinet, and in Canada the equivalent person is known as the clerk of the Privy Council. Each of these people plays an important role not just in terms of proximity to the prime minister, but also as the figurehead who can speak out on behalf of the civil service as a whole in each country when required.

The other position that Figure 3 shows as streaking ahead in terms of press coverage is that of Treasury secretary—the bureaucrat in charge of the

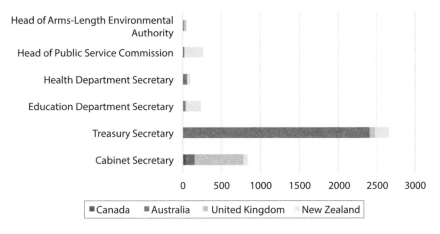

FIGURE 3. Press coverage by position, calendar years 2010–2013

department that minds the government coffers. I have written elsewhere on the kind of 'Antipodean exceptionalism' that seems to allow mandarins from Australia and New Zealand a greater freedom to comment and engage on the public record (see Grube 2012). Nowhere is that more in evidence than in the position of Treasury secretary. As a number of my interviewees discussed, Treasury departments are seen as holding a special position by virtue of their specialist knowledge.

There are clearly also systemic nuances in each country deriving from the individual strengths and responsibilities of various institutions. In New Zealand, the head of the State Services Commission has a strong independent profile. This is deliberate and by design. The New Zealand State Services Commission has a much greater role in management and appointments right across the public service than does its equivalent in other jurisdictions. The head of the commission plays a leading part in selecting and recommending candidates for appointment to become heads of government departments and agencies. It is therefore unsurprising that the role represents the single biggest New Zealand category in terms of press coverage, and is significantly ahead of the coverage that its counterparts can muster in other countries.

When you delve deeper into these data, you also find that press coverage follows particular events which act like magnets. For example, the Australian Treasury secretary's profile in the media as highlighted in these graphs is dramatic. A good portion of that reflects the fact that—as already discussed—the Australian government asked then Treasury secretary Ken Henry to conduct what became known as the 'Henry tax review'. This generated an enormous amount of coverage in 2010 in particular. Yet even that doesn't tell the full story. Henry's successor, Martin Parkinson, also attracted many hundreds of hits, as did Henry on topics other than his tax review. Both men chose to make full use of their profile to exercise a very public style of leadership.

Crises can also propel an individual into the public spotlight and create peaks of unsought public profile. For example, the New Zealand data show a particularly high count on articles mentioning the head of the Education Department. This reflects a tremendous row in 2012, involving the leadership of the department by Lesley Longstone, who was only in office for a little over a year. Longstone faced criticism for her leadership style, but according to press reports also had to contend with a minister seen as not performing strongly herself. This forced Longstone into taking a more public role. As *Guardian* journalist Max Rashbrooke put it, 'In Longstone's case, that accountability translated, rightly or wrongly, into having to front up to the media to defend key decisions, after Parata [the minister] failed to show—something that UK permanent secretaries, for example, would rarely, if ever, have to do' (Rashbrooke 2013).

It is possible to argue that in Australia and New Zealand, a 'Washminster' system of public leadership is already evolving. There is a higher level of media reporting of senior civil servants, and a wider expectation that they will adopt a public role of their own. There remains deep controversy about the how far such a public face should extend but little doubt that it is now an embedded part of public bureaucratic leadership. But certain variables can still make an enormous difference, and amongst these is the degree to which the government of the day is willing to try to restrict opportunities for public outreach, as the case of Canada highlights.

As all Canadian interviewees attested, the Harper government in Canada tried extremely hard to control government communication with a vice-like grip. They could do little about civil servants having to appear in front of parliamentary committees to be questioned, but they could certainly put in place procedures to stop leaders from proactively building public profiles of their own. The success of that approach is highlighted in Figure 4. In the four years in which New Zealand mandarins scored over 600 name 'hits', UK civil service chiefs over 700, and Australian bureaucratic heads over 2,500, Canada could barely muster fifty. As I discuss below through interview data with Canadians, a culture of restriction around public comments did undoubtedly have an impact.

I turn now in the sections below to look at this media puzzle through the eyes of the mandarins who have had to work within it. Through questions about the different ways in which they connect with the media, I build up a series of categories of interaction based on how leaders across the four

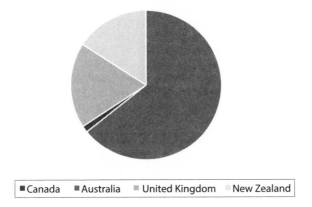

■ Canada　■ Australia　▪ United Kingdom　▫ New Zealand

FIGURE 4. Total press coverage by country

countries saw themselves and what they were trying to achieve through their public engagements. It is an issue that without exception everyone interviewed had thought a lot about, and had some concerns about. Few were willing to attest that they themselves had ever overstepped the line to become political advocates, but many thought that their colleagues had. As Figures 3 and 4 show, even those in Australia, New Zealand and the UK who believed that they had been circumspect in fact received plenty of media coverage. I begin by looking at those occasions on which leaders had made the conscious decision that they should front up and take the lead on a public policy issue.

Consciously Taking the Public Lead on Big Issues

Many bureaucratic leaders, especially those whose service had been the most recent, were willing to step forward in public if it was part of getting the job done. In an age of outcomes-based assessments, reaching out through the media can be a necessary part of 'cutting through'. For example, the former CEO of an arm's-length government agency in Australia made it clear to his communications staff from the outset that public leadership would be part of his approach. '[I]f there was any issue that was sufficiently important that they in their judgement felt would be useful for me to talk to, I made it clear that I was available . . . I think my predecessor just didn't like doing that so he avoided that' (author interview, Australia, 2015). For one former UK leader of a similar organisation, the drive was all about actually getting the outcome that was needed. 'Our view was we had to make a difference . . . We had to use an integrated approach so we didn't favour one part of the community from another and we employed and trained professionals to do the job. Occasionally we ruffled feathers, occasionally we were wrong, but more often than not we were right' (author interview, UK, 2015).

Not all opportunities were as proactively embraced. One normally very cautious former permanent secretary of a line department in Australia recalled having to step up because things weren't going well. '[T]hat was when I was backgrounding journalists, because we were getting a flogging in the media and we knew we had a good case. And [the minister] wasn't . . . particularly good' (author interview, Australia, 2016). Even when ministers were perfectly competent, politically astute public servants could see the value in providing non-partisan media briefings to take away some of the political sting. As one told his minister when dealing with the need to update the media on a matter with lots of complex components, 'I'll do that.

I'll call a media briefing and I'll do it in great detail. And they'll all just be bewildered' (author interview, Australia, 2015).

All mandarins are aware that there is a 'line'. There are political borders that you shouldn't cross, although some feel that if you don't make the occasional incursion you probably aren't living close enough to the edge. But even Australians know they have to avoid going too far. 'Well I guess, even though you might be in this independent statutory authority you still operate in a political environment and you've got to be cognisant of that, and then you've got to work out, well how do I work in this political environment without becoming political . . . and I think we do see examples of statutory authorities becoming political. In my view that's to be avoided' (author interview, Australia, 2015).

Many interviewees, especially in Australia, reflected that they had been willing to appear in public because it was in the interests of their minister that they do so. If they were directly asked to do it, most felt that it would be difficult to say no. One reflected on just such an occasion, on which things went off the rails.

> I suspect that my more cautious former colleagues would just refuse to do that, I suspect others . . . who are more gung-ho would be prepared to do that if they see themselves as a bit more of a player, but I was asked to do it by [name omitted] and I thought the circumstances were sufficient that it was going to protect me but [it] leaked within an hour and so it became a major issue. (Author interview, Australia, 2015)

Even when things went according to plan, there was always the need for these mandarins to ask themselves whether what they were doing was in fact appropriate. 'I have to be realistic, the reason for that was it was a good way for [name omitted] to fly the kite without his fingerprints all over it on this stage. . . . When it seemed to go well, very quickly they came and embraced that policy. So very occasionally like that there is a value in a public servant floating ideas, seeing what sort of response you get, but it's very much the exception' (author interview, Australia, 2015).

The challenge of course is not just the act of going public, but the fact that this is not what Westminster civil servants traditionally signed up for. Being thrust into the limelight is a nerve-wracking experience, replete with anxious preparation, sweaty palms and robust feedback. One interviewee found out that politicians do watch when public servants go on air, and are quick to provide their assessment afterwards. 'I had to go on breakfast television because the minister was unavailable or something, and I'd get pretty instant feedback from the minister or the prime minister's office' (author interview, Australia, 2015). Often requests came at short notice. '[The minister] was tied up and couldn't do it. He rang me up eight o'clock the night before, on Sunday night, and said, "Can you do this tomorrow morning?" Get a sleepless night . . . got up early, into a suit, along to the bloody studio, and you know . . . they had an ambush there' (author interview, Australia, 2015).

So bureaucratic leaders aren't walking around with their eyes closed. They know they can expect to face hostile questioning from reporters when they front the media. It is of course one thing to expect it, and quite another to then be able to deal with it effectively. One strategy that some mandarins adopted was to build strong connections with the media from the outset. Their descriptions below show that this did not always lead to better outcomes, but it did connect them into a world that might otherwise have seemed more intimidating.

Building Connections with the Media

Mandarins know that it pays to stay connected to the outside world. A politically astute civil servant is seldom found with her or his head in the sand. Most of my interviewees had made sure that they knew who the main journalists shaping opinion in their area were. As one Australian put it, 'I would always try and work on the basis that I cultivated good relationships, I knew most of them by their first name' (author interview, Australia, 2015). Off-the-record discussions and briefings are not uncommon—not necessarily in a Machiavellian scheme to control the story, but certainly to make sure that the underlying information journalists are using for stories is factually correct and defensible. Every public agency and department now has a media and communications section. There are professionals helping leaders to shape the public face of the organisation. As one Canadian remembered, '[I]f you wanted to on occasion get your story out you might try to do a one-on-one, or someone might set up a one-on-one interview, but that would all be professionalised in a sense [through] the communications professionals' (author interview, Canada, 2015).

Some mandarins made these connections at the outset to shape the reporting of issues in their department or agency. According to one Australian, 'I certainly was at pains, right at the beginning . . . I was certainly encouraged to, and I did provide briefings to a range of senior journalists from the press gallery about the plans to reform the [name omitted] Department' (author interview, Australia, 2015). This did not mean that leaders engaged uncritically with journalists. They went in with eyes open. One Canadian said he had been very wary.

> There was no sort of habit of private lunches in quiet places, disgorging all the secrets of the state to some chosen columnist or something. That said, a number of the media people do work hard at trying to get that kind of a relationship with senior public servants, and in some cases they do have it, sort of traditional sort of notion of a quiet lunch with a martini and, blurb, it all comes out. But no, I never really did that. (Author interview, Canada, 2015)

It may not have been quiet lunches with martinis, but bureaucratic leaders know how important building strong networks can be and most worked hard to facilitate this. Even without clandestine meetings and brown envelopes, there were opportunities to engage that some were keen to seize, as this Australian describes.

> I had relationships with journalists who I respected, which were just contacts around Canberra, at social events and so on, they would be cultivated in that way and I would occasionally talk to them in that sort of environment . . . off the record. An occasional lunch, either at their invitation or once or twice at mine to try to inform them about what was happening. And my relationships were generally pretty good; they were not abused that I can remember or not misused by the journalists that I'm thinking of. (Author interview, Australia, 2016)

Each individual has a clear personal idea of what the job should entail. Some think it includes engaging with the media, whereas others believe that this in itself is already something of a political act. A Canadian interviewee described keeping as much of a distance as possible. 'Yeah, I mean my rule was, public servants do not speak on the record to the media, that's the job of ministers' (author interview, Canada, 2015). And the same leader reflected that when journalists were spoken to off the record, it was seen as a way not to burnish one's own individual reputation, but rather to clarify the government's agenda 'Certainly I would talk to them from time to time but it was never about me, it was always about "Do you really understand this issue that you're writing about?" . . . I would never say, "Well I think this is the sort of political dynamic"' (author interview, Canada, 2015). And of course the benefits flow both ways, as one Australian interviewee pointed out. Journalists need good and reliable sources, which a well-placed bureaucratic leader could most certainly provide. 'I would say on the whole it was good journalists, particularly their chief political correspondents, who would always go out of their way to keep a good relationship with me because occasionally I could be helpful, I could give them genuine background on an issue' (author interview, Australia, 2015).

At the other end of the spectrum, the former head of an arm's-length government agency saw interacting with the media as part of what it means to be a public leader. 'I talk to the media. I had people in [the] English and French press that I talked to, I briefed on a regular basis, they could call me, I did interviews, I had my picture in the paper, I talked to the media a lot . . . Sometimes the media themselves wanted a little bit more of a controversy. So I talked to the media, I didn't bother with the communications policy, I didn't have any issues' (author interview, Canada, 2015). That doesn't mean that even arm's-length agency heads don't need to be careful. As one New Zealander recounted, appearing alongside a politician in the media can give a political flavour to what follows, as they found out when they ended up on the same radio programme. 'And we all sort of filed away a little note for the future: whenever you're going on to any radio programme, television programme, or whatever, check who else is going to be talking . . . and insist you will not be opposing, or alongside a politician. And so, yeah, that was always one of my rules of survival after that' (author interview, New Zealand, 2016).

Many of those who had decided not to establish media relationships felt that there would have been advantages in having done so. Reflected one Australian, 'I probably didn't do enough of that. There are others in the game much better at that than me. I had a couple. I wouldn't say I cultivated them but, you know, I knew I could ring them' (author interview, Australia, 2015). But the same leader emphasised that it had been an exercise of personal choice, not a lack of media interest, that had driven this approach. 'I could be contacted, and was, a lot, but I was always pretty careful about what I said. I never, ever leaked anything or went on background to set a tone or anything. I never did that. I wasn't confident in that area. I didn't do it. I think players now do that more' (author interview, Australia, 2015). Another Australian lamented a lack of connections as having hurt them publicly, but expressed no regrets about having made this 'ethical' decision. '[I] t might have helped if I had have bothered to cultivate a relationship with the media . . . I consciously didn't do it . . . I didn't see why senior public servants should be cultivating or need to be cultivating journalists. That is the job of the minister' (author interview, Australia, 2015).

A UK mandarin agreed that bureaucratic leaders were indeed now cultivating journalists, but that this was the unavoidable consequence of appearing in public more often.

That's exactly what's happening and the more and more that civil servants are in the public domain and of course now if you give evidence as I've done to select committees, you're on the television. You can hear yourself quoted the next morning on the radio and you didn't know. I've gone to a meeting and they said I heard you on the radio this morning and thought I didn't give a radio interview and it was a tiny clip that the media had decided it was handy for whatever programme they were using. So somebody woke up to hear me on the *Today* programme. So you are thrust into the limelight because of something you say when you're giving information to a committee. So I can absolutely understand why you want to make sure there is going to be journalists who understand you, are on side with you or, if you get yourself in a corner, won't necessarily come out attacking you. They might even help you of course. (Author interview, UK, 2014)

The inconvenient truth is, of course, that no matter how well prepared mandarins are, and no matter how much they cultivate good relationships with the media, sometimes things go wrong. Various interviewees described how they were pursued through the media with degrees of intensity that they found shocking. Most modern politicians are no longer surprised by the viciousness that can emerge when the heat is on, but for bureaucratic leaders this is a newer experience.

When Things Go Wrong

Whether bureaucratic leaders choose to engage with the media or not, the media are going to come looking for them when they smell a story. When something's gone wrong and there are signs that administrative mistakes have been made, journalists will come knocking. It's their job. But what is the job of mandarins, in response? Should they come out swinging, stay professionally factual and minimise the damage, or simply refuse altogether to comment? On the whole, there is not a lot of love for the media within the higher echelons of bureaucracies. As one Australian bemoaned, they had tried to explain a complex situation to reporters only to find that 'the media demonstrated it was completely unable to grasp the subtleties of that and had just wanted a story' (author interview, Australia, 2015).

The problem is always that when organisations wait to react to something when it goes wrong, rather than being proactive in their engagement, they can get caught off guard. The more complex the issues, the more a sense of disengagement can hurt, as one Australian explained. 'We had difficulties with the media. I think we didn't handle the media at all well . . . [We had] what was perceived as a secretive sort of approach. So that didn't go down well. You had very uninformed journalists trying to write about a difficult issue. Hadn't been briefed. So I think the handling of the media by us . . . was pretty poor' (author interview, Australia, 2015). Of course, being proactive doesn't necessarily mean that something won't blow up in your face. A Canadian interviewee reflected how surprised they were when their dry briefings became media stories. 'I was surprised by it, because what I was saying, generally speaking, I thought the public would have known already. I mean, I wasn't going around telling state secrets' (author interview, Canada, 2016).

The sense that things can go wrong even when people are on the front foot is magnified when something blows up unexpectedly. As one British leader of an arm's-length agency put it, '[T]he reactive stuff is usually the negative stuff. Something's gone wrong, what idiot's responsible? Let's get them on television and make him look like a fool' (author interview, UK, 2015). That capacity for reputations of civil servants to be ripped apart by the intensity of the media gaze caused some interviewees to fear for the future of the profession. 'It's very draining and very worrying and I think it's putting a lot of people off the thought that they want to be in leadership positions . . . because they've seen other people—certainly their character, their integrity, their reputation—pulled apart in a kind of a feeding frenzy' (author interview, New Zealand, 2016). The same interviewee described it as 'weathering the storm' when there is simply no way to actually re-align the story.

> I think all you could say to your comms team is, look, we're going to have to weather the storm as best we can but you do have to try to say to the formal media journalists who cover this part of the public service, there's more to this than meets the eye and it's more complex than you might think and we are going to be looking for a moment to try to background you on that complexity, but that's the most you could do, that's the most you could do. You just have to stand there and do your best basically and sometimes your best's not good enough.

These are of course the moments when tradition would have it that politicians should step in and take the blame. After all, they are the elected bosses in whose names decisions are made. But as one British interviewee delightfully noted, you should not always expect to turn around and find that your minister is covering your back. 'Oh, all the time . . . They'll just suddenly not be there. You'd be straining at the face of opposition and crisis and protest and it was your minister right behind you and all of a sudden, he isn't there anymore . . . He's climbing back [from] it, while he's encouraging you out on the limb' (author interview, UK, 2015). Sometimes, alas, it is the job of a senior official to take the blame when politicians are too gun-shy to do so, as one New Zealander colourfully explained. '[H]ave you heard the phrase "swallow a dead rat"? I'm better at it than any other public servant in the country, I reckon, because of my years at [name omitted] and the [name omitted] office' (author interview, New Zealand, 2016).

Precisely because the civil servant's name appears in the press when things do go wrong, another New Zealander was all in favour of appearing on the public record to correct any misconceptions. When I asked whether that didn't make him a 'participant' in the public debate, he saw no problem if it did. 'Yeah, but can you not be a participant? If your advice is forced to be in the public domain, then you are a participant. So, best they understand what you said, and why you said it, and the nuances around that. I'm certain about this' (author interview, New Zealand, 2016). If bureaucratic leaders don't succeed in correcting media misapprehensions and things go spiralling totally out of control, they may face little choice but to 'consider their position'. Another New Zealander described how such a situation might arise.

> Once an issue has become sufficiently politicised, in that case the issue had become highly politicised, then there was a whispering campaign starting. In that case I did talk to some journalists about a couple of situations, but the thing had spiralled pretty much out of control, and once it gets to a certain level of it spiralling out of control, that's when a public servant has to say, do I stay or do I go . . . it's high status games and you, perhaps, need to take some counter-measures, but in the end if you lose the confidence of a minister, absolutely lose it, you've got to think about what you're doing. (Author interview, New Zealand, 2016)

So the stakes are high. Missteps under pressure can see small cracks turn into fissures waiting to swallow up the careers of those trying to deal with an issue. Political scalps do occasionally roll, but bureaucratic leaders seldom walk away unscathed. At worst, they have to themselves resign or be pushed, as the Lesley Longstone example from New Zealand demonstrated. Given the consequences, it is perhaps hardly surprising that many of my interviewees still saw public engagement through the media as something to be pursued only when no other choice remains.

Not If I Can Help It

Right across the four Westminster-system countries, there was no shortage of leaders who expressed their allegiance to the traditional goal of avoiding the media altogether if it was possible. I have labelled this group the 'not if I can help it' group, as they tried their best to stay out of the limelight. But as most revealed during discussion, it's a rule that is fiendishly difficult to stick to in practice. It simply isn't always possible to 'help it'. Nevertheless, the starting point for these mandarins remains the maintenance of anonymity. One Australian insisted that it wasn't their place to be the public face. 'I guess I could if I wanted to, but I don't want to and I don't think it's a good idea. I could use this position to start advocating for certain policies' (author interview, Australia, 2015). Another long-serving Australian reflected that, 'For most of us, most of the time, we've taken the view in the last thirty years that I know of, the less often you're in the media, the more comfortable it is' (author interview, Australia, 2015). A Canadian fully agreed, explaining how they tried to emerge unscathed from oversight committee hearings. 'Your goal as a public servant is not to say anything that gets your name in the paper. I think that's fair to say. I don't recall that I ever was quoted by name as a result. It would be on the television though. You could watch it, it would be televised on occasion' (author interview, Canada, 2015).

Even some heads of arm's-length agencies were cautious about choosing when to get out into the public gaze. A British head referred to choosing the moments carefully, deciding on quality rather than quantity of intervention.

> Once in a blue moon, when you've got something really important to say to the system as a whole, you want to stand up and say it, but generally speaking, for the day-to-day regulatory decisions, you don't want to be out there shouting at people in public. You want to be having the conversation behind closed doors. (Author interview, UK, 2015)

Much of this remains a matter of personal choice, as leaders make decisions based on a combination of values, traditions and personal preference. A UK former permanent secretary confirmed having instructed the department that a dialogue with the media should be avoided. 'No, the media was . . . interesting—the media was always the bridge too far. I remember one or two very, very interesting debates we had around the permanent secretaries' table about that . . . We were very clear in the department that except in very exceptional circumstances, I wouldn't speak to the media' (author interview, UK, 2015). As the subsequent discussion demonstrated, exceptional circumstances do sometimes arise, dragging bureaucratic leaders into an unwanted limelight.

This realisation of the inevitability of media contact is reflected in the fact that many bureaucratic leaders now undertake media training. For some, this is not just about how to handle reporters, but also about how to avoid wading into reputational traps when faced with aggressive questioning by oversight committees. Some make a very positive case for training as being part of the natural re-alignment of bureaucratic leaders as heads of outward-focused organisations. In other words, if public leadership is the new reality for civil servants, there are opportunities to go with the flow.

> [T]he last thing you want is the public servants to feel as if they've got to be so out of the limelight that they're boring and hopeless at managing marketing. They've got to be quick, they've got to be agile, they've got to be clever, all of those things which are part of the marketing approach, have got to be part and parcel of your professional arrangements. And if you think about it purely in terms of traditional anonymity which gives rise to images of the public service as this boring, clumsy, bureaucratic thing, [that] is totally inconsistent with what modern communications require for smart management. (Author interview, Australia, 2015)

But media training is also about avoiding the pitfalls, and knowing when to keep the elected arm of the political executive informed. Politicians hate being blindsided, and all the bureaucratic leaders interviewed saw it as part of their job to avoid such scenarios. The leader of an Australian arm's-length agency stressed the need to have a good communications team on the job. 'I had a pretty good media team and they had a pretty good nose for what might be sensitive politically as well. Sometimes it was me saying, "We'd better let the minister's office know about that", but perhaps more often it was the media people saying, "This could be front page news, we'd better let the [minister's] office know"' (author interview, Australia, 2015).

Whether leaders see themselves as cautious or gregarious, almost all did at some stage find themselves on the other end of a telephone with a member of the fourth estate. It might have been simply to provide background information, or to quell a rumour. For the more forthright it was for on-the-record comments on the public issues of the day. As political communications professionals regularly attest, in the modern media environment, not to engage at all is a recipe for disaster. If you don't seek to frame the story, it may frame you. And few leaders, including bureaucratic ones, can afford to take that risk.

But hanging over that particular decision-making matrix is the attempt by some governments to exert control over all communications precisely at the point when it is becoming more difficult and less desirable to do so. For example, in Canada under the Harper government, the rules were well known. 'Nobody talks to a journalist without it going through a minister's office/the Communications shop, and in most cases the only people who talk to the media are the Communications people. And that's been a very big change, and in the Harper government' (author interview, Canada, 2015). And yet, as examples like the furore over the resignation of Canada's chief statistician in 2010 show, communications control is a temporary illusion that comes at a high price when it breaks down.

Under the kind of 'Washminster' leadership framework outlined in chapter two, 'media skills' must be placed right at the centre of what is required for modern bureaucratic leaders to be effective, on either side of the Atlantic. Those skills can be deployed in a non-partisan way; in fact it is a requirement in both the USA and Westminster-system countries that leaders not engage in party political disputes. But leaders cannot control perceptions. Most acknowledge that it would be naïve to think that their own intention to offer politically neutral judgements based only on evidence always comes across that way in public or through the media.

> I used to take a pride that in general people couldn't know when I did speak publicly on a policy whether I had briefed for it or against it or somewhere in the middle, that what they would hear from me is what the motives and the purpose of the policy was and how it was going to be implemented. Now, it is true that most people would see you doing that to support the policy; I thought it was about implementing the policy and I can think of instances when the media quite wrongly thought that actually I supported this where I didn't. (Author interview, Australia, 2015)

The lesson from Washington and the handling of the Gulf of Mexico oil disaster is the same lesson as is reflected in the experience of Westminster mandarins: 'the media' is a complicated animal. It can bite as easily as it can praise, and it has proven remarkably reluctant to act as a lapdog, despite many scholarly claims to the contrary. The mainstream media, albeit increasingly joined by online-only sources such as Breitbart and Huffington Post, still help to drive political agendas. They provide an outlet for public executives seeking to inform and explain. Equally, they can rip apart careers in a matter of hours when things go wrong.

The interview data from Westminster-system countries, backed by the quantitative picture of press coverage, show that whilst the challenges are the same as in the USA, there are different variables that can change the playing field. The first thing to emphasise is that whilst all mandarins retain the power to reach out as 'rhetorical bureaucrats', many choose to use that power sparingly. Governing in public may be the new normal, but it's still possible to fight the tide. Many Canadian leaders in particular emphasised this in their interview answers. There were also New Zealanders and British leaders who were adamant that it was not their role to speak to the media, and they would not do so if it unhelpfully placed them in the public spotlight.

Secondly, some Westminster-system countries are more advanced than others in shaping public personas for bureaucrats. Australians and New Zealanders are on the whole out in front. It is perhaps no coincidence that in both of these jurisdictions, permanency of tenure gave way several decades ago to fixed-term contracts of employment. The entire Australian senior executive service is hired on contracts—with time periods that have varied from three to five years depending on government preference. The jury is still out in terms of the scholarly debate over whether this has changed the nature of bureaucratic leaders, away from being as frank and fearless as they once were. One thing that is clear is that it has not turned them into creatures of the shadows. They are frequently out there in public, and longitudinal studies are needed to further test whether they are acting inappropriately, as partisan agents, or shaping more independent personas to further policy debates that politicians seem unwilling or unable to engage with themselves.

In Canada, and to a lesser extent in the UK, reticence remains. There have been quite visible cabinet secretaries, like the gifted communicator Gus O'Donnell, but equally many leaders who choose to stay as close to the backroom as they can. And yet, as Figure 3 suggests for the UK, even after O'Donnell's retirement in 2011, the new cabinet secretary Jeremy Heywood also continued to score highly in terms of being named in the press. This reflects the pivotal role played by the cabinet secretary in the UK system, as being the connection point between the civil service and the political executive. When something goes wrong politically that a prime minister doesn't want to have to sort out, the cabinet secretary is often asked to do it. In Heywood's case, this included being asked to investigate allegations that the government chief whip, Andrew Mitchell, had called police officers at the Downing Street gates 'plebs' in 2012. From little things big things grow, and from this one alleged comment grew the entire 'Plebgate' scandal that saw Heywood receive widespread press criticism for the way he conducted his investigation, whilst Mitchell himself was forced to resign.

The third variable, along with individual choice and systemic factors, is the amount of licence governments are willing to grant bureaucrats in interacting with the media. As the Canadian case demonstrates, it is certainly possible for governments to create a culture in which senior civil servants are very aware that any proactive media engagement of their own is discouraged. The flipside, of course, is that when things do go wrong, the subsequent explosions of crisis can seem greater because of the pressure built up behind them. The row between clerk of the Privy Council Wayne Wouters and the parliamentary budget officer Kevin Page in 2012 is a case in point. Several exchanges of letters between the pair—hardly a revolutionary act in most bureaucracies—sparked significant discomfort for both Wouters and the government more broadly.

The data both on press coverage and from interviews with bureaucratic leaders themselves show that conditions in the twenty-first century no longer match those of the age in which the traditions characteristic of a Westminster-type civil service were first formed. Bluntly, there is no longer a backroom in which to hide, even if leaders wished to do so. The choice now concerns whether to get out on the front stage, to try to keep ahead of events and drive media narratives from the outset, or whether to await developments, by adopting a defensive posture. Both are still possible, and both can be successful, judging by current practice. My argument here is that the conditions underpinning the reality of 'governing in public' aren't going away any time soon. The 24/7 news media aren't about to return to a slower pace, and the reach of social media seems unlikely to contract. Equally, it is inconceivable for now that any government would argue for a diminution in levels of accountability and transparency with regard to the behaviour of senior bureaucrats.

So the direction of travel is clear, and it would be a brave bureaucratic leader who thought that the media could not impact on her or his professional life in the years ahead. In the era of governing in public, bureaucratic leaders need the skills to proactively build public faces of their own. They need connections with key media sources that they can reach out to. Often this will be off the record, to provide information or a new perspective. Sometimes it will be fully on the record, in the blinking glare of a crisis. Occasionally it will be in the teeth of direct criticism from elected politicians looking for someone else to carry the can. Whatever the scenario, it's tricky and needs preparation. No CEO of a publicly listed company in the twenty-first century would be unaware of how the media can shape a public face. Public sector executives need to join them. The risk matrix has shifted. The greatest risk now attaches to those who reactively wait for the media anvil to fall from the sky before trying to get out of the way. Public executives can do better than that, as many are showing already. They're building the skills to protect their own backs when politicians are no longer willing to do it for them.

7

Over-sharing in Public?

THE CHALLENGE OF SOCIAL MEDIA

I'm now a C-List celebrity in Kim Kardashian: Hollywood. Come join me and become famous too by playing on iPhone! (Accidental tweet from US Environmental Protection Agency's Office of Water, 21 July 2014)

The US Environmental Protection Agency is a pretty outward-looking kind of place. As at 30 April 2018, their Twitter account had 589,000 followers and had delivered some 14,600 tweets into the world since it joined the Twittersphere in May 2008. Not bad for government work. And this is communication with a purpose. The EPA has led the charge amongst US government agencies over the past decade in using its public face to shape public opinion. It is stringently non-partisan, as indeed it must be under United States law, but it weighs in on some of the biggest policy issues of our time. Climate change, pollution, energy use and environmental degradation—the EPA makes sure that its analysis is out there to feed data and evidence into the heat of deeply political debates. But just as importantly, it presents its information in ways that tell a story. More than just airing dry statistics, the EPA under both Democrat and Republican administrations has presented information in order to persuade people.

The EPA's social media profile demonstrates just how much the bureaucracy is now in the persuasion business. Its Twitter account is a vital tool for changing people's minds and influencing how they view the world. It does this in a number of ways. First, it provides a platform for the EPA's head—the 'administrator'—to shape and build her or his own public profile. Second, it allows the EPA to demonstrate how engaged it is in really practical things, like crisis relief during emergencies. Third, it provides a voice for the translation of esoteric scientific data into concrete policy directions. But, as the rocky road the organisation has travelled under the Trump presidency demonstrates, none of this is easy or uncontroversial.

Recent administrators of the EPA have all used the Twitter account to 'introduce' themselves to the wider public. Scott Pruitt, Trump's nominee for the post, was sworn in on 17 February 2017 and remained in office until resigning amidst a sea of controversy in July 2018. The EPA used Twitter to publicise both Pruitt's arrival and his views once in post. This included both the prosaic and the perplexing. The tweet of welcome on 17 February seemed innocent enough: 'We'd like to congratulate Mr. Pruitt on his confirmation! We look forward to welcoming him to EPA.' Yet even this launched the Twittersphere into a frenzy of memes and mockery based on the presumed discomfort for the EPA of having Pruitt as their new head, given that he had sued the organisation on multiple occasions as attorney general of Oklahoma. It did of course get more interesting in the months that followed, with Pruitt's leadership of the organisation coming under heavy criticism on both ethical and environmental grounds.

The EPA's Twitter account throughout remained a useful vehicle for painting a particular picture of Pruitt's character and interests for the public. This included for example tweeting, on 15 August 2017, a link to an interview on *Who TV* focused on Pruitt's views about baseball. On 5 June 2017 it tweeted links to interviews given by Pruitt in support of President Trump's decision to withdraw from the Paris climate agreement. The Twitter presence provides a platform for heads of the EPA to build their own profiles and support the policy agenda of the president who appointed them. This is also exactly what happened under the Obama administration, just perhaps with less controversy given the stronger alignment of the Obama administration's policies on matters like climate change with the perceived mission of the EPA as an environmental campaigner. The administrator during the second Obama term, Gina McCarthy, was an avid tweeter as head of the Agency—as exemplified by the *Washington Examiner* story on 'EPA Administrator McCarthy's top ten greatest tweets' (Chaitin 2015). These included a 22 April

2014 effort covering the advice she'd received in preparing to throw the ceremonial first pitch for a Boston Red Sox game.

So the EPA's public face includes an established (if frequently controversial) role in building the profile of the leader of the organisation through Twitter. The second focus of its social media outreach is on dealing with emergencies. In late 2017, the extraordinary impact of hurricanes Harvey and Irma dominated the EPA's Twitter feed and Facebook site, as they gave advice and reassurance to the people of Texas and Florida in particular. Advice on avoiding generator fumes, storing sufficient drinking water and how to deal with flooding was shared on a daily basis. Appearing alongside were reassuring images of EPA professionals out doing their job.

The third focus of the EPA's social media profile, in times of less immediate environmental crisis, has been on sharing scientific data and evidence about environmental impacts. Here we see examples like the 31 July 2017 tweet about nutrient pollution as a pressing problem. There are details about grant funds and congratulatory call-outs to organisations that have worked in innovative ways to meet one challenge or another. On 31 October 2016, there was information on how teaching children to wash their hands thoroughly can help to prevent lead poisoning. There are even introductions to some of the EPA's scientists, such as, on 5 October 2016, research ecologist Jana Compton.

As in other spheres, what US public agencies like the EPA are doing on Twitter tends to be out in front of what is happening in Westminster-system countries, but the distance between them is by no means as great as one might think. Despite the theoretical difficulties I outline below, Westminster-type departments and agencies have on the whole begun to embrace social media. But it has been a haste filled with caution, to put it in slightly oxymoronic terms. Politicians get very nervous around social media. There is seldom such a thing as a small mistake. And when politicians are nervous, so are bureaucratic leaders. The stakes are simply too high to allow mistakes to happen. And as Donald Trump demonstrated so emphatically within a day of becoming president, social media accounts can be told to shut down when they overreach.

Like other agencies and departments, the EPA has its own social media policy. Its goal is clearly stated. 'It is EPA's policy to use social media where appropriate in order to meet its mission of protecting human health and the environment' (Jackson 2011a, 2). Quite where discussion of baseball by successive administrators fits into that is less clear—demonstrating the wide interpretations that agencies are willing to allow in building a profile for their leaders that can subsequently be harnessed in the organisation's cause. The document makes clear that it sees social media as a way of reaching out beyond the EPA itself. 'The benefits of using social media in support of EPA's mission include increased ability for the Agency to engage and collaborate with partners, notably the American public' (Jackson 2011a, 1). The accompanying guidance on 'Using Social Media to Communicate with the Public' urges employees to '[r]emember that you are "speaking" for the Agency when you are working in your official capacity' (Jackson 2011b, 2). This means that people should not be using social media to engage in 'any partisan political activity', and nor should they 'say anything online that you would not say in a speech in your official capacity' (Jackson 2011b, 2).

To contrast American practice with current approaches in Westminster-system countries, this chapter proceeds firstly by drawing out the tension between the speed of social media communications and the traditionally slow civil service authorisation processes. In order to conceptualise how civil servants might be able to balance that tension effectively, I draw on the work of John Kane and Haig Patapan on the Aristotelian idea of prudence and the extent to which it provides a guide to careful judgement when engaging on social media. To finish, the chapter then compares the formal rules on social media use for civil servants in Australia, Canada, New Zealand and the UK, to see what room is actually available for prudent creativity in using social media to publicly connect with citizens.

The issue, as with so much of the 'governing in public' environment, is the speed of social media as compared to the much slower natural speed of government. As discussed in the previous chapter, the speed of response required from politicians is now very rapid indeed. As Tony Blair reflected in 2007 in his address to the Reuters Institute,

> The news schedule is now 24 hours a day, 7 days a week and it moves in real time. . . . You have to respond to stories also in real time. Frequently the problem is as much assembling the facts as giving them. Make a mistake and you quickly transfer from drama into crisis. . . . Things also harden within minutes. I mean you can't let speculation stay out there for longer than an instant.

That was in 2007. A decade later, the speed at which news moves, and the speed of the response required, have continued to multiply. Social media have driven what Rodrigues and Niemann (2017) dub 'incessant political communication'. Some politicians have tried to harness that speed by using social media to cut into the news cycle at will (see Katz et al. 2013 for the

Obama presidency, and Marland et al. 2015 for Canadian observations). President Trump's Twitter account is a daily manifestation of how that can work to drive the news cycle. For bureaucracies and their leaders, a desire to avoid undue controversy, and a traditional reticence in public outreach, make that kind of overt and instant attempt to shape the news through social media more problematic, as I discuss below.

Hierarchical Tensions

For civil servants in Westminster systems, the challenge of social media is that they create horizontal communication patterns in what remains fundamentally a hierarchical system. Under the conventions of a Westminster parliamentary democracy, civil servants answer to ministers, who in turn answer to parliament—and through parliament to the people. It is a system designed to operate through clear vertical flows of both information and authorisation. A system based on ubiquitous engagement with social media at multiple levels is fundamentally at odds with this traditional hierarchical model. Instead of information being passed up the chain and released through elected politicians at the top, it seeps into the public domain from multiple sources. What was once an information pipeline with ministers at its head becomes instead an information colander.

Current practice shows that bureaucracies are on the whole pushing forward regardless. In the twenty-first century, government policy doesn't just encourage public servants to be open and proactive in their relationship with the public—it demands it. The sheer breadth and reach of social media platforms such as Twitter, Youtube, Facebook, Instagram and others have created new options for public servants to engage with a form of outreach that carries both enormous potential and enormous risk.

The Westminster system was created in the days when information flows were slow and certain. Under Westminster convention, ministers are responsible for the actions of their departments, and yet today the idea that they could keep up with the immense flow of information being placed into the public domain, even by their own departments, is laughable. Even permanent secretaries and assistant secretaries would be hard pressed, with the incredibly complex demands on their time, to authorise every tweet, Facebook post, internet blog and Instagram picture that emerges from their buildings. Of course, for most of these communications, the type of information being shared is not particularly controversial. But the nature of social media means that it potentially only takes one small slip on a Twitter posting for a public servant to be landed in a remarkably embarrassing and difficult situation.

The embrace of social media seems on the surface to be perfectly in keeping with contemporary political commitments to transparent governance, right-to-information laws, and a citizen-centred public service. If governments are there to serve the people, why not talk to them through the medium that they now use? But it also fundamentally changes the relationship between a minister and her or his department. Instead of the minister being the face and voice of public communication, the department becomes porous, with information coming into the public domain from multiple levels, targeted at different audiences. The protective shield of ministerial responsibility that once guaranteed the anonymity and impartiality of public servants is set aside, with bureaucrats communicating directly with the public, often under their own names, with all the attendant risks and personal public accountability that such a change entails.

When I talk about 'social media' here, I mean something more than simply utilising the internet for the passing of information to a passive receiver. Contemporary social media reflect the advances inherent in what has been termed 'Web 2.0', towards seeing the internet as a place where users can be creators of information as well as receivers (see Morison 2010). To quote New Zealand government guidelines on social media use, '[f]undamentally it is about conversation'; social media constitute 'a set of online technologies, sites and practices which are used to share opinions, experiences and perspectives' (Government Information Services 2011, 4). In other words, social media are fundamentally a two-way form of interactive communication.

The rise and rise of social media has generated increasing academic attention over the past half-decade. The literature on how governments can or should use social media has largely focused on questions around how they can best be utilised to better connect citizens with their governments (see Chadwick 2011 for a summary of this literature; Bertot et al. 2012; Kavanaugh et al. 2012; Paris et al. 2013). This has been coupled with consideration of how far public servants can use social media to make personal political comments outside the workplace. The literature in this latter area is focused largely on employee rights and employment law cases which have tested how far employers are justified in acting against employees who make private posts in their personal rather than official capacity. This aspect of the topic has also attracted wide attention in the popular media, through a number of high-profile cases of employees posting strong critiques of the governments they serve. For example, a former immigration department official in Australia faced a five-year legal battle for anonymously criticising immigration policy on Twitter (see Dingwall 2018a), whilst in the UK, a civil servant was sacked in 2011 for ridiculing government ministers on Twitter under a pseudonym (see Watt 2011).

In the field of public administration, scholarship has focused on discussions around 'e-governance', and in particular the shift towards what has been termed 'digital-era governance' (DEG) (see Dunleavy et al. 2006; Margetts 2008; Coleman and Blumler 2009). Amongst the elements of DEG, according to Margetts (2008), are the 'reintegration' of government services, a 'needs-based holism' that focuses on providing information in the ways that citizens actually want it and increased 'digitisation' leading to e-processes replacing more traditional paper-based alternatives. Similarly, work by Morison (2010) on the United Kingdom has examined the ways in which the move towards 'Gov 2.0' offers new ways for public servants and citizens to interact, whilst recognising that the citizen-centred focus of official rhetoric isn't necessarily always reflected in practice. In America, works such as Ines Mergel's 2013 book *Social Media in the Public Sector* have struck a largely positive note on how social media can lead to more open and engaged styles of government.

Governments are certainly aware that social media use does not come without risks attached. Bureaucracies across the Westminster world have put in place new rules and guidance as they attempt to reconcile the potential power and reach of social media with the traditions of impartiality, anonymity and hierarchical control that have been central to the Westminster system for over a century. In the following pages, I examine the rules in place in Australia, New Zealand, Canada and the United Kingdom. Just how far are civil servants able to go in building a public profile in their official capacity? The reason this matters is that the formal rules reflect the extent to which governments are either actively embracing social media, or merely tolerating their presence. As one Swedish study shows, local officials are much more likely to use social media as passive consumers, to monitor what is going on, rather than adopting them as an active tool for communications outreach (see Djerf-Pierre and Pierre 2016). Where there is active discomfort within organisations about the use of social media, the challenges for leaders keen to reach out more proactively into public debate become more intense: they are having to re-shape cultural norms in the process.

Prudence and Public Value

In 2006, Kane and Patapan argued that the reforms encompassed within New Public Management (NPM) had liberated bureaucracies from traditional command-and-control models, but had done so without correctly understanding the extent to which the need for prudent judgement was being dispersed to a much wider range of officers. In essence, the traditional Westminster model of a bureaucracy gave the mandarins at the top wide discretion, but required little in the way of similar levels of judgement from junior officers who followed mandated and long-established internal processes. For the people at the top, prudent judgement was central to the successful exercise of discretion. Following Aristotle, Kane and Patapan argued that prudence 'was demonstrable only in the concrete judgements made by an intelligent individual acting in specific circumstances. It was never the simple application of impersonal, universal and certain laws' (2006, 712).

Faced with a choice between supporting civil servants in making individual judgements or seeking to tightly regulate their behaviour, modern governments have sought to have it both ways. They have encouraged the emergence of a less risk-averse breed of administrative entrepreneur (Van Wart 2003), whilst at the same time generating an ever-widening array of guidance documents to govern the behaviour of public servants in every conceivable situation. As the empirical material below demonstrates, public servants are being encouraged to use social media to reach out to the public—to be entrepreneurial communicators—and yet at the same time to be hyper-vigilant about saying anything that might compromise the bureaucracy or the government.

In essence, public servants are being told to be adventurous and cautious at the same time. These contradictory urges are encapsulated within a raft of internal rules designed to regulate their behaviour, often with unintended consequences. For example, an exploratory case study by Chadwick (2011) demonstrates that the operation of tight rules to police what happens online, and the fear of litigation if rules are overstepped, can contribute to public servants becoming risk-averse in ways that limit the effectiveness of the online initiative being undertaken. On the flipside, bureaucrats who act as moderators of online forums can find themselves cast in the role of censors, projecting a so-called 'shadow of control' over a supposedly open forum (Wright 2006; Edwards 2002; Wright and Street 2007).

The pace and reach of social media mean that bureaucracies are operating outside their traditional comfort zone. It's easy to see why prudent judgement is the only skill that matters when it comes to wrestling with the electronic public. For example, when public servants join blog discussion groups in order to challenge misinterpretations of government policy, they are arguably pursuing public value, but in a way that means millions of people can choose to follow the discussion, and place their own interpretations and perceptions on what an official has said. It's taking the search for public value out of the confines of small group discussions in meeting rooms and into the public domain. Arguably, a higher level of personal judgement is required, one that reflects the higher risks of public embarrassment that are involved.

Rules governing the relationship between public servants and social media appear at two levels. The first is as part of the more generic rules that govern bureaucratic behaviour and communication. These are the broad 'codes of conduct' that have now been enacted in almost all modern democracies in some form or other. Such codes cover broad responsibilities and values like honesty, integrity and impartiality. The second level, which is the predominant focus here, are the rules and guidelines aimed specifically at social media, to try and keep up with the myriad opportunities and problems that the ever-widening array of platforms provides. In the sections that follow below, I examine the guiding documents currently in place in Canada, the United Kingdom, New Zealand and Australia in turn, before broadening into a comparative discussion of the challenge that social media use poses to the structure of a Westminster-system public service.[1]

Canada

The Canadian government's *Policy on Communications and Federal Identity* is available through the Treasury Board of Canada Secretariat—which carries responsibility for the majority of public service guideline documents. The current version was promulgated in 2016 by the new Trudeau government, replacing the former *Communications Policy of the Government of Canada*. As para. 4.4 of the current *Policy on Communications* makes clear, digital communication is now simply what the public expects.

Canadians increasingly use technology to communicate in their daily lives, and expect to interact with the government in the same way. Using new communications approaches that stem from the rise of digital technologies, balanced with using traditional methods, enables the Government of Canada to reach and engage with Canadians effectively and efficiently in the official language of their choice, regardless of where they reside. (Treasury Board of Canada Secretariat 2016)

More information, specifically on the use of social media, is supplied in the *Policy on Acceptable Network and Device Use*. The policy provides as appendices lists of acceptable and unacceptable uses of devices and networks. The examples of 'acceptable use' listed in Appendix B include internal government communication, and the watching of work-related video content such as parliamentary committee hearings. The list goes on to refer to a range of specific social media platforms and tools, including Twitter, Slide-Share and LinkedIn. Public servants are encouraged to '[f]ollow thought leaders and government officials on blogs or micro-blogs such as Twitter', and to themselves '[t]weet, re-tweet or share links to professional activities and events, or interesting and relevant articles' (Treasury Board of Canada Secretariat 2013, Appendix B). This freedom extends to online discussion groups, where public servants can '[r]ead, contribute to, or edit articles in work-related wikis, online forums or discussion groups' (Treasury Board of Canada Secretariat 2013, Appendix B).

Terms such as 'work-related' and 'interesting and relevant' are not defined in the definitions section of the document, leaving significant room—as ever—for individual interpretation by public servants. The most relevant examples of 'unacceptable use', and the ones that have generated the greatest public debate through court cases, are the uses seen to be breaching the public servants' 'duty of loyalty', through criticism of the government. These include activities that are illegal, such as '[r]evealing sensitive government information without authorization' (Treasury Board of Canada Secretariat 2013, Appendix C). But they also include activities that are in breach of public service policies and guidelines without necessarily being illegal or criminal. These activities can occur both when public servants are acting in their official capacity and when they are using networks in their own time within the 'personal use' provisions.

In their official capacity during work time, a public servant cannot 'make public comments about government policies, except when acting as the official spokesperson, or . . . engage in political activity that could impair his or her ability to perform duties in an impartial manner' (Treasury Board of Canada Secretariat 2013, Appendix C). Similarly, bureaucrats cannot represent 'personal opinions as those of the organization, or otherwise [fail] to comply with organizational procedures concerning public statements about the government's positions' (Treasury Board of Canada Secretariat 2013, Appendix C). In terms of 'limited personal use', public servants can check a weather forecast or use social media sites to connect with family and friends, but cannot cause congestion to information channels by circulating chain letters or sending bulk emails of a personal nature.

The *Guideline on Acceptable Network and Device Use* (which follows up in support of the broader policy document) embraces social media as publicly-facing communication tools to be harnessed. The guideline distinguishes between 'professional use', 'personal use' and 'official use', and sets out ways for departments to monitor the operation of the policy. Some of the language of the guideline's predecessor, which had focused more on avoiding 'negative perceptions' and how to respond to 'on-line vandalism', has been set aside in this latest version.

In summary, the Canadian rules support the use of social media by public servants, but in relatively risk-averse ways. The emphasis is more on caution than innovation. Bureaucrats are encouraged to follow 'thought leaders', rather than to become thought leaders themselves. It is an approach that sees social media as an additional tool rather than as a unique avenue through which public servants can proactively pursue public value.

This caution was very much reflected in my interviews with individuals who have operated at the top of the Canadian public service. For example, one interviewee discussed the difficulties in using social media to solicit input from the public.

> [W]e made the conscious decision to keep our traditional way of so-liciting input, which was to put out public notices and invite input because what do you do with somebody's Twitter comment, or you know, through Facebook. How do you take that 140 characters seriously when you're asking very detailed, technical questions? (Author interview, Canada, 2015)

Another confirmed the sense that civil service Twitter feeds were likely to be quite 'boring' (author interview, Canada, 2015), to avoid controversy, and might be used by public service heads as a way of communicating with the wider organisation, rather than to debate public policy ideas. As in other areas, even those who were concerned about the impact of social media acknowledged the inevitability of its impact. '[I]t's very difficult to function in the world today in a public policy world, and being able to disregard things like the new social media; it's just a fact of life. But it has given, I think, some greater degree of a public face to senior mandarin types' (author interview, Canada, 2015).

Canadian interviewees continued to reflect on the degree to which the Harper government in particular was trying to control all communication, and how this stopped social media from achieving its potential as an outreach tool to citizens. One noted that social media posts were just re-worked versions of more traditional communication forms like media releases. '[T]hey produce the social media versions of them and they all go through the same approvals and they're all pat pieces, standard stuff and there's nothing really particularly fresh or authentic about it' (author interview, Canada, 2015). The same person thought that this was in the end unworkable, given the technological shift and wider need for engagement with citizens. '[F]rom a public service point of view and whether it's Australia, UK or Canada, if you continue to live in a command-and-control, risk-averse environment and you don't allow your public servants to talk to anybody about anything, you're dead' (author interview, Canada, 2015).

Another interviewee shared a similar sentiment about current Twitter usage in Canadian government being 'inane', but believed that this will inevitably have to change over time. 'They'll either give up the Twitter or they're going to have to make it real, in which case there'll have to be risks that sometimes it'll be something that's not so inane' (author interview, Canada, 2015). The capacity to communicate has essentially outstripped the capacity for civil service traditions to keep up. As another Canadian interviewee argued, the system is in a state of flux. 'I don't think any government . . . have figured this out. Politically you're seeing it all the time. Ministers are tweeting and they're doing all that but how do public servants—how are we using social media and all those interactive tools to gain more knowledge but doing it in a way that isn't seen as, again, moving into the space of what our politicians normally would do? It's a tricky issue for all of us right now' (author interview, Canada, 2015).

United Kingdom

In the UK, a *Social Media Guidance for Civil Servants* was released in May 2012 as part of the UK government ICT strategy, and updated in October 2014. The foreword in the document by the then minister for the cabinet office, Francis Maude, presents social media as a way of engaging 'actively with the public' so that the civil service can 'reach out to the people it serves' (Cabinet Office 2014). The opening statement shows that social media are no longer seen simply as internal communications mechanisms that the wider public can tune in to if they want, but more as an outward-looking communications tool that can underpin more participative styles of democratic interaction between civil servants and the voters they serve.

The *Guidance* as a whole encourages a very proactive and engaged social media approach by the civil service. Rather than simply monitoring social media sites, the emphasis is on civil servants participating. 'There are many benefits to using social media. It helps government to communicate with the public; to consult and engage; and to be more transparent and accountable. As civil servants, we are becoming increasingly digital in the way we operate.'

The *Guidance* and the accompanying 'Social Media Playbook' emphasise that there is much to be gained for the public sector by engaging in social media. There is less sense than in the guidelines from other countries that social media are something for civil servants to be scared of lest they bite them in unwelcome ways.

> Social and digital media usage is constantly increasing. The quality of interaction and demographics of our audience should influence our choice of how and when to communicate. The more we can learn about online communities, the better we can engage with them. Going to where our audience already is can save both time and money. (Cabinet Office 2014)

The degree of proactive engagement extends not just to the delivery of services, but also to the active solicitation of advice on policy.

> Online engagement can be very helpful when developing policy. This could include something as simple as asking questions for crowd-sourcing views or drawing attention to consultation events. For example, a LinkedIn blog can be used to gauge the opinion of people in the business community. (Cabinet Office 2014)

The *Guidance* emphasises that civil servants retain their duty of impartiality in the online social media environment as much as they do in any other aspect of their working lives. 'Social media is a public forum and the same considerations would apply as, say, to speaking in public or writing for a publication either officially or out of work'.

The inherently dynamic nature of the medium, where things can go viral in a matter of minutes and mistakes can be amplified exponentially, means that the professional judgement of civil servants in what they choose to post must be acute. The *Guidance* acknowledges that this can be a difficult balancing act.

In social media the boundaries between professional and personal are often more blurred—so it's important to be particularly careful. As civil servants we are (of course) free to use social and other digital media in our own time. But we always need to be mindful of our duties not to disclose official information without authority, and not to take part in any political or other public activity which compromises, or might be seen to compromise, our impartial service to the government of the day or any future government. (Cabinet Office 2014)

The balancing act becomes even more difficult when civil servants are commenting in either their personal or official capacity on issues that are directly relevant to government policy. The *Guidance* suggests that civil servants 'must take care about commenting on government policies and practices and should not do so without the proper authorisation. We should avoid commenting altogether on politically controversial issues and avoid making any kind of personal attack or tasteless or offensive remarks to individuals or groups'. It also shows an awareness that the startling pace of social media can make their users forget that it's much easier to put something up than it is to take it down. As the guidelines point out, 'once something is posted online it's very difficult to remove it'.

In summary, the UK approach to social media use by civil servants reflects a comparatively enthusiastic embrace. Civil servants are positioned not only as followers, but as active participants in online communities. The rules, whilst emphasising the usual cautions, recognise that social media can allow civil servants to proactively pursue public value in how they interact with citizens. Just how warm that embrace of the citizenry through social media should be was something of a debating point amongst the UK civil service leaders interviewed for the current project.

One former head of an arm's-length agency noted that social media were a factor contributing to the transparent world that 'governing in public' has foisted upon civil servants. 'There's nothing you can do that you can assume will be kept confidential . . . So you might as well write, think and speak as if every single word you're going to say is going to be in the public domain. It's the only safe way' (author interview, UK, 2015). The same interviewee had experienced the sharp end of social media after giving a TV interview that had proven to be controversial, leading to an outbreak of criticism on social media. '[T]hey were tweeting every twenty minutes and it was hugely personal. It was all about me, not about what I'd said or I'd done, called for my resignation endlessly . . . You begin to think, shit this is never going to end' (author interview, UK, 2015).

A similar view was taken by another UK interviewee, for whom social media were the final straw that had broken the back of anonymity; so
bureaucratic leaders had to get used to facing these new pressures. 'I think
the genie's out of the bottle . . . Not to the point where we act as though we
are quasi-politicians. I think that is completely wrong. But I think we do
have to be comfortable in our own skin with being public figures' (author
interview, UK, 2015). The more cynical interviewees took the same view as
Canadians, that really there was nothing of substance being put on Twitter
because it was too dangerous to do so. 'My impression is, [name omitted]'s
Twitter account is pretty boring . . . which is what you want it to be. Absolutely dead down the middle and slightly pious . . . I don't see how you can
do anything else' (author interview, UK, 2014). All interviewees were aware
that they were balancing the risks of social media use against the benefits,
and for many the benefits were not sufficient to sway them. One former
permanent secretary explained it this way: 'Twitter, Facebook, just seem
to me that that would lay me open to just too much conversation and the
chance that you would just say the wrong thing almost by accident. There
are other ways I can communicate without having to go on Twitter' (author
interview, UK, 2015).

New Zealand

Of the four jurisdictions under study, New Zealand has the most developed
range of tools to assist public servants as they engage with social media.
The available documents are grouped under the heading of *Social Media in
Government*, and include a *High Level Guidance, How to Handle a Mishap,
Hands-on Toolbox* and a case study of successful use of social media. Similarly to the UK approach, there is considerable encouragement for public
servants to see social media as an important avenue through which to engage
in 'conversation' with New Zealanders. The *High Level Guidance* stresses
at the outset that, '[i]n contrast with traditional media, the nature of social
media is to be highly interactive' (Government Information Services 2011, 3).
The *Guidance* asserts that '[s]ocial media is a dialogue that happens between
Government and its citizens' (4).

The *Guidance* stresses the importance of having in place staff who can
act as 'authorised authors' to utilise social media quickly and responsibly.
The need for speed in social media use is emphasised. 'Nothing kills the
effectiveness of a social media project more quickly than slow response
times where each and every statement or 'tweet' needs to go up the chain

of command to be approved before publication' (7). In setting out the need for swift and authoritative social media updates, the *Guidance* undoubtedly sets out established best practice in social media use. But at the same time it highlights the inherent tension between the traditionally hierarchical structure of a Westminster public service and the modern demands of social media.

The Westminster system of government, with its enshrined doctrine of ministerial responsibility, is based on things going 'up the chain of command'. Traditionally, anonymous public servants quietly worked in the background to build or implement policy, with work continually fed up the administrative line to the departmental permanent secretary and ultimately the minister. Social medias' need for speed alters this fundamentally, exchanging the hierarchical process for a horizontal one. Trusted public servants are given authorisation to independently exercise their judgement and publish as and when they deem appropriate. What is more, the New Zealand guidelines stress that '[you should] identify yourself as a public servant if you are responding on behalf of your organisation' (Government Information Services 2011, 7). Anonymity is not only no longer protected, but actively discouraged, because of the very nature of social media.

As in the UK, the *Guidance* does not attempt to hide the dangers that are present for the individual and collective reputations of the public service when people participate online. They stress that the same rules and codes of conduct apply in all public situations. 'Staff should participate in the same way as they would with other media or public forums such as speaking at conferences' (8). It is stressed that public servants must expressly 'seek authorisation to participate in social media on behalf of your agency' (8). In other words, the encouragement for the public service to become more engaged through social media does not extend to a carte-blanche approach that encourages every employee to hit the public message boards on any matter that they wish.

Nevertheless, the *Guidance* also recognises that there is no clear line, once information is public, between personal and official messages. 'Be aware that participating online may attract media interest in you as an individual, so proceed with care regardless of what capacity you are acting in' (8). This danger of attracting media interest is particularly acute for those who are senior leaders within the public service. The New Zealand *Guidance* provides 'Special advice to Chief Executives' who can garner a public and professional profile by using social media under their own name.

One of the most serious drawbacks for Chief Executives is the amount of time social media takes up and the risk that, if they are not familiar with social media, Chief Executives might come across as too formal and, therefore, inauthentic. (9)

The capacity for things to go 'horribly wrong' is acknowledged by the provision in the New Zealand suite of documents of guidance on 'How to Handle a Mishap'. The kinds of risks and mishaps outlined include the use of 'questionable humour' by public servants when posting, misinterpreted messages and the unintended early release of information or documents (Government Information Services 2012, 3–4). Especially when coping with the speed and complexity of social media, a vital role remains for the individual judgement of public servants.

> They are often the challenging area for Government agencies because there are no specific rules and processes to follow for each situation. People responding to social media on behalf of the agency need to rely on a set of general behavioural guidelines and judgements made at the time. (Government Information Services 2012, 4)

And those judgements sometimes need to be made in a hurry, with the *Guidance* noting that 'approved authors' should be able to respond after hours if need be (2012, 5). To minimise the chance of a 'mishap', the *Guidance* suggests that public servants also proactively 'identify key influencers within your social media base and keep them happy—who has the most followers and what does the influencer appear to find most valuable within the social media realm?' (5).

From a social media control point of view, it is undoubtedly good advice. But from a Westminster system of government point of view, should it really be the role of public servants to keep key social influencers 'happy'? Furthermore, in providing information to a social media platform, public servants could very easily release information whilst policies are still being developed. 'When employees post on their social networking sites about projects they are working on or policies their agencies are developing, they don't necessarily realise they are posting government confidential information' (Government Information Services 2012, 8). In other words, much of what public servants do in terms of policy development is not really suited to a social media type of interaction, given the continuing role of ministers as the ultimate source of policy authorisation.

In summary, the New Zealand case presents rules that show understanding of the unique demands of a social media environment. They recognise that turnaround times need to be at the speed expected of social media, which is why authorised authors need to be available at all hours to be able to provide immediate responses without having to clear them with managers up the line. The rules suggest that public servants actively engage in social media management by knowing who 'key influencers' are and keeping them 'happy'. It's a proactive approach to avoiding trouble and responding quickly, but it stops short of encouraging public servants to reach out ahead of existing opinion to create new online communities.

Do these rules connect with the realities of practice? On the whole the answer is 'yes'. There was a sense amongst interviewees for the present project that the New Zealand system has been acclimatised to transparency for longer (the Official Information Act dates back to the early 1980s), meaning that ministers are less anxious about the civil service engaging with social media. That was particularly so because of New Zealand's relatively small size. 'I think it's one of the plusses [of] being a small country. . . . [It] means that the public sector guys, in a way, have a bit more space to be their own person, to be seen that way and not be tarred with a particular government brush' (author interview, New Zealand, 2016). There was still caution from some. 'I could only see pitfalls in that to be honest. The risk and reward ratio just wasn't good enough for me to spend the time and effort that it would have taken. I mean, I had comms people whose job it was to do stuff' (author interview, New Zealand, 2016). Another felt that the rules did not allow civil servants to defend themselves in an environment where they could be lambasted on social media. '[I]t's very difficult I think for the chief executives and the senior public servants because they still are bound by loyalty and obedience to their minister and generally they have to respond with their gloves on to a bunch of people who have got their gloves off' (author interview, New Zealand, 2016).

Australia

The Australian guidelines, as set out by the Public Service Commission, have been frequently updated in the last decade as the complexities of social media have increased. The most recent revision, in August 2017 (quoted below), drew forth widespread media criticism alleging that the government was going too far to muzzle its public servants. Like their counterparts, the Australian guidelines emphasise that public servants should view remarks on social media in the same way as any other public comment, in terms of their responsibility to remain impartial. 'In general, APS employees must not make public comment that may lead a reasonable person to conclude that they cannot serve the government of the day impartially and professionally' (Australian Public Service Commission 2017, 2).

The guidance acknowledges that some public servants may engage in public comment outside their APS role, but in a way that still relates to their professional competence. The general provision for public servants to make private comments is broad. 'As members of the Australian community, Australian Public Service (APS) employees have the right to participate in public and political debate' (2). But underneath this general provision lies a web of complexity and caution.

The nature of the guidance reflects the difficulties inherent in promulgating guidelines that can actually provide clear boundaries for public servants. 'Deciding whether to make a particular comment or post certain material online is a matter of careful judgement rather than a simple formula' (2). Ultimately what the guidance demonstrates is how difficult it is for public servants to become public actors without crossing the established bounds of public service impartiality. Under Westminster convention, public servants are anonymous servants of the government of the day for a reason. As soon as they enter the public domain, others can interpret their comments in whichever way they see fit. Even if public servants are striving to be apolitical in their comments, they cannot control how others will perceive and portray them. The 24/7 news media are constantly in need of stories to maintain their momentum, and any perception of a misstep by a public servant can quickly be portrayed as criticism of the government.

The opportunities presented by social media have changed the public administration playing field, whilst also increasing the underlying risks that public servants take when going public. That risk gets deeper the higher up the ladder of responsibility a public servant resides. As the guidance states, members of the Senior Executive Service face extra scrutiny of their public statements because of their leadership positions.

> As a general guide, the more senior you are in the APS the more likely it is that people will believe you are privy to the real workings of government. Your opinions will carry more weight and have a greater capacity to affect the reputation of an agency or the APS. Senior APS employees, or employees with a particularly high-profile or specialist role, need to be especially careful in considering the impact of any comments they might make. (4).

In the Australian context, similarly to the other jurisdictions under comparison here, there is an unequivocal starting point that there is a direct public benefit to be gained from public servants engaging with social media. In this, the guidance follows the findings of the 2010 report by the Australian government's 'Gov 2.0 Taskforce'—*Engage: Getting on With Government 2.0*—which supported 'robust professional discussion as part of their duties or as private citizens'. The danger, as noted in the guidance, is that social media are not the same as other platforms for public comment. Public servants need to exercise particular care.

> The speed and reach of online communication means that material posted online is available immediately to a wide audience. It can be difficult to delete and may be replicated endlessly. It may be sent to, or seen by, people the author never intended or expected would see it. (2)

These dangers exist not only when employees are posting in their official capacity under their own name, but also when they choose to post in an unofficial capacity using an alias.

> You may not have identified yourself as a public servant but many of us now have a digital footprint that makes it easy to find out who we are and, often, where we work. Posting material anonymously or using a pseudonym doesn't guarantee your identity will stay hidden. Even if you don't identify yourself you can still be identified by someone else. . . . It is simply common sense to assume that anything you write or post can be linked to you and your employer—whether you intend it or not. (6)

In summary, in Australian government the emphasis overall is on control and avoiding overreach by public servants on social media. Rather than being encouraged to actively pursue public value, Australian public servants are exhorted to make sure first and foremost that their behaviour does not overstep any boundaries. In interviews for this project, recently retired senior public servants were very aware of the level of political anxiety around this issue, and tended towards caution. It chafed for some, whilst seeming perfectly appropriate to others. The cautious responders highlighted the inability to actually control social media. 'I have to say that for a whole range of reasons Twitter and Facebook require the most careful management. If you allow on Twitter and Facebook a public exchange you find there are all sorts of things you can't control on that and if it's on your Facebook site even though you didn't write it you are held responsible for allowing it to happen' (author interview, Australia, 2015). Even where there is political will in support of engaging with social media, the most experienced departmental secretaries were very wary. One remembered,

In fact we had a secretaries' discussion once, under Rudd, when Rudd was suggesting that perhaps secretaries ought to get a bit more active in social media. And [name omitted] raised it in the secretaries meeting, and I remember virtually all the rest of us said, 'What a stupid idea.' . . . I mean it would be all very well for Prime Minister Rudd when we were saying good things about him, [but if] people were saying what he was doing was a lot of crap he wouldn't be too happy. (Author interview, Australia, 2016)

Younger secretaries felt slightly more positive in seeing social media as a part of outreach in the modern governance environment that just needed to be handled well. '[I]t's a bit like email used to be before Twitter and Facebook. People can put things in emails which are not a good look if they turn up in the newspaper, and that's what can happen with Twitter, but if it's appropriately managed it is a legitimate tool because often in departments you have to engage with stakeholders in order to implement programmes' (author interview, Australia, 2015).

The Prudent Pursuit of Public Value

Any idea that governments and public servants could simply ignore social media, or opt out of their use, is clearly fanciful. Nevertheless, social media offer new challenges to the way a public service operates within the confines of a Westminster system. Importantly, these challenges extend beyond how to make best use of social media to connect with people, and even beyond the problems of individuals overstepping the mark in their personal use of social media. At the core conceptual level, social media challenge the fundamental hierarchical structure that governs ministerial accountability within a Westminster-type system. Contentious public policy decisions are always inherently political. That is why it is left to democratically elected ministers to make them and announce them. Social media create risks because of their ability to divert traditional patterns of information flow in ways that may create political and public controversy, whilst opening up new forums for debate which are inherently hard to control.

What the policies, guidelines and standards examined here don't sufficiently grapple with are the political dangers involved when public servants overstep the mark. By engaging publicly in an official capacity through social media, public servants are walking into policy conversations that are inherently contentious and political, a space in which public servants have traditionally been warned not to walk. The New Zealand guidance suggests that there is a 'need for care around party political comment' (Government Information Services 2011, 10) but this does little to address the potential for social media use to get public servants into 'political' trouble.

Political communication is the obsession of twenty-first century politics. Political leaders surround themselves with media advisers because they know that they cannot allow themselves to lose control of their communications environment for even a moment. The 24/7 news cycle, and the wider impact of social media, means prime ministers are increasingly centralising government communication within their own offices to avoid contradictory messages. Stray words are seen as dangerous. And yet, the potential for public servants to generate uncontrolled communications is magnified dramatically once departments are encouraged to deeply engage with social media in an official capacity.

As more communications go out without direct ministerial authorisation or knowledge, ministers will have no choice but to publicly criticise their own departments when messages go wrong. The social media guidelines examined here suggest that governments are applying the established conventions of Westminster-type public services to social media as if they were just the same as any other form of public outreach. To quote the UK *Guidance,* for example, 'Staff should participate in the same way as they would with other media or public forums such as speaking at conferences' (Government Information Services 2011, 8). Public servants are told to remain impartial, and to refrain from behaviour that would lead to any loss of public confidence in the bureaucracy. This suggests that social media can be managed without any fundamental change in approach. In reality, social media normalise mass communication by multiple public servants at multiple levels. Even with expectations in place that public servants need authorisation to become accredited to use social media officially, the system cannot control the content of every tweet and Facebook post.

In a comparative sense, all the guidelines and rules examined here begin at the same point. They see social media as an important tool that government departments and agencies can and must incorporate into their work. Social media represent a positive to be actively embraced, albeit with eyes open as to the potential risks. From that starting point, different jurisdictions make different judgements as to how far they are willing to allow public servants to use their own prudence to add 'public value' (without specifically using the term) through their social media use.

The United Kingdom rules, and to a lesser extent those in New Zealand, are the most positive—even enthusiastic—in tone about what can be achieved through social media. The rules in these jurisdictions exhort public servants to get involved in online conversations, rather than focusing on warnings of the dire consequences if things go wrong. Both jurisdictions still provide the standard cautions about not overstepping political lines, but do not let that overshadow the general rule that social media should be vigorously engaged with. The benefits of 'communicating 1-to-many' are extolled, as are the opportunities for civil servants to become 'a catalyst for the creation of online communities' (Government Digital Service 2012, 3). Social media are presented as 'dialogue' (Government Information Services 2011, 4), which should not be slowed down by the cumbersome authorisation procedures of traditional bureaucracy. Essentially, the rules in the UK and New Zealand are set up on the basis that public servants can be trusted to exercise prudent judgement in how to go about interacting with social media.

The Canadian and Australian guidelines certainly do encourage the public service to make use of social media, but are overall more tentative and risk-averse in their encouragement. There is no talk here of leading the creation of online communities, with a much greater focus on preventing breaches of public service obligations of impartiality. As the media reports on the new guidelines promulgated by the Australian Public Service Commission in 2017 indicate (see McIlroy 2017), the desire to control public service behaviour is trumping the willingness to take risks in order to better communicate with citizens. The need for hierarchical control and authorisation is trumping the opportunities for horizontal patterns of engagement.

In essence, social media allow public service departments and the individuals within them to create their own unique public profiles, separate from those of the ministers they serve. As a result, public servants are no longer sheltered behind the anonymity provided by the bricks-and-mortar walls of large departments. The various guidance documents encourage public servants to get involved and engaged in a two-way dialogue with citizens. This is a fundamental horizontal levelling of the hierarchical tradition of Westminster-type bureaucracies. Departments, and individuals within departments, are becoming direct communicators with the public, without the traditional filters that protect ministerial accountability and public service anonymity. This is particularly so at the 'pointy end', where departmental permanent secretaries and their equivalents are having to engage as public figures in their own right. Rather than creating social media rules that simply apply established Westminster principles to this evolving area, governments may need to reconceptualise their view of how 'public' a modern public service needs to become.

This presents governments with a stark choice in the social media field. If they wish to authorise entrepreneurial communicators within the public service, they must provide protection rather than blame when things go wrong. It is hard to be more adventurous when the safety net has been removed. Alternatively, if they wish to maintain a 'business-as-usual' approach to official social media use, then clearer hierarchical controls need to be written into the guidelines, so that authorisation and accountability flows can easily be traced. At the moment, the guidelines being promulgated by Westminster-system governments are having it both ways—encouraging engagement but counselling extreme caution—with the risks settling squarely on the shoulders of public servants rather than of their ministerial masters.

That is why a Washminster approach offers new opportunities. In keeping with other aspects of leaders' public face, it includes a commitment to taking personal responsibility for what goes out on social media. In essence it means departments providing ministers with a degree of plausible deniability, and taking the public blame if anything goes wrong. Instead of ministerial resignations, there might be bureaucratic ones. But in return, social media can be used—as they are in America—to build the kind of public profile that departments and departmental leaders need to be successful in the era of governing in public.

Again, this would represent a significant break from the traditional Westminster system. But I argue that, as in other areas, it's happening anyway. Departments and their leaders are being dragged into using social media, because there is now little choice. Soon it will make as much sense for a modern bureaucrat to shun social media as it would for their predecessors to have refused to use the telephone to replace telegrams. But unlike the telephone, the digital revolution allows communication not just one-to-one, but one-to-millions, which takes the bureaucracy into uncharted waters. A Washminster approach would allow bureaucratic leaders to join the public debate, with both eyes open, and contributing to the ideas marketplace in non-partisan ways. It's not for the faint-hearted.

8

Reminiscing in Public

Cygnet is a quiet little place. Idyllic in many ways. The kind of place travel writers would call 'sleepy'. It has an annual folk festival, tearooms and a thriving arts scene. It's nestled in the Huon Valley in the Australian state of Tasmania, an area once known as the heart of the nation's apple industry. All in all, Cygnet is not the kind of place one would consider a natural epi-centre of intrigue and political conflict. Yet in the late 1970s, it gained a new resident who would bring both with him, in the person of the British former MI5 operative Peter Wright.

Wright had worked at the UK's spy agency in the heady days of the Cold War in the 1950s and '60s. He was a contemporary of people whose names are now infamous—men like Kim Philby and Anthony Blunt, whose post-humous notoriety continues to grow. Wright enters our story here because, whilst whiling away his retirement in the rural tranquillity of the Tasmanian countryside, he decided to pen his memoirs. The book lit a fire under the feet of the British establishment. Entitled *Spycatcher: The Candid Autobiography of a Senior Intelligence Officer*, Wright's volume detailed his life in the intelligence service from 1949 to 1978. It included an airing of potentially in-cendiary accusations that a former senior colleague, Sir Roger Hollis, might have been a Soviet spy.

The book launched Wright to prominence well before it actually hit the news-stands because of the manic efforts of the British government to stop its publication. In a fine early example of how senior civil servants can find themselves pulled into very political matters, the Thatcher government sent then cabinet secretary Sir Robert Armstrong out to 'the colonies' to try to stop the book from ever seeing the light of day. Armstrong's appearance as a witness in court proved a sensation, largely because of the intensity of his nine-day cross-examination by the future Australian prime minister Malcolm Turnbull. The British government lost its case in Australia, and subsequently also in the UK when the judges decided that the book's publication in Australia rendered any attempt to further block its publication in the UK a waste of time. Even in the days before the internet, news could not be isolated and ring-fenced in the Southern Ocean.

Wright and his publishers Heinemann Australia could hardly have devised a more successful marketing campaign. Both he and his book became household names, and the memoir sold two million copies as it took the publishing world by storm. Importantly for our purposes here, in arguing against the book's publication, the British government had insisted that former intelligence officers were bound by a lifelong duty of confidentiality. In other words, Wright should have taken his secrets to the grave. The judges in the House of Lords in fact agreed in large part with that assertion, but argued firstly that the publication of the work overseas rendered insistence upon it pointless in this case, and secondly that the idea of whether it was in the public interest to release something was really a matter for debate in individual cases. As one of the judges, Lord Goff, put it in the judgement,

> [T]he basis of the law's protection of confidence is that there is a public interest that confidences should be preserved and protected by the law, nevertheless that public interest may be outweighed by some other countervailing public interest which favours disclosure. This limitation may apply, as the learned judge pointed out, to all types of confidential information. It is this limiting principle which may require a court to carry out a balancing operation, weighing the public interest in maintaining confidence against a countervailing public interest favouring disclosure. (Attorney General v. Guardian Newspapers Ltd (No. 2) 1988, 29)

But the judges in this case were not convinced that the public interest provided a defence for Wright's actions. In the words of Lord Jauncey of Tulichettle, 'The publication of *Spycatcher* was against the public interest and was in breach of the duty of confidence which Peter Wright owed to the Crown. His action reeked of turpitude.' (40)

This response to Wright's book is an extreme example of the idea that public servants should keep their secrets to themselves. Clearly his is a special case, because of the security concerns that attach to the work of intelligence agencies. But the case also provides a wonderful demonstration of the extent to which Westminster tradition frowns on the idea of making a profit from public service. One need only look at the distaste which has greeted Tony Blair's post-prime ministerial selling of his consultancy services around the world to sense the discomfort with which traditionalists view such behaviour. It is a level of distaste that is substantially increased when directed at former civil servants seen as trading on the knowledge gained from their previous privileged positions at the heart of government.

The other noteworthy point about the Wright case is that it marks an important stepping-off moment, as since then the British intelligence services have embraced a culture of much greater openness and transparency. Whilst in the mid-1980s the full force of the British state was mustered to stop Wright's book, by 2001 the former head of MI5 Stella Rimington was publishing her own autobiography a mere five years after leaving her post at the head of this once most secretive organisation. It was the culmination of her remarkably open leadership style, which began in 1991 when she was identified in newspapers and on TV as being the head of an organisation that had never previously confirmed details of its office holders. But as Rimington herself reflected during media interviews coinciding with the publication of her autobiography *Open Secret*, there remained tremendous discomfort within government about such things. She described to *The Guardian* how revealing it was to suddenly be fighting government from the outside as she was forced to change and cut information from the memoir in response to its official vetting in Whitehall. 'I think I understand better what people outside feel when they're trying to deal with the state, or particularly with the secret state . . . you do just get a feeling of how persecuted you can feel when things are going on that you don't actually have any control over' (Norton-Taylor 2001).

The slow, careful and hard-fought approach to publishing memoirs in the UK has not been matched in Washington, where there has been much less reticence from former administrative leaders who decide to publicly reflect on their time in office. For many sub-cabinet presidential nominees, serving as leaders of the bureaucracy has not necessarily been their lifetime's calling, but just another station on the route. Producing a memoir to some extent marks a rite of passage from government service to whatever comes next. This has certainly been the case for many high-profile politicians. The shelves of leading booksellers are groaning under the weight of political memoirs from authors who claim to have changed the world in the service of their country. But the second shelf down also contains significant writings from people that have served in different agencies and departments and have stories to tell.

Take Alan Greenberg. His memoir of 2010 recounted his life as a senior executive in the US General Services Administration. So far it sounds like a tough sell. But Greenberg's great talent for indiscretion turned it into a fascinating read. *Confessions of a Government Man: How to Succeed in Any Bureaucracy* was an entertaining engagement with the challenges and characters of government. It humanised what can often appear like a remotely-controlled machine. Russell Train was head of the Environmental Protection Authority in the 1970s, and his memoir *Politics, Pollution, and Pandas* was widely praised for its insights into how government worked in the Nixon and Ford administrations. There was certainly no chorus from critics claiming he had defied a convention against publication. And of course, former heads of the Federal Reserve such as Alan Greenspan and Ben Bernanke have won wide acclaim for their memoirs, which have also proven to be bestsellers.

United States ambassadors regularly push out books reflecting on their careers in the foreign service. And even more interestingly, there has been a consistent flow of memoirs from heads of the FBI and the CIA. Louis Freeh, Robert Gates and Allen Dulles all produced insider accounts of their time in the hot seat. All such books are controversial when they're released. All garner reviews and critiques from pundits, commentators, politicians, friends and foe alike. Sometimes they cause national headlines and debates about competing narratives of past government disasters. But few authors have been attacked simply for having had the temerity to write at all.

The book by L. William Seidman is a case in point. Seidman had served multiple presidents, and most notably in terms of his book, he had served as chair of the Federal Deposit Insurance Corporation (FDIC) from 1985 to 1991. He was known as a straight shooter, a reputation burnished as he led the response to the Savings and Loans scandal that saw the FDIC and the newly created Resolution Trust Corporation (RTC) seek to address the overhang of billions of dollars in bad loans left by failing financial institutions. Here was a man who knew that writing a memoir also meant ruffling some political feathers. And he didn't care, as the opening section of his recollections made clear.

> I share the goals of most memoirists: to immortalize my contribution to society; even scores with my enemies; provide financial security for my old age; confirm the taxpayers' worst suspicions about their government;

and generally leave a record of my adventures for the benefit of future historians. Perhaps some useful points can be made for those interested in how our government works, and how those in public service can best attempt to accomplish their missions for the common good. (Seidman 1993, xv)

The *New York Times* included the memoir as one of its 'notable books of the year' for 1993. It was notable in part for the people it criticised by name, including President George H. W. Bush's chief of staff, John Sununu, and former secretary of state Henry Kissinger—and even the president himself. It was bold, it was controversial, and it received mixed reviews.

But since then, in this age of disruption, things have ratcheted up another notch. With the inauguration of President Trump in the United States, political discourse has taken on a much sharper edge of personal attack, well encapsulated in the furore over the publication in April 2018 of James Comey's memoirs. The recollections of the FBI chief sacked by Trump immediately topped bestseller lists across the globe. It was the book nobody could ignore. President Trump himself certainly had no intention of ignoring it, tweeting his own character assessment of Comey ahead of the book's publication. 'James Comey is a proven LEAKER & LIAR . . . He leaked CLASSIFIED information, for which he should be prosecuted. He lied to Congress under OATH. He is a weak and untruthful slime ball . . . It was my great honor to fire James Comey!' (tweet on 13 April 2018).

The book described in detail Comey's meetings with the president and his own assessments of Trump's qualities and behaviour. This included reflections on some of the more puerile debates from the election campaign about the allegedly small size of Trump's hands (Comey confirmed they were smaller than his own), and Trump's famously elaborate hair. But it also included dramatic comparisons between the president of the United States and a mafia boss. 'The silent circle of assent. The boss in complete control. The loyalty oaths . . . The lying about all things, large and small, in service to some code of loyalty that put the organization above morality and above the truth' (Comey 2018, 251).

The book was as divisive as all other aspects of the relationship between the two men. Media commentators and reviewers varied between those who lauded Comey's courage in stating the truth, and those who disapproved both of the publication of the memoir at all, and of what it revealed about the author's own character. 'What a sickly, sanctimonious, self-reverential piece of work this is', declared one review in *The Times* (Webb 2018). *New York*

Times critic Michiko Kakutani noted the key tension between the political nature of Comey's memoir and the apolitical nature of his job.

> It's ironic that Comey, who wanted to shield the F.B.I. from politics, should have ended up putting the bureau in the midst of the 2016 election firestorm; just as it's ironic (and oddly fitting) that a civil servant who has prided himself on being apolitical and independent should find himself reviled by both Trump and Clinton, and thrust into the center of another tipping point in history. (Kakutani 2018)

It is in this aspect of the case—the nature of what it means for a civil servant to act 'politically'—that Comey's memoir holds the greatest interest here. He acted within the existing American tradition that public servants when they retire can write a memoir without being in breach of a fundamental duty against disclosure. What Comey's memoir did, however, is push this qualitatively to a new level for a non-elected sub-cabinet public servant. The book was about as political as a memoir can be. It offered a moral, ethical and political judgement on the president of the United States. It was a book of and for its times.

In keeping with the arguments I've made here, Comey embraced a form of public leadership which added to the public debate. But a crucial aspect of a Washminster framework of leadership is the application of prudent judgement about when and how to speak out. His memoir offered a moral critique, rather than new evidence that would help elected politicians form an evidence-based view about the Trump administration. It was certainly an act of persuasion, but one centred on politics itself rather than on policy or process.

In the United Kingdom, memoirs by government officials seldom reach such heights of notoriety. The introduction of the Official Secrets Act 1989 following the *Spycatcher* case, not to mention the multiple changes to the security apparatus of the state since 9/11, have ensured that quite so blatant a set of revelations by a spy as that of Peter Wright would now face higher hurdles. But the mindset underlying non-disclosure goes much deeper than legal obligations. It is part of the unspoken code of the mandarin; part of the bargain. In return for access to the highest echelons of political decision-making, senior civil servants should not (as a rule) write memoirs about their life in government. It is a belief with a long history, but is another area where the public face of the bureaucracy is breaking through the surface of its traditional anonymity.

There are for example the 'celebrated' memoirs of Sir Christopher Meyer, British ambassador to Washington during the fraught early years of this millennium when the UK and the US were considering their options for the invasion of Iraq. Not only did Meyer publish his remembrances only a few short years after they occurred and whilst Tony Blair was still in power, but he indulged in some instances of genuine indiscretion. He revealed his thoughts on government policy, and gave frank assessments of senior ministers. He also dared to make his memoir an interesting read as regards tone and style. Under the title *DC Confidential,* the book was in many ways a challenge to two conventions. Firstly, it was a civil servant reflecting directly on the political decisions and reputations of the ministers he had served. And secondly, it was wide-ranging enough to be more than just an administrative memoir, and became instead a hotly contested political narrative.

Published in 2005, the book caused a minor sensation. Deputy Prime Minister John Prescott and Foreign Secretary Jack Straw, amongst others, called for Meyer to stand down from his new job as chair of the Press Complaints Commission. Broadsheet and tabloid newspapers leapt on Meyer's colourful descriptions in the memoir of some of Blair's ministers as political 'pygmies'. Some hit back in kind. John Prescott, mocked in the memoir as being a 'mastiff with his hackles up' wrote an open letter to Meyer castigating him for his decision to publish. Quoted widely in the press, the letter described Prescott's alarm 'that you are perfectly happy to profit from tittle-tattle, betraying confidences and by character assassination', and suggested that Meyer himself had been known as the 'red-socked fop' in Washington (BBC 2005).

Meyer's memoir was just one of the many that came out during and shortly after the Blair government's time in office, with ministers, advisers and civil servants all stepping up to the plate. The level of furore was sufficient to cause the Public Administration Committee in the House of Commons to investigate the rules around the publication of memoirs. Their 2006 report drew out the tension inherent between the need to learn openly from the past and the necessity of maintaining trust between politicians and bureaucrats.

> [M]emoirs and diaries tell us a great deal about the workings of government. They are a source of interest to the general reader, valuable for the citizen, and a resource for future historians . . . On the other hand . . . Ill-judged and instant memoirs can undermine that confidentiality, and erode the trust which is necessary for ministers, officials and advisers to work together. (PASC 2006, 1)

The report set out a list of recommendations for potential restrictions that could usefully be placed on the publication of memoirs. Specifically, for civil servants, the tenor of the report was to stress that they owe an obligation not to profit from their position in a way that embarrasses the ministers they served. 'Civil service guidance and codes emphasise the confidential relationship between ministers and public servants. Public servants are only able to produce saleable reminiscences as a consequence of their position in a non-political public service. Former ministers have largely kept their side of the bargain; public servants should be expected to keep theirs' (22–3). Under the current UK rules, and by convention, potential memoirs must first be submitted to either the Cabinet Office or the Foreign and Commonwealth Office for 'screening', to make sure there is nothing too outrageous or confidential to be released.

The Public Administration Committee suggested that the government set up an advisory committee to adjudicate on memoirs submitted for vetting, arguing essentially that there is too much vested interest for governments in acting as the referees for material regarding themselves. It also suggested that where authors use official material, the copyright for that should be vested in the Crown, the Crown then relinquishing copyright once the book was cleared for publication. 'This new system will not prevent any author publishing anything he or she wishes, but it will reduce the incentive to spice up memoirs with gratuitous material' (PASC 2016, 45). The government formally responded to the committee's report more than a year later, in November 2007. It accepted most of the comments and recommendations without rancour, but did not want to relinquish the capacity to decide the fate of memoirs to an external advisory body.

One result was a revision to an internal guideline for diplomats known by the scintillating title of 'Diplomatic Service Regulation 5'. The Public Administration Committee subsequently reviewed this, and suggested that the government had moved from a system that was too forgiving to one that was too tough. 'It is too stringent to expect people to seek clearance for anything they say that draws on any experiences they had in their entire careers. Were the rules to be applied literally, they would (among other things) prevent any live TV or radio commentary from former diplomats for the rest of their lives' (PASC 2008).

The long and the short of it is that publication of memoirs all hinges on whether the government agencies charged with reading them think they are innocuous enough to be let through. There is a built-in institutional disincentive to write anything too controversial. And for the most part it seems to work. In the words of the Committee, 'In reality, then, the FCO's response is not to attempt to enforce its rules. As Sir Peter Ricketts said, he relies on good sense and judgement. Sometimes, as with Sir Christopher Meyer, that approach may be unsuccessful, but in general we share Sir Peter's confidence that former members of staff are aware of their continuing obligations of confidentiality' (PASC 2008, 9).

The extent to which former officials are willing to weigh their obligations of confidentiality against a wider desire to contribute their reflections for posterity is well demonstrated in the case of the former UK ambassador to the United Nations Jeremy Greenstock. His book—entitled *Iraq: The Cost of War*—was published in 2016, but had actually been written much earlier. As Greenstock writes in the foreword,

> In 2005 I wrote and submitted for publication a book about my involvement, as UK Ambassador to the United Nations and later as UK Special Envoy for Iraq, in the lead-up to the Iraq invasion of March 2003 and in the aftermath on the ground in Baghdad. In July of that year, Jack Straw, then Secretary of State for Foreign and Commonwealth Affairs, asked me to delay publication until the Ministers involved had left office. He also expressed unhappiness with the concept of Government servants publishing comment on their official work. (2016, ix)

Ultimately, Greenstock held back the book until 2016 to also allow the Chilcot inquiry into the UK's role in the Iraq War to present its report. He wrote of his hope that 'the passage of time makes my decision to publish less problematic' (2016, ix).

The issue, as it always is in government, is that what constitutes 'the line' depends on who you ask, as a recent Australian case illustrates. Senator John Button was a long-serving Australian Labor party politician, most famous for the tariff reforms he instituted as industry minister in the 1980s. In 2012, his son James Button released a memoir entitled *Speechless: A Year in My Father's Business*. Button junior is a journalist and writer who had been recruited by the Department of Prime Minister and Cabinet to write speeches for the then prime minister, Kevin Rudd, in 2009. The book describes the triumphs and tribulations of trying to write non-partisan speeches within a department, and the frustrations of not being able to get close enough to the prime minister to build an understanding. It provides reflections (generally positive) on different politicians and public servants by name.

The book was applauded by some Australian public servants as a warm insight into the realities of government, whereas others suggested it had overstepped the conventions of confidentiality that restrict personal memoirs of this kind. In Australia, the potential sanctions are serious ones under

Section 70(2) of the Crimes Act, which penalises public servants who reveal things they had a duty to keep to themselves. It's broad, and scary, although in this case the department in question did not refer the matter to the police. But this doesn't mean there was no criticism, both privately and in public. In public, the secretary of the Department of Prime Minister and Cabinet and the public service commissioner issued a joint media release expressing their concern at the breach of confidentiality.

> We want to make it clear the importance we attach to maintaining the Australian Public Service's [APS] culture of confidentiality . . . We do not think that confidentiality ought to be sacrificed in the interests of telling an inside story about politics and/or the public service (as cited in Burgess 2012).

The release went further.

> It is a matter of regret and disappointment, in particular, that Mr Button has published details of conversations with the former prime minister. . . . The unauthorised disclosure of such conversations is, in our view, corrosive to the relationship of trust that must exist between ministers and the APS. Preservation of this relationship is essential in maintaining the APS's tradition of impartiality and its reputation for being apolitical and professional. (as cited in Burgess 2012)

The media release was widely reported through the press, leading defenders to emerge in equal number. Respected ABC journalist Annabel Crabb reflected that there was a culture of information protection at work in the public service. 'To this day, the quickest way to freak out a public servant is to ring him or her on a direct line. Those who don't immediately hang up in terror will generally make it clear straight away that they are not authorised to speak, and that a special place in public sector hell would await them should they ever appear in some sort of publication' (Crabb 2012). On Button's case in particular, she noted the irony that he had been roundly criticised in public for writing a book that actually painted a very sympathetic picture of public servants and what they were trying to achieve. But to be fair to the mandarins involved, they were simply protecting the principle that it was their job to uphold. The question is really whether the principle is still a useful and feasible one.

I explored the Button case with many Australian mandarins in my interviews, and there was a divergence of views. Some thought it provided a great window into the public service without giving anything away. Said one, 'First of all it was written well and it operated at all sorts of levels, but in terms of how public service worked, I thought this is great. This is an outsider briefly on the inside' (author interview, Australia, 2015). Another was adamant in failing to see what the fuss was about. 'I've got no problems with James Button . . . Just ridiculous, just ridiculous, there is nothing in that that makes me unhappy' (author interview, Australia, 2015). Others were more circumspect, saying either the equivalent of 'I wouldn't have done it', or that the rule against publishing memoirs exists, and until it's changed it should be obeyed.

Across Australia, New Zealand, the UK and Canada, the views from mandarins on what is appropriate tend to fall into three camps. First, there are those who feel it is ethically wrong for public servants to gain a benefit from their proximity to government decision-making. This is the 'under no circumstances camp'. A separate line of argument, shared between this camp and some of their slightly more liberal colleagues, is that in principle it would be acceptable to write a memoir, but only if the author was exceptionally careful to say nothing 'political' and nothing that reflects on information they gained whilst in service. This is the 'too boring to publish' camp, and probably represents the largest group. At the other end of the spectrum there are those who cautiously embrace the right to publish, on the grounds that it will provide a learning opportunity for other civil servants. This is the 'OK if you're careful' camp. A very few even take this further, to suggest that someone needs to place an 'authoritative' version of events on the public record, because otherwise hazy and incorrect memories will become the dominant historical narrative.

'Under No Circumstances'

On the whole, these mandarins tend to be those who have served the longest, and are perhaps most imbued with Westminster tradition. They are against publication on principle, and some developed their ideas during an age of stronger trust between ministers and civil servants, when publishing would have felt like stabbing your minister in the back. One such Australian framed it that way. 'I wouldn't like after all these years to breach confidences or to re-tell history in a way that was disappointing to the minister of either party that I'd been working for' (author interview, Australia, 2016). It was simply part of the deal. As one Canadian put it, 'Well I guess I'm pretty old school on that . . . I would never feel right myself writing memoirs, because I feel that's a part of the deal I made' (author interview, Canada, 2015). It is a matter of trust, as echoed by another Canadian. '[I]t certainly would never be my intention to write a kiss and tell book. I've had ministers say, "What did you advise my predecessor?" and have to say, "Sorry Minister, can't tell you that, that's their secret, just like if somebody in the future asks me, I'll tell them I can't tell them what I told you" because then they'll know if you took advice or not' (author interview, Canada, 2015).

On the whole, the country with the strongest disinclination for the publishing of memoirs remains the United Kingdom. The original home of the Westminster system has retained a sense of propriety about what is and is not the 'done thing'. Many expressed it essentially as an article of faith. 'I've always been quite cynical of people—as I put it—who found their conscience after they left. My view . . . was and is that it was a fantastic privilege to serve right at the centre of government . . . To be privileged to offer advice and it did seem to me that it's a breach of that trust and confidence [to publish a memoir]' (author interview, UK, 2015). Some in this group were quite animated about the poor judgement shown by Christopher Meyer in publishing his memoir. 'To be frank, I think what Meyer did was despicable. I am quite old-fashioned about that and actually I think the way he did it as well, there were just some ghastly comments' (author interview, UK, 2015).

An Australian expressed it as a personal ethical judgement to be made. 'Well I mean, it comes down to your own personal sense of values, doesn't it, what's appropriate and what's not appropriate' (author interview, Australia, 2016). A Canadian also presented his stance as a strong personal conviction. 'I can understand the rationale for doing it as a contribution to the public policy process or as a tool for educating public servants coming up through the system, but I've always had this quirky view that public servants should not cash in on their public service, and that is, for me, the reason why I've never written' (author interview, Canada, 2015). But the same person was certainly not doctrinaire about it. When pressed as to whether he was against others putting pen to paper, he responded that it's a 'free world', and rather delightfully added that '[o]ne of them is coming over to dinner tonight, actually' (author interview, Canada, 2015).

Another Canadian made the same ethical point, but as the discussion continued swung around in favour of publication. Whilst able to see the ethical argument around the 'question of integrity that there would be things that would be inappropriate to reveal publically', the same interviewee then went on to defend the need for protecting the integrity of the civil service by making things public.

So part of me thinks well if it's back to that question it's literally who else is going to speak up if these institutions are being damaged or being shifted or constrained in ways that are not what the original bargain was? . . . All systems are better with a certain transparency and if you thought there was going to be some transparency on key questions it might actually be a good thing. So I guess, I do think it's a problem for it to be too far under wraps and where precisely the line needs to be. I haven't thought enough of it except it does strike me that there are things that senior public servants, in the aid of the institution, not in a self-serving way, should be able to share. (Author interview, Canada, 2015).

The convention against publication is a tradition passed through the Westminster DNA, although few mandarins could recall actually having seen it specifically outlawed. 'I would say there is a view that having been a public servant, you don't suddenly retire and start dissing everything that the government's doing. I mean, it's not stated anywhere. Maybe it is for all I know, but you know, there just is sort of that expectation' (author interview, Canada, 2015).

An extension of the ethics-based argument is that the act of publishing a memoir would so dramatically impact on the level of trust that makes government work that it becomes untenable. 'I mean, if I were to write a book it would only be interesting if I dumped a load on three or four ministers . . . and I reckon I could' (author interview, Australia, 2016). Or, put another way, 'I mean how can ministers trust you if they think that in a few years you're going to be writing a memoir, a warts-and-all sort of memoir, which inevitably shows the decision-making process in a lesser light?' (author interview, Australia, 2015). As another reflected, it's about trust not just in the wider processes of government, but also in the individual relationships between ministers and their bureaucrats.

If ministers thought that you were making a note of what was being said to use in a public statement or a book at some stage in the future then that would really erode the trust, and in some cases there's not a lot of trust there to start with, but it would really erode the trust. (Author interview, Australia, 2015)

This sentiment also came through particularly strongly in the UK, although it was undoubtedly in evidence across all four countries. Said one mandarin, '[If] I feel that you'll write down everything and within six months of leaving the job you'll be doing a book it's going to impact on my relationship with you. I just think it's about trust and it's not . . . appropriate. I may be old-fashioned but that's the way I am' (author interview, UK, 2014). Or, as another put it, '[M]y worry is that if everybody believes the civil service are going to publish a memoir fairly soon afterwards, nobody will ever trust it. You know, people will keep everything to themselves and [there] will not be a sharing of information' (author interview, UK, 2015). And it flows both ways, with one mandarin recalling what happened when ministers were planning their own memoirs whilst still on the job. 'It's interesting, I remember talking to a very senior civil servant who talked about working with a minister who was quite obviously going to write his memoirs and was literally writing as they had their meeting' (author interview, UK, 2015).

'Too Boring to Publish'

Civil servants are on the whole a charmingly self-deprecating lot—in the way that only a group of people well aware of their own worth can afford to be. They are high-quality professionals, trained through long experience in the arts of government. They can polish a strong policy memo, whisper in a minister's ear, gently guide the performance management of their staff, and on occasion stand toe-to-toe with ministers and share a few home truths. Yet they will assure you that all of that—at least the parts that they would be empowered to write about—would simply be too boring for words.

One laconic Australian dryly observed, 'A couple of people are pressing me to write something. I'm just too lazy, I think' (author interview, Australia, 2015). A Canadian took a similar view that there just wasn't time to gather memories on the job. 'I mean I didn't have time to write my own Christmas cards, much less take notes for memoirs' (author interview, Canada, 2015). This kind of self-deprecation was in evidence across all four countries, as this UK reflection demonstrates: 'No I'm not that full of myself actually. I don't think many people—I mean I've got some interesting stories but they're alright for a half-hour after dinner speech but they're not really sufficient to trouble the publishing world' (author interview, UK, 2015). Another interviewee, when asked whether the writing of memoirs is a positive thing, suggested, 'Well, if that's a personal question my memoirs would be so damn boring' (author interview, Australia, 2016). 'Boring' is the word that appears ubiquitously, as though government memoirs are the equivalent of filling in some run-of-the-mill IRS form. 'When the odd publisher has approached me about writing a book all I've said is that's all very well, but the very things that would make a book interesting are the things that would not appear in a book, and thus the book would be indescribably boring' (author interview, Australia, 2015). A Canadian made the same observation, that in effect, the interesting material would have to be missed out. 'So, . . . somebody says, "When are you going to write your memoirs?" and I said, "All the stories I have to tell I really can't tell them." I really can't be out there and make those issues public and those are the most interesting ones' (author interview, Canada, 2015).

Are these mandarins in fact right, that their memoirs would just be too boring? As James Button's book in Australia shows, you don't have to tell state secrets to write a book worth reading. I argue that this convention is a hangover from the age of anonymity. When the civil service was neither seen nor heard and just quietly got on with running the country, it made good sense not to countenance some kind of rush to publication upon retirement. When civil servants are now increasingly spending part of their career in the public eye, however, and politicians write memoirs explaining how they saw the big political decisions of their time, why not have another version out there? Of course no one should be empowered to disclose state secrets—and nor could they, because it's a criminal offence. But need that be the same as leaving out interesting non-partisan observations on the exercise of political power?

For example, much ink has been spilled by academics, advisers and former ministers on how Australia responded to the global financial crisis during the Rudd government. This was a vital period of quick-fire policymaking, and everyone seems to have their take on whether the policy response was a disaster or a miraculous success. The then Treasury secretary, Ken Henry, is often seen as one of the architects of the plan that was put in place. Would it not be fascinating for students of government to read an account from him on the policy challenges then faced, without it becoming some sort of finger-pointing exercise between political players? At the very least it would not be boring.

'If You're Careful'

This final group covers those who feel that they have something to tell posterity. Not in the vainglorious way associated with some political memoirs, but in a way that helps us build collective memories about what went right and what went wrong. Even more than that, it's about prying open a window sufficiently for people to be able to see how government actually works. The average citizen probably doesn't really get to see most of what government is. They see tips of icebergs, represented by politicians, or the street-level bureaucrats stamping their social security form at the front counter. The rest is hidden from view, and the memoirs of politicians often do little to bring it to light, because the magnifying glass is trained so strongly on their own political analysis. As one Australian interviewee expressed in frustration, 'I don't think you should breach confidences but I find it a tragedy that the story can't be told so that people understand how governance works' (author interview, Australia, 2015). Another was concerned that the risk-averse nature of the bureaucracy is not actually in the best interest of the public. 'And my nervousness is that you take the prudent thing so far and you fail a whole series of public interest [tests]' (author interview, Australia, 2015).

Most in this group agreed that whilst they might lean towards publication, some distance from events was warranted to allow the sense of political battle to blow over first. 'And the confidences with the minister, you know, you really have to respect that period of time. And that's sort of part of the deal. Other than that I don't think it stops you from writing anything, I mean nobody's ever told me about a prohibition' (author interview, Canada, 2015). This sense that time would cure any ills attaching to publication was strongest in Canada, with many expressing the view that 'once you're out of it and had a decent time out, I think writing your story—everybody's writing their story, so why can't public servants; senior public servants?' (author interview, Canada, 2015). Another Canadian agreed. 'Well I think you have to use discretion frankly, I mean I don't think it should be sort of like a tell-all exposing kind of thing' (author interview, Canada, 2015). Basically, this group agree that if you're careful, publication is acceptable.

> I wouldn't have any—I wouldn't see as a former public servant, any barrier to writing memoirs. I haven't given it a lot of thought, but I think it's a kind of a reasonable thing to do. I think you'd have to . . . exercise some judgement in terms of the nature of—well I mean you wouldn't want to give away Cabinet confidences and you'd want to be careful about that I think. (Author interview, Canada, 2015)

The Canadian interviews were undertaken just after a former Canadian diplomat and ambassador to China, David Mulroney, had published a book on China entitled *Middle Power, Middle Kingdom: What Canadians Need to Know about China in the 21*st *Century.* Many of the Canadian interviewees raised this book in conversation, and its appearance helped to frame their thoughts on whether it was a reasonable thing to have done. Most argued that the book had been well received, and that whilst it may have been critical of government policy at some points it was not inappropriately or invasively so. It encapsulated the overall Canadian sense that it was useful for former public servants to contribute to public debates, as long as they displayed some sense of prudent judgement in doing so.

At the furthest end of this group are those who recognise that memoirs are important for demonstrating not just how government works, but also how history will judge what happened. One Australian leader who had been closely involved in a highly controversial piece of policymaking viewed it that way. 'I guess one of the reasons I'm tempted to write it is I think that if I don't write it then there'll be another version that will come out which may or may not be accurate, and I think it is important for the truth [to be told]' (author interview, Australia, 2015). But this was in no way about a settling of scores, and these interviewees were under no illusions that it would be other than a difficult balancing act. 'I think it's probably appropriate, but it would need to be done in a way that was very factual. It will take a lot of judgement, I think, to write those things' (author interview, Australia, 2015).

Some of the longest-serving UK mandarins expressed similar sentiments, but perhaps more carefully. Their argument was that, essentially, once enough time had passed, there were things to be communicated for history's sake, provided it was done cautiously. One put it this way: 'I don't think there should be a complete ban on civil servants publishing memoirs. I've just finished writing my own life story . . . but I've been careful in that not to betray ministerial confidences or to take a political line' (author interview, UK, 2014). Another even went slightly further, but again couched within a strong sense of the need for very careful judgement.

> But I've come to the view—I mean, so much has been published by politicians and by special advisors, that I think I owe it to history to make sure that what I can contribute is also available. So I will do something that in time is available, but I'm not going to do it in a rush and I'm not going to—my instincts at the moment is not to do kiss-and-tell. Although there are moments when I am strongly tempted. (Author interview, UK, 2014)

Nobody expressed any explicit reservations about the need to have books vetted by central departments to clear them for publication, although some saw it as a formality. One mandarin who has written a book reflected that 'I did clear it before publication and I think it would have been a bit irresponsible not to. If somebody had said well, for political reasons we don't want you to talk about this, then I think I would have said, sod it, I'm publishing anyway' (author interview, UK, 2014).

To Memoir or Not to Memoir

Almost without exception across the four countries, retired mandarins were happy to share their knowledge in other ways. So rather than writing memoirs, they would give guest lectures at universities, and teach on public policy courses for civil servants. Many in fact made the jump to formally take up academic positions, freeing them slightly more to write books in their field. Some would also come back as mentors and collaborators to speak to young civils servants on the job. In Australia, it is also now the norm for senior public servants to give a valedictory speech on the occasion of their retirement, reflecting back on their career and the changes in the nature of government that they have witnessed (see IPAA 2016; Wanna et al. 2012). So there is definitely an argument to be made that institutional memory about how government works and should work is being shared, even in places where memoirs are few and far between.

But there is also a wider question about transparency and public accountability. A well-written memoir which actually engages with policy questions in a non-partisan way, and reflects on mistakes that were made, would surely reach a wider audience. For one thing, up-and-coming politicians might be tempted to read it, whereas they are distinctly unlikely to be included in the type of quiet outreach that mandarins currently use to pass on knowledge to the next generation of civil servants. Citizens would also have the opportunity to see the complexities of government in a new light. I'm not for a moment suggesting that this would result in some kind of national education on the meaning of government, but it would throw open a new window onto why things happen as they do.

The biggest and most pressing concern is around the impact on the relationship of trust between mandarins and politicians. My perhaps provocative question is whether the conditions of modern governance now mean that this relationship is essentially illusory already. In the space of a few decades, the kind of close working relationship that was the norm has been fractured by changing conditions. The widespread arrival of partisan special advisers within ministerial offices has created a firewall between departmental civil servants and the ministers they serve. Very few bureaucrats in Westminster countries are able to build up as close a level of access as the ministerial staff who are literally sitting in the next office along from their ministers. The civil service has lost its monopoly on the provision of policy advice, and is frequently publicly attacked by the government for not being innovative and creative enough. And when things go wrong, too often today it is the

bureaucracy that is hung out to dry. If ministers and advisers are busily scrib-
bling notes for their memoirs during meetings, is it realistic for civil servants
to believe that they still operate in a regime based on intimate levels of trust?

One long-serving UK mandarin highlighted such changes as providing a
strong reason why writing memoirs may now be justified.

> I think my career . . . is a bridge from the time when civil servants did not
> write about themselves or draw attention to themselves, and ministers
> writing their books did not talk about them. [It] spans that period to a
> period when ministers and their special advisors feel entirely free to talk
> about them and to be rude about them. But they are still expected not to
> defend themselves. (Author interview, UK, 2014)

So, as in so many other areas described in this book, we are moving
towards a Washminster system by stealth anyway. We are perhaps clinging
onto notions of trust that no longer accurately reflect the structures of modern government. In Washington, no such reluctance applies. When people
move in and out of government as presidential appointees, there is almost
an expectation that they will get out and publish a book to mark their transition point. There is a hungry market for political memoirs, including those
by non-partisan leaders who held central positions of power. Perhaps the
Westminster world is not yet ready for this kind of full-throated embrace of
individual disconnect between civil servants and elected representatives—
and it may well be undesirable. But a Washminster hybrid is in part about
recognising that things are changing already. Loosening the prohibitions
around memoirs might be a part of re-shaping how the relationship between
ministers and civil servants works, in response to those changes.

9

Conclusion

WALKING THE TIGHTROPE

On 17 September 2017, the British press was full of the details of a dispute between the head of the UK Statistics Authority, Sir David Norgrove, and British Foreign Secretary Boris Johnson. So what had the keen Brexiteer done to upset Britain's top numbers man? Johnson had written an opinion piece in *The Daily Telegraph*, seeking to recapture the debate over what Britain's future outside the EU might look like. The piece was classic Johnson, full of high-flying rhetoric seeking to craft a transformational message to pull Brexit negotiations out of the transactional mire they had become trapped in. Seen by many commentators as a shot over the bows of Prime Minister Theresa May, the Foreign Secretary's intervention dominated the news cycle for twenty-four hours at least.

In his piece, Johnson laid out a positive conception of a post-EU Britain. The imagery was splashed about with abandon, seeking to freshen a debate that had grown stale. He decried those weak-willed doubters who believed that Brexit might yet be snatched from the grasp of those who had voted for it. 'They think that we will simply despair of finding the way out of the EU and sit down on the floor and cry—like some toddler lost in the maze at Hampton Court'. He referenced the 'arc of history' that would allow historians to make sense of why Britain first joined, and then chose to leave, the EU. Britain should have confidence in its future connections with the world, not least because it educates so much of it. 'It is an astonishing fact that of all the kings, queens, presidents and prime ministers in the world, one in seven was educated in this country' (Johnson 2017). Heady stuff. But 'one in seven' was not the piece of arithmetic that drew the ire of the head of the UK Statistics Authority. His focus was on a number that had first become an infamous part of the original Brexit referendum debate a year earlier: £350 million.

Those three numerals had in mid-2016 become synonymous with claim and counter-claim about what the UK would save when it left Brussels for good and took its cash with it. The Leave campaign had stamped the number on the side of a large red bus, promising that this extraordinary sum would be wrenched back from the hands of European bureaucrats in order to be spent on the constantly underfunded NHS (National Health Service). Remain campaigners pilloried the figure as a fantasy designed to sway voters with promises of untold wealth that would never materialise. It was this number—£350 million—that Johnson brought back from the dead in his opinion piece, by reviving the claim that it would help to revolutionise the NHS.

> And yes—once we have settled our accounts, we will take back control of roughly £350 million per week. It would be a fine thing, as many of us have pointed out, if a lot of that money went on the NHS, provided we use that cash injection to modernise and make the most of new technology. The NHS is one of the great unifying institutions of our country.

More than any other part of Johnson's approximately four thousand words, it was the re-introduction of £350 million into the public debate that galvanised opinions. And most importantly for our purposes here, it roused the head of an arm's-length government agency to pick up his pen and write to the Foreign Secretary. Norgrove wrote that he was surprised indeed to have had this figure thrust into the public domain once more. It is a letter that was short, sharp and accusatory. In full, it read,

> Dear Foreign Secretary,
>   I am surprised and disappointed that you have chosen to repeat the figure of £350m per week in connection with the amount that might be available for extra public spending when we leave the European Union.
>   This confuses gross and net contributions. It also assumes that payments made currently to the UK by the EU, including for example for the support of agriculture and scientific research, will not be paid by the UK government when we leave.

It is a clear misuse of official statistics.
Yours sincerely
Sir David Norgrove

It was that last line that cut the deepest. It turned what was a *debate* about numbers into a definitive statement that the Foreign Secretary had gone too far in his 'misuse of official statistics'. 'How did the letter get out into the public domain?', I hear you ask. Was it quietly leaked by some mischief-maker? Far from it. It was released through the official Twitter handle of the statistics authority. Now of course, Norgrove had the choice to give his advice quietly—to privately advise the Foreign Secretary that he was using the wrong number. But in the age of governing in public, would this have been enough? Was Norgrove simply doing his duty, as an independent civil servant, by calling out his government for publicly pushing a half-truth? Johnson certainly didn't think so. So exercised was Johnson by Norgrove's intervention that he wrote back. Johnson accused Norgrove of wilfully mis-representing his position. The letter is too long to reproduce in full here, but even an edited version gives a flavour of the controversy.

Dear Sir David
    I must say that I was surprised and disappointed by your letter of today, since it was based on what appeared to be a wilful distortion of the text of my article . . .
    What is beyond doubt is that, upon withdrawal, we will have complete discretion over the £350m per week and that huge sums will indeed will be available for public spending on priorities such as the NHS. I believe that would be a fine thing.
    If you had any concerns about my article, it would of course have been open to you to address the points with me in private rather than in this way in a public letter. As it is, if you seriously disagree with any of the above, I look forward to hearing your reasoning.
    Boris Johnson, Secretary of State for Foreign & Commonwealth Affairs

It is the public nature of Norgrove's original letter that Johnson specifically draws attention to. He was aggrieved that the traditional Westminster modes of operation—in which mandarins quietly give advice to ministers—had been circumvented. The reality is that the conditions under which those traditions emerged have changed. Norgrove wrote in public because he has a role as a public leader of a government agency. He consciously and proactively decided to enter public debate to make a point about the way a minister was choosing to employ statistics. Whilst the media jumped on the exchange as an ugly spat, it was in fact simply a manifestation of how modern public sector leaders now work. Claims and counter-claims are made in public, or sometimes leaked to the media, rather than being argued out in backrooms. There was nothing constitutionally wrong with Norgrove's intervention—he was exercising the power of rhetorical bureaucracy to frame Johnson's article as 'misusing' official statistics. He made a personal leadership choice. Equally, there was nothing wrong with Johnson's original article, nor his decision to publicly take issue with Norgrove's representation of it. Both men operate in a political world. Both have leadership responsibilities, and both are seeking to inform the public in a way that paints their own case in the best light.

This is a Washminster system in action. Yes it's messy, but it's also enlightening. It empowers bureaucrats to engage on important policy questions, and enables politicians to fight their corner in return. The line that must not be crossed is the line of non-partisanship. There was no evidence here that Norgrove intervened on partisan grounds. His letter did not admonish a Tory government and instead praise the Labour party for its use of statistics—such a move would have been untenable. The decisions on Brexit economics remain the government's to make. Norgrove's decision to publicly 'fact check' aspects of that debate can only help to sharpen the level of accountability that both Norgrove and Johnson face. That is how it should be.

At the outset of this book, I promised a narrative that was not only empirically compelling, but normatively useful. It's time to deliver on that promise. If we want public executives to continue to provide informed contributions to public debate, but without crossing the line to become some kind of unelected 'guardians' of public policy (see Rhodes and Wanna 2007), we need to develop rules of the road that both politicians and bureaucrats can live with. A Washminster hybrid that allows people like Sir David Norgrove to speak out, and people like Boris Johnson to take him to task.

To begin with, bureaucratic leaders already have more power than they have actively chosen to exercise. Specifically, they possess the power to persuade—to use the knowledge, information and experience they possess to seek to change the minds of the public and politicians about particular issues. Once this could best be done behind closed doors. Things could be argued out over a sherry at number 10 Downing Street, or over a game of tennis in Theodore Roosevelt's White House. The old saying about laws and sausages held true—nobody wanted to see them being made. That reality has changed. Governing now occurs in the full glare of transparency. Every action and reaction entails a jostling for public perception, as Elizabeth Birnbaum and Thad Allen know only too well from trying to negotiate the challenges of the BP oil spill.

An awareness of this now exists in Westminster-system countries, just as in the USA. It's the risk matrix used by Martin Parkinson and David Tune in Australia when deciding whether or not to publicly challenge a prime minister's use of 'Treasury advice'. It's the risk balanced up by Jeremy Heywood in the UK when he decided how to respond to a request from the prime minister that he run an inquiry into an extraordinarily political scandal like 'Plebgate'. It's the same calculation made by New Zealand mandarins when they decide which issues they need to fight on, and which ones simply require them to 'swallow a dead rat' and move on. But of course not every issue is the same, and not every bureaucratic position provides the same institutional incentives and protections when it comes to speaking out.

So first, let's sketch out the fundamentals of the Washminster hybrid that is already emerging. To begin with, the Westminster tradition of ministerial responsibility is hanging on by the skin of its teeth. Very few ministers are willing to resign for a mistake made by a bureaucratic leader within their department. Far more likely is that the minister would promise to fix whatever problem is occurring, and if need be would move or remove the senior official who had let the team down. This is even more the case when dealing with arm's-length agencies that might come within a minister's portfolio, but are less clearly under her or his direct responsibility. In other words, bureaucratic leaders are having to fend for themselves when the going gets rough. This won't be news to American agency heads who have faced that scenario for decades, but it does demonstrate a discernible shift towards independent levels of responsibility for mandarins in Westminster-system countries.

Second, the idea that mandarins do not comment publicly in their own defence is under challenge, whilst not yet in total freefall. Individual cases demonstrate that some bureaucratic leaders are willing to directly contradict elected politicians if they are backed into a corner. If politicians misuse information, they will be called out for it—as was done by the Australian Treasury and finance secretaries during an election campaign, and by the UK's former ambassador to the EU on his way out of the door at the start of 2017. Heads of arm's-length agencies—such as Sir David Norgrove, Lord Smith or Prof. Gillian Triggs at the Australian Human Rights Commission— are already in reality operating under a system where they run their own lines under their own independent authority. My prediction is that under the impact of the factors driving the shift to 'governing in public', more heads of government agencies will more readily defend themselves. But this does come at a cost. Once they are willing to publicly take issue with the government, they are opening themselves up to legitimate decisions by politicians to return fire. Whilst public debate may be the winner, it will mean that bureaucratic leaders in particular will need to develop new public leadership skills and thicker hides.

Third, there is a gentle move towards a greater preparedness by some mandarins to pursue the kind of 'public value' agenda espoused by Mark Moore, based on US governance models. Traditionally, civil servants have no agenda other than that of the government of the day, at least in theory. They are servants of the elected government, indivisible from those they serve. But the public value conception provides a framework in which mandarins can begin to conceive of a wider independent responsibility. It's the kind of mindset that let leaders like Gus O'Donnell in the UK, Ken Henry in Australia, John Whitehead in New Zealand and Wayne Wouters in Canada talk in speeches about the longer-term policy challenges that politicians of all political stripes will be facing. Things like climate change policy, or demographic shifts, or long-term economic trends.

Now, each of those leaders was also occasionally attacked for allegedly overstepping the mark; but each also showed the ability to hold his own and continue speaking out in measured ways. All four of those leaders have retired in the last few years at a time of their choosing, and they have done so with their reputation as non-partisan public servants intact. They were politically astute enough to be able to dance through the politics of policy minefields without compromising their essentially independent role. But each was also very much at the apex of the civil service in his respective country, and that undoubtedly emboldened them in a way that a more up-and-coming leader might be wary of.

Most fundamentally, the shift towards a Washminster system is encapsulated in the decline in the anonymity of bureaucratic leaders in Westminster-system countries. As my interviewees stressed time and again, the need to appear before oversight committees to be questioned has been a large part of that change. It is certainly the part that is most front-of-mind for those who have gone through the experience. But equally, factors like more intrusive media, a faster-paced communications environment, the rise of social media, the transparency of freedom of information regimes and ministers being more publicly combative with their civil servants have combined to emphasise the shift. Individually, none of these factors is decisive. But in combination, they have pushed and pulled mandarins into the public domain. As former cabinet secretary Lord Richard Wilson wrote over a decade ago, senior civil servants are increasingly treated 'as if we were figures in our own right rather than servants of the government' (2003, 372), which in itself constitutes a shift in the genetic make-up of Westminster-type bureaucracies.

The shift is real, and it's accelerating. In response to this collection of new pressures, mandarins have on the whole chosen one of two courses. The traditionalists have held tight to the Westminster conventions that once protected them. They steadfastly refuse to engage publicly, and for many this reticence has served them well. The second group has embraced the changes, to essentially re-shape a leadership approach that takes advantage of the new opportunities by being less risk-averse. If they are going to be dragged into the public domain, these mandarins have decided, they might as well have something to say while they are out there. This means that they do find themselves more in the media, and more often in conflict either with their own government or with its political opponents. But it also means that they can shape the wider policy debate in ways of their choosing. They have recognised the power of the rhetorical bureaucracy and activated it.

What I propose below is to see a Washminster framework as a spectrum of practice rather than a binary distinction. Very few sub-cabinet leaders in America are actively seeking to thrust themselves into the midst of every possible debate, and very few Westminster mandarins would absolutely refuse to speak publicly under any conditions whatsoever. All realise the futility of pretending that civil servants can merge back into the shadows any time soon. But equally, all recognise the madness of seizing a level of bureaucratic celebrity that sees them spending their days in pitched public arguments with politicians. Instead, bureaucratic leaders need the room to form prudent judgements about when to hold their cards close and when to lay them on the table.

So in each individual instance, leaders have to calculate where on the spectrum to place themselves, in order to act in the most prudent manner. There are fine judgements to be made. Let's assume that the extreme anonymity end of the spectrum equates to hiding under the duvet with the lights off, and the extreme publicity end equates to standing on a soapbox in Times Square denouncing the president. In between lies an ocean of possibilities. I propose below a list of six variables for bureaucratic leaders to consider as they make their calculations on whether or not to enter the fray.

Each of the variables in Table 2 requires a degree of conscious assessment when leaders are weighing up whether they should have something public to

TABLE 2. Factors to weigh up in deciding whether to speak out in public

Variables	Questions for mandarins to ask themselves
Position held	Does the leader have a particular expertise to bring to bear by virtue of the position she or he holds?
Type of agency the leader represents	How arm's-length from government is the agency?
Level of public/media interest	Is this likely to be a front page story?
	Is there a high level of salience around this issue that makes 'average' citizens interested in it?
Level of political contention/debate on the issue	Is this an issue where bipartisan consensus exists?
	What is the level of political rhetoric from elected leaders around this?
Level of organisational interest for the leader's own organisation	Does the organisation that the leader represents 'have skin' in this policy game?
Ethical or moral judgements involved	Is there an ethical or moral imperative to say something?
	What would the consequences of silence be?
Level of 'public value' involved	Is there a 'public value' argument to be made— does participation in the debate create 'public capital' in needed areas?

say about a particular issue. I'm not proposing to quantify that assessment, as any number placed on it would be arbitrary given the complexity of the calculation actually involved. As ever with individual judgement, it is more art than science, tempered by experience and clarity of thought about what's at stake. But let me explain what I mean by each variable in a little more detail.

Position held and Agency type: These first two variables are closely interlinked, and envisage leaders asking themselves two questions. The first is whether it is accepted that the person holding the position has a degree of expert knowledge to bring to bear on an issue. So for example, a Treasury secretary or a parliamentary budget officer will be seen as having a particularly valuable opinion when dealing with economic matters. Their views on the state of medical research would be less relevant. The second question relates to the kind of position the speaker holds. Especially in Westminster systems, there is a clear distinction to be made between those officers who have a statutory set of powers that allow them to operate at arm's-length from government, and those who are leading the core bureaucratic departments of government. The latter have traditionally had the closest relationship with ministers, and would conventionally be the most reluctant to take a public stance without the clear blessing of their minister. The heads of independent authorities charged with environmental management, or business regulation, or the management of statistics, perhaps have less to lose. The leaders of core departments need to work closely with ministers and their ability to do so will determine their future career options in many cases.

So for that latter group in particular, the specific extra question to be asked is whether to seek ministerial clearance before speaking out on an issue. It costs nothing to ask, and there is nothing that ministers hate more than surprises, so seeking permission would seem the prudent course. If it is refused, mandarins will then need to examine the remaining variables to see whether publicly engaging is warranted even at the risk of courting ministerial displeasure. As New Zealand and Australian experience shows, smart ministers have little to fear from allowing their bureaucrats to take a public role in solving problems that would only become more politicised if left to ministers alone to deal with.

Public and media interest: This is obviously a vital variable. As discussed in the opening chapter, the kinds of event that see senior public servants talking to their own organisations about ways to improve are unlikely to have much wider salience. Equally, a piece introducing a new leader when they take on a role isn't likely to lead to citizens hurling objects at their televisions in disgust. But the line is in fact finer than it seems. Leaders need to consider every statement they make as potentially a public one. What may seem like a little internal morale-boosting exercise can all too quickly develop into something else. For example, in 2007 the then Australian Treasury secretary Ken Henry made a speech to an internal gathering of Treasury bureaucrats which was interpreted as being critical of the policy approach of the government of Prime Minister John Howard. A set of internal comments very quickly became a public crisis.

Interest of course relates not just to the type of forum and audience, but also the topic discussed. In-depth discussions about changes to accounting software are going to struggle to break the surface of public consciousness even with the benefit of a little colourful language from a speaker. But again, one has to be careful: many seemingly innocuous IT changes have become major public meltdowns once they are seen as having wasted government money. There are myriad cases of new pay systems and file management systems that have become multi-million-dollar nightmares for the bureaucratic leaders who first championed the change.

Political contention: Astute public executives pride themselves on their political awareness. Like an angler sensing a tingling in the line as a fish nibbles, experienced bureaucrats should know when they are about to reel in a piece of political dynamite. But it takes a deft touch to deal with such situations. Time and again, senior public executives have found themselves attacked, either by their own ministers or by political opponents, for having inserted themselves into an issue that political parties are fighting about with vigour. This is where building and maintaining a reputation as an independent public figure provides some level of protection. For example, in the space of a few months in 2013, the then Australian Treasury secretary Martin Parkinson was accused by both major parties of acting as a partisan for the other— which suggests that he was in fact simply walking a line of his own.

Organisational interest: Every public executive heads up an organisation of some kind. Whenever such a leader speaks out, she or he does so as the representative of that organisation. For this reason, it's important to consider whether the organisation actually has some skin in the policy game that warrants the taking of a public position. Has a politician or an external organisation actually asserted something about your organisation that you see as untrue or as a slur? When the head of the Canadian Statistics Authority Munir Sheikh publicly quit his post in 2010, it was because he believed that the government had incorrectly characterised the advice it had received from the Authority about the census. It was an issue clearly within the bailiwick of the organisation Sheikh led, and the government's assertion that the Statistics Authority supported its actions in dismantling the long-form census clearly reflected on the organisation as a whole, to the point where Sheikh felt he had to speak out.

Similarly, when the Treasury and finance secretaries in Australia publicly rebuked the prime minister in 2013 for misusing Treasury advice, it was because the prime minister had publicly stated that the figures he was relying on had come from Treasury. In other words, he had been trying to draw on the kudos of the Treasury to add some authority to his arguments about the opposition party's policy costings. This is different from the decision Sir David Norgove made, to chastise Boris Johnson because Johnson had not publicly stated that he was relying on figures from the UK Statistics Agency. In other words, Norgrove did not have as much skin in the game, from an organisational perspective, as his Canadian and Australian counterparts had in the examples I've cited. This doesn't mean that he shouldn't have acted; simply that he was weighing up other variables when he did so.

Ethical and moral judgement: Not every ethical quandary facing leaders comes in the form of crisp dollar bills in a brown paper bag in exchange for their silence. Moral complexity comes in a variety of shapes, and involves leaders making some tortured choices based on what they perceive a good leader should do. James Comey illustrates this dilemma perfectly. A look at my list of variables suggests that he waded into the most politically contentious issue imaginable in making statements about Hillary Clinton's emails just weeks from a presidential election. Media interest could hardly have been higher if he had personally set the Capitol on fire. And yet he still acted. As his congressional testimony in the aftermath revealed, he made the calculation that he had a responsibility to reveal what he was doing. To him, it would have been ethically untenable not to have revealed the re-opening of an investigation into one of the candidates for the presidency. Yet, as many Democrat critics have since protested, he didn't take the same view at the time on the investigation of alleged links between Russia and the Trump campaign. It's impossible to say definitively whether Comey was 'right' or 'wrong', because it was ultimately a matter of personal judgement. Like many others, he has found himself attacked by both major parties as acting as a partisan for the other. Whether he was or was not partisan, Comey was arguably imprudent in intertwining his decision-making so fully with his own ethical judgement as to elevate his responses to Trump and to Clinton's emails into a moral question on which he would be the final arbiter.

The undeniable fact is that ethical and moral judgements—whilst they might be based on evidence—rely on the exercise of the independent assessment of the person making the judgement. When public executives defend their decision to intervene, or not, in public debate, they are framing their own actions in a particular way to try to persuade their audience that they had no choice but to act as they did. These are exercises in rhetorical bureaucracy. It is a matter of mounting a persuasive defence on a public stage. It happens in Washington as it does in Westminster systems, but it also frequently proves to be something of a 'nuclear option' in terms of its impact on career prospects.

Public value: In deciding whether to take a public position on an issue, public leaders make decisions as to whether they are on balance likely to build 'public value' for citizens. Is the likelihood of adding to a political dispute worth it, in light of the potential public policy gains? For example, public executives who comment on climate change are wading into what has become a very hotly contested political topic in America, the UK and Australia. And yet,

Complete Silence	Low Profile	Publicly Reactive	Publicly Proactive	High Voltage Intervention	Off the Deep End
Not answering your door and phones turned off.	Appearing before a select committee when called; Factually answering off-the-record questions from journalists.	Issuing a factual media release, or doing interviews in response to questions and in consultation with your minister.	Making a public foray without being asked, on issues that are important but not politically contentious.	Commenting publicly on high salience issues knowing it will result in controversy.	Stand on the street corner swearing at passers-by while live-streaming to the internet.

FIGURE 5. A spectrum of public behaviour

there is an argument to be made that airing policy disputes in this field is likely to create public value in the longer term. It's just another judgement that leaders have to make on a case-by-case basis.

So as public executives weigh up how far to engage in building a public profile, it's perhaps useful to think of sliding a judgement scale along a spectrum and comparing the cases and decisions that others have made. Figure 5 captures in pictorial form the different places on the spectrum that leaders can conceive themselves as inhabiting.

How far individual leaders will go either way on the spectrum will depend on the nature of the issue, and the balance of the variables outlined above. Almost all mandarins interviewed for this book would happily operate amongst the first three (leftmost) settings without much concern. The braver embracers of the new 'governing in public' environment happily slid even further right to the 'publicly proactive' box. 'High-voltage' interventions are saved for rare situations. That is the kind of territory for leaders who are either looking for trouble, or have decided they can't avoid it and so may as well embrace it on their own terms. That is where we could place James Comey and his Clinton email interventions, or Martin Parkinson's intervention in the 2013 Australian election, questioning the prime minister's use of Treasury figures. This is the place where leaders really do start to walk out on the wire without a safety net. Many seemingly safe interventions on the left-hand side of the spectrum end in tears, but often unforeseeably so. High-voltage interventions once made cannot be controlled, and the end game is difficult to foresee.

Public leadership remains an vastly complex job. Every holder of elected political office in the world knows this. So do the bureaucratic leaders who operate alongside them to carry out the work of the modern state. They are all dancing under a magnifying glass. Transparency, accountability, the 24/7 news media, social media, networking needs and angry citizens have combined to make governing in public the new normal. The jury is still out on how public executives can best pick their way through that minefield and deliver the kind of public leadership that is now required of them, without losing the trust of either their ministers or the wider citizenry.

It is the contention of this book that adopting a Washminster framework of leadership offers the best way forward, as senior civil servants seek to operate effectively in the age of disruption. As politics gains an even sharper personal edge, and traditional aspects of the relationship between elected representatives and non-elected administrative leaders come under pressure, new styles of engagement are emerging. If more accountability, transparency and creativity are being demanded of public servants, they must be allowed the room in which to embrace those new styles of engagement. They are 'governing in public', and conventions governing their behaviour need to catch up with that empirical reality.

APPENDIX

Media Searches

As outlined in chapter six, I undertook searches of media sources to gauge the level of publicity that different bureaucratic positions have been able to attract in the United Kingdom, Canada, Australia and New Zealand. Using the *Factiva* database as the search vehicle, I selected three newspapers in each country to search through (see Table 3). Where possible, for comparative purposes, I selected one newspaper seen as 'left-leaning', one seen as 'right-leaning' and a popular tabloid in each jurisdiction. I focused on a specific four-year timespan to provide a comparable dataset across the four countries that would be wide enough to even out the discrepancies likely in any given year should there have been a spike of media interest about a particularly contentious policy debate. So all searches were across the four calendar years from the start of 2010 to the end of 2013.

I also selected a range of bureaucratic positions, to make the comparisons as meaningful as possible (see Table 4). So I focused on the heads of central agencies, the heads of specific 'line agencies' (specifically Health and Education) and the heads of the Civil Service Commission in each country. I also included the head of an arm's-length environmental regulation body in each country, to see if the combination of arm's-length status with the highly topical nature of environmental policy would result in particular press interest. There are of course many mechanisms for undertaking this kind of comparative analysis. I could have chosen social media, or television appearances. I

TABLE 3. List of newspapers searched by country, 2010–2013

Country	Newspapers selected
United Kingdom	*The Guardian*; *The Daily Telegraph*; *The Sun*
Australia	*The Sydney Morning Herald*; *The Australian*; *The Daily Telegraph*
Canada	*National Post*; *The Gazette*; *The Toronto Star*
New Zealand	*The Dominion Post*; *The Press*; *The New Zealand Herald*

TABLE 4. List of positions searched by country, 2010–2013

United Kingdom	Cabinet Secretary
	Treasury Secretary
	First Civil Service Commissioner
	Permanent Secretary, Department for Education
	Permanent Secretary, Department of Health
	Both CEO and Chair of the Environment Agency
Australia	Secretary of the Department of Prime Minister and Cabinet
	Treasury Secretary
	Public Service Commissioner
	Secretary, Department of Education and Training
	Secretary, Department of Health
	Chairman and CEO, Great Barrier Reef Marine Park Authority
Canada	Clerk of the Privy Council
	Secretary of the Treasury Board
	President of the Public Service Commission
	Deputy Minister of Health Canada
	Deputy Minister of Employment and Social Development Canada
	President of the Canadian Environmental Assessment Agency
New Zealand	CEO of the Department of Prime Minister and Cabinet
	Treasury Secretary
	Chief Executive and Secretary for Education
	Chief Executive and Director-General of Health
	State Services Commissioner
	CEO of the Environmental Protection Authority

chose the press because it is the most readily accessible source that affords the opportunity to make controlled comparisons. It offers a snapshot, rather than a definitive statement about the different levels of interest that different leaders are able to attract.

NOTES

Chapter 1: Introduction

1. The literature on politics and public administration offers up many different terms for describing administrative leaders. I therefore use terms like 'senior administrator', 'public executive', 'senior civil servant', 'mandarin' and 'bureaucratic leader' interchangeably throughout the book. All are intended to refer to the same kind of non-elected senior leadership role.

2. This is not to say that transparency is uncontentious, or indeed as ubiquitous as we might think. For an excellent discussion, see: Roberts 2006; Lord 2006.

3. Mandarins of course face myriad duties, of which speaking truth to power is only one aspect. See Wilson 2003; Rhodes and Weller 2001; Barberis 1996; Aberbach et al. 1981; Davis and Rhodes 2014.

4. For just a flavour of the breadth of this scholarship, particularly as it relates to administrative leadership, see Van Wart et al. 2015; Boin 2001; Boin and Christensen 2008; 't Hart 2014.

5. See files BA6/61–BA6/93.

6. Speech entitled *The Role and Character of the Civil Service*, the fifth annual lecture under the 'Thank-Offering to Britain Fund', 24 June 1970. The National Archives, BA6/72.

7. For a discussion that examines 'New Political Governance' in the context of previous changes and current behaviour by Canadian deputy ministers, see Lindquist and Rasmussen 2012.

Chapter 2: Governing in Public

1. For a discussion of the range of reasons why governments choose to delegate authority to unelected bodies, see: Elgie 2006.

2. For coverage of how the capacity to reach out directly to the public is even stronger within independent agencies, see Breger and Edles 2015.

3. Lloyd also continued to draw controversy, with the merit protection commissioner making a finding that he had breached Australian public service values in emailing a document to an outside think tank—the Institute for Public Affairs. (See Dingwall 2018b for a media report on the issue).

Chapter 3: Writing in Public

1. *Papers on the Re-Organisation of the Civil Service*, London, printed by George E. Eyre and William Spottiswoode, 1855, 75. Forming part of the Trevelyan Papers archive held at the University of Newcastle, United Kingdom, shelf designation CET 49.

2. Ibid., 76.

3. As part of his role at the Treasury, Trevelyan carried responsibility for the British government's relief efforts in Ireland—efforts that he discussed and defended in his book. His approach

in this regard was immensely controversial, and he was the target of passionate criticism both from Irish contemporaries and historians since. A historiographical battle continues to rage over whether he was a cold-hearted bureaucrat who starved Ireland in its hour of need, or rather a benevolent civil servant who did everything he humanly could to avert the catastrophe (see Haines 2004; Woodham-Smith 1962; Trevelyan 2012).

4. Stopforth v. Goyer. *Ontario Reports (Second Series) Reports of Cases Determined in the Courts of Ontario*, Vol. 20, Ontario, Canada Law Book Limited, pp. 262–81, 272 (emphasis added). The Court of Appeal ultimately found that the minister in the case—Goyer—had acted within his rights in naming Stopforth.

5. An earlier version of this case study formed part of a co-authored article in the journal *Governance* in 2016, entitled 'Promiscuously Partisan? Public Service Impartiality and Responsiveness in Westminster Systems'. I am grateful to my co-author Cosmo Howard for his permission to reproduce some of that material here.

6. Public Administration Select Committee, *Oral Evidence: Civil Service Impartiality and Referendums, HC 1149*, London, 1 May 2014, 3. http://data.parliament.uk/writtenevidence /committeeevidence.svc/evidencedocument/public-administration-committee/civil-service -impartiality-and-referendums/oral/8504.html (accessed 1 September 2017).

7. Ibid., 4.

Chapter 4: Leading in Public

1. In the UK this is usually the cabinet secretary; in Canada the clerk of the Privy Council; in Australia and New Zealand the secretary of the Department of Prime Minister and Cabinet.

Chapter 7: Over-sharing in Public?

1. In my discussion of government social media policies, I refer to documents which are correct as at April 2018. This remains a fast-moving area, as governments continually look to update policy documents to keep pace with the challenges of social media use.

REFERENCES

AAP [Australian Associated Press] 2010a. 'Top PM officials to front Senate insulation inquiry', *Australian Associated Press General News* 26 February. Consulted 13 December 2013 via *Factiva* database.

AAP [Australian Associated Press] 2010b. 'Garrett rejects royal commission calls', *Australian Associated Press General News* 15 July. Consulted 13 December 2013 via *Factiva* database.

ABC [Australian Broadcasting Corporation] 2010. 'Department head says sorry for insulation deaths', *ABC News* 22 February. Consulted 13 December 2013 via *Factiva* database.

ABC 2013. 'Kevin Rudd accuses Coalition of a $10billion', *Radio National—The World Today with Eleanor Hall* 29 August. Available at http://parlinfo.aph.gov.au/parlInfo/search /display/display.w3p;adv=yes;orderBy=customrank;page=0;query=Content%3AWong %20Content%3ARudd%20Content%3ABowen%20Date%3A29%2F08%2F2013;rec=9 ;resCount=Default (accessed 2 November 2015).

Aberbach, J. D., Putnam, R. D. and Rockman, B. A. 1981. *Bureaucrats and Politicians in Western Democracies.* Cambridge, MA: Harvard University Press.

Advertiser 2010. 'Garrett rejects insulation inquiry', *The Advertiser* 16 July, 9. Consulted 13 December 2013 via *Factiva* database.

Alexander, C. 2010. 'Bureaucrats kept damning report from Garrett', *Australian Associated Press General News* 22 February. Consulted 13 December 2013 via *Factiva* database.

Alford, J. 2008. 'The Limits to Traditional Public Administration, or Rescuing Public Value from Misrepresentation'. *Australian Journal of Public Administration* 67(3): 357–66.

Armstrong, R. 1985. *The 'Armstrong Memorandum'.* Available at http://www.civilservant.org.uk /library/1996_Armstrong_Memorandum.pdf (accessed 2 August 2017). Updated 1996.

Atkins, J. and Finlayson, A. 2013. '". . . A 40-Year-Old Black Man Made the Point to Me": Everyday Knowledge and the Performance of Leadership in Contemporary British Politics'. *Political Studies* 61: 161–77.

Atkins, J., Finlayson, A., Martin, J. and Turnbull, N. (eds.) 2014. *Rhetoric in British Politics and Society.* Basingstoke: Palgrave Macmillan.

Attorney General v. Guardian Newspapers Ltd (No.2) 1988. UKHL 6 (13 October 1988). Available at http://www.bailii.org/uk/cases/UKHL/1988/6.html (accessed 6 November 2018).

Aucoin, P. 2012. 'New Political Governance in Westminster Systems: Impartial Public Administration and Management Performance at Risk'. *Governance* 25(2): 177–99.

Austin, J. 1962. *How to Do Things with Words.* Oxford: Clarendon Press.

Australian Government 1989. *Government Guidelines for Official Witnesses before Parliamentary Committees and Related Matters.* Canberra. Available at http://www.aph.gov .au/Parliamentary_Business/Committees/Senate_Committees?url=wit_sub/gov_full .htm (accessed 10 June 2013).

Australian Public Service Commission 2017. *Making Public Comment on Social Media: A Guide for APS Employees.* Canberra. Available at http://www.apsc.gov.au/publications-and-media /current-publications/making-public-comment (accessed 12 September 2017).

Barberis, P. (1996) *The Elite of the Elite: Permanent Secretaries in the British Higher Civil Service.* Aldershot: Dartmouth.

Bass, B. M. 1985. *Leadership and Performance beyond Expectations.* New York: Free Press.

BBC 2005. 'Meyer should quit PCC: Prescott', BBC News Online 20 November. http://news .bbc.co.uk/1/hi/uk/4453632.stm (accessed 31 October 2018).

Beeby, R. 2010a. 'Union warned Govt on inadequate safety plan', *The Canberra Times* 27 February, 6. Consulted 13 December 2013 via *Factiva* database.

Beeby, R. 2010b. Senate inquiry hits out at Govt's 'systematic failures', *The Canberra Times* 16 July, 5. Consulted 13 December 2013 via *Factiva* database.

Bell, S. 2011. 'Do We Really Need a New "Constructivist Institutionalism" to Explain Institutional Change?' *British Journal of Political Science* 41(4): 883–906.

Bennister, M. 2013. 'Tony Blair's Oratory', in R. Hayton and A. Crines (eds.), *Labour Party Oratory from Bevan to Brown.* Manchester: Manchester University Press, 156–71.

Bertot, J. C., Jaeger, P. T. and Hansen, D. 2012. 'The Impact of Policies on Government Social Media Usage: Issues, Challenges, and Recommendations'. *Government Information Quarterly* 29: 3–40.

Bevir, M. and Rhodes, R.A.W. 2001. 'Decentering Tradition: Interpreting British Government'. *Administration and Society* 33: 107–32.

Blyth, M. 2002. *Great Transformations: Economic Ideas and Institutional Change in the Twentieth Century.* Cambridge: Cambridge University Press.

Blyth, M. 2013. 'Paradigms and Paradox: The Politics of Economic Ideas in Two Moments of Crisis'. *Governance: An International Journal of Policy, Administration, and Institutions* 26(2): 197–215.

Boin, A. 2001. *Crafting Public Institutions: Leadership in Two Prison Systems.* Boulder, CO: Lynne Rienner.

Boin, A. and Christensen, T. 2008. 'The Development of Public Institutions: Reconsidering the Role of Leadership'. *Administration and Society* 40(3): 271–97.

Bourke, L. 2014. 'Labor attacks Treasury Secretary Martin Parkinson after he says it can't "oppose all reform", ABC Online News 4 July. http://www.abc.net.au/news/2014-07-03/labor-attacks -treasury-secretary-after-budgetreply-criticism/5569762 (accessed 31 October 2018).

Bovens, M., Schillemans, T. and 't Hart, P. 2008. 'Does Public Accountability Work? An Assessment Tool'. *Public Administration* 86(1): 225–42.

Bowen, P. 2013. 'Basis for Preparation of PBO Costings'. Media Release, 29 August 2013. Available at http://parlinfo.aph.gov.au (accessed 2 November 2015).

Breger, M. J. and Edles, G. J. 2015. *Independent Agencies in the United States.* Oxford: Oxford University Press.

Breusch, J. 2010. 'Combet steps in as Garrett', *The Australian Financial Review* 27 February, 2. Consulted 13 December 2013 via *Factiva* database.

Bridges, E. 1953. *Portrait of a Profession: The Civil Service Tradition* (The Rede Lecture, 1950). Cambridge: Cambridge University Press.

Burgess, V. 2012. 'PS chiefs chafe at disclosures', *The Australian Financial Review* 21 September, 9. Consulted 28 September 2017 via *Factiva* database.

Burns, J. M. 1978. *Leadership.* New York: Harper & Row.

Button, J. 2012. *Speechless: A Year in My Father's Business.* Melbourne: Melbourne Uinversity Press.

Cabinet Office 2014. *Social Media Guidance for Civil Servants*. Available at https://www.gov.uk/government/publications/social-media-guidance-for-civil-servants/social-media-guidance-for-civil-servants (accessed 12 September 2017).

Campbell, A. 2007. *The Blair Years: Extracts from the Alastair Campbell Diaries*. London: Hutchinson.

Carpenter, D. 2001. *The Forging of Bureaucratic Autonomy: Reputations, Networks and Policy Innovation in Executive Agencies, 1862–1928*. Princeton: Princeton University Press.

Chadwick, A. 2011. 'Explaining the Failure of an Online Citizen Engagement Initiative: The Role of Internal Institutional Variables'. *Journal of Information Technology and Politics* 8(1): 21–40.

Chaitin, D. 2015. 'EPA administrator McCarthy's top ten greatest tweets', *Washington Examiner* 29 August. Available at http://www.washingtonexaminer.com/epa-administrator-mccarthys-top-10-greatest-tweets/article/2571068 (accessed 11 September 2017).

Cillizza, C. 2010. 'MMS director Elizabeth Birnbaum took the hit', *Washington Post* 30 May. Available at http://www.washingtonpost.com/wp-dyn/content/article/2010/05/28/AR2010052801950.html (accessed 15 September 2017).

Clement, J. 2017. 'I'm a scientist. I'm blowing the whistle on the Trump Administration', *Washington Post*, 19 July. Available at https://www.washingtonpost.com/opinions/im-a-scientist-the-trump-administration-reassigned-me-for-speaking-up-about-climate-change/2017/07/19/389b8dce-6b12-11e7-9c15-177740635e83_story.html?tid=a_inl&utm_term=.a45166e61e25 (accessed 14 September 2017).

Coleman, S. and Blumler, J. 2009. *The Internet and Democratic Citizenship: Theory, Practice and Policy*. Cambridge: Cambridge University Press.

Comey, J. 2016. 'Letter to Congressional Chairs', 28 October 2016. Available at https://www.nytimes.com/interactive/2016/10/28/us/politics/fbi-letter.html (accessed 30 August 2017).

Comey, J. 2018. *A Higher Loyalty: Truth, Lies, and Leadership*. London: Macmillan.

Committee on Oversight and Government Reform 2015. 'DOJ IG: Handling of Sexual Harassment and Misconduct Allegations', April 14 2015, Serial No. 114–17. Available at https://www.gpo.gov/fdsys/pkg/CHRG-114hhrg94542/html/CHRG-114hhrg94542.htm (accessed 26 July 2017).

Coorey, P. 2010 (with L. Hall). 'The incredible shrinking minister', *The Sydney Morning Herald* 27 February, 1. Consulted 13 December 2013 via *Factiva* database.

Crabb, A. 2012. 'Let's free up the private world of public servants', ABC online analysis site 'The Drum', 26 September. http://www.abc.net.au/news/2012-09-25/crabb-release-the-bureaucrats/4279164 (accessed 28 September 2017).

Crosby, B. C., and Bryson, J. M. 2005. *Leadership for the Common Good: Tackling Public Problems in a Shared-Power World*. San Francisco: Wiley.

Crosby, B. C. and Bryson, J. M. 2017. 'Why Leadership of Public Leadership Research Matters: And What to Do about It'. *Public Management Review* 20(9): 1265–86.

Daily Express 2017. 'Sir Ivan Rogers couldn't be trusted and civil servants must obey leaders, claims IDS', *The Daily Express*, 4 January. Available at http://www.express.co.uk/news/uk/750075/Sir-Ivan-Rogers-EU-ambassador-Brexit-not-trusted-Iain-Duncan-Smith (accessed 31 October 2018).

Daly, M. 2015. 'White House: No vote of confidence for embattled drug chief', *Associated Press Newswire* 17 April. Consulted 27 July 2017 via *Factiva* database.

Davis, G. and Rhodes, R.A.W. (eds.) 2014. *The Craft of Governing: The Contribution of Patrick Weller to Australian Political Science*. Crows Nest, NSW: Allen & Unwin.

Davis, J. H. 2015. 'Michele Leonhart, head of D.E.A., to retire over handling of sex scandal', *New York Times* 21 April. Available at https://www.nytimes.com/2015/04/22/us/michele-leonhart-top-dea-official-is-expected-to-resign.html (accessed 27 July 2017).

Denhardt, J. V. and Campbell, K.B. 2006. 'The Role of Democratic Values in Transformational Leadership'. *Administration and Society* 38(5): 556–72.

Department of Justice 2015. 'Attorney General Statement on Retirement of Michele Leonhart', 21 April. Available at https://www.justice.gov/opa/pr/attorney-general-statement-retirement-michele-leonhart (accessed 27 July 2017).

Department of the Interior 2010. 'Statements of Secretary of the Interior Ken Salazar and S. Elizabeth Birnbaum', 27 May. Available at https://www.doi.gov/news/pressreleases/Statements-of-Secretary-of-the-Interior-Ken-Salazar-and-S-Elizabeth-Birnbaum (accessed 15 September 2017).

Dillman, D. L. 2007. 'Enduring Values in the British Civil Service'. *Administration and Society* 39(7): 883–900.

Dingwall, D. 2018a. '"Thoughtcrime": Immigration official sacked for tweets wins compensation', *The Sydney Morning Herald* 18 April. Available at https://www.smh.com.au/public-service/thoughtcrime-immigration-official-sacked-for-tweets-wins-compensation-20180418-p4za8z.html (accessed 31 October 2018).

Dingwall, D. 2018b. 'John Lloyd breached code of conduct over email to think tank, inquiry finds', *The Canberra Times* 8 August. Available at https://www.canberratimes.com.au/politics/federal/john-lloyd-breached-code-of-conduct-over-emails-to-think-tank-inquiry-finds-20180808-p4zwc2.html (accessed 31 October 2018).

Djerf-Pierre, M. and Pierre, J. 2016. 'Mediatised Local Government: Social Media Activity and Media Strategies among Local Government Officials 1989–2010'. *Policy and Politics* 441(1): 59–77.

Doig, J. W. and Hargrove, E. C. 1987. *Leadership and Innovation: A Biographical Perspective on Entrepreneurs in Government*. Baltimore and London: Johns Hopkins University Press.

Duncan Smith, I. 2013. 'Margaret Thatcher's legacy is a better country and a safer world for my girls', *The Daily Telegraph* 10 April. Available at http://www.telegraph.co.uk/news/politics/margaret-thatcher/9985862/Margaret-Thatchers-legacy-is-a-better-country-and-a-safer-world-for-my-girls.html (accessed 31 August 2017).

Dunleavy, P., Margetts, H., Bastow, S. and Tinkler, J. 2006. *Digital Era Governance: IT Corporations, the State, and e-government*. Oxford: Oxford University Press.

Edelman, M. 1964. *The Symbolic Uses of Politics*. Chicago: University of Illinois Press.

Edwards, A. 2002. 'The Moderator as an Emerging Democratic Intermediary: The Role of the Moderator in Internet Discussions about Public Issues'. *Information Polity* 7(1): 3–20.

Elgie, R. 2006. 'Why Do Governments Delegate Authority to Quasi-Autonomous Agencies? The Case of Independent Administrative Authorities in France'. *Governance* 19(2): 207–27.

Elgie, R. 2014. 'Executive Leadership in Semi-Presidential Systems', in R.A.W. Rhodes and P. 't Hart (eds.), *The Oxford Handbook of Political Leadership*, ch. 31.

Ellis, M. 2013. 'Lack of common sense that cost us £50 million: Fury at West Coast rail farce', *The Daily Mirror* 26 February, 16. Consulted 13 December 2013 via *Factiva* database.

Fawcett, P. and Marsh, D. 2014. 'Depoliticisation, Governance and Political Participation'. *Policy and Politics* 42(2): 171–88.

Finlayson, A. 2007. 'From Beliefs to Arguments: Interpretive Methodology and Rhetorical Political Analysis'. *British Journal of Politics and International Relations* 9: 545–63.

Finlayson, A. and Martin, J. 2008. '"It ain't what you say . . .": British Political Studies and the Analysis of Speech and Rhetoric. *British Politics* 3: 445–64.

Fischer, F. 2003. *Reframing Public Policy: Discursive Politics and Deliberative Practices*. Oxford: Oxford University Press.

Flinders, M. 2008. *Delegated Governance and the British State: Walking Without Order*. Oxford: Oxford University Press.

Flinders, M. 2011 'Devolution, Delegation and the Westminster Model: A Comparative Analysis of Developments within the UK, 1998–2009'. *Commonwealth and Comparative Politics* 49(1): 1–28.

Flinders, M. and Wood, M. 2014. 'Depoliticisation, Governance and the State'. *Policy and Politics* 42(2): 135–49.

Freeman, T. and Peck, E. 2007. 'Performing Governance: A Partnership Board Dramaturgy'. *Public Administration* 85(4): 907–29.

Friedman, J. and Friedman, S. 2012. *Rethinking the Rhetorical Presidency*. Abingdon: Routledge.

Fulton .1968. *The Civil Service, Vol. 1. Report of the Committee 1966–68*. London: HMSO.

Government Digital Service 2012. *Social Media Guidance for Civil Servants*. London: Cabinet Office. Available at https://www.gov.uk/government/publications/social-media-guidance -for-civil-servants (accessed 6 January 2014).

Government Information Services 2011. *Social Media in Government: High-Level Guidance*. Wellington: Department of Internal Affairs. Available at https://webtoolkit.govt.nz/guidance /social-media/high-level-guidance/ (accessed 7 January 2014).

Government Information Services 2012. *Social Media in Government: How to Handle a Mishap*. Wellington: Department of Internal Affairs. Available at https://webtoolkit.govt.nz /guidance/social-media/how-to-handle-a-mishap/ (accessed 8 January 2014).

Gowan, P. 1987. 'The Origins of the Administrative Elite'. New Left Review 162: 4–34.

Grattan, M. 2010. 'Treasury's unleashed rock star', *The Age* 14 May, 15. Consulted 6 September 2017 via *Factiva* database.

Grattan, M. 2013. 'Public servants say "No Minister"'. *The Conversation* 29 August 2013. Available at https://theconversation.com/day-25-public-servants-say-no-minister-17663 accessed 31 October 2018).

Greber, J. and Coorey, P. 2013. 'Treasury torpedoes Budget attack', *The Australian Financial Review* 30 August, 1.

Greenaway, J. 1992. 'British Conservatism and Bureaucracy'. *History of Political Thought* 13(1): 129–60.

Greenstock, J. 2016. *Iraq: The Cost of War*. London: Heinemann.

Gribben, R. 2013. 'Bungled West Coast rail contract to cost taxpayer £50m, say MPs', *The Daily Telegraph* 26 February, 7. Consulted 13 December 2013 via *Factiva* database.

Grube, D. 2012. 'A Very Public Search for Public Value: "Rhetorical Secretaries" in Westminster Jurisdictions'. *Public Administration* 90(2): 445–65.

Grube, D. C. 2013. *Prime Ministers and Rhetorical Governance*. Basingstoke: Palgrave Macmillan.

Grube, D. C. and Howard, C. 2016. 'Promiscuously Partisan? Public Service Impartiality and Responsiveness in Westminster Systems'. *Governance* 29(4): 517–33.

Guardian 2017. 'Sally Yates fired by Trump after acting US Attorney-General defied travel ban', *The Guardian* 31 January. Available at https://www.theguardian.com/us-news/2017 /jan/30/justice-department-trump-immigration-acting-attorney-general-sally-yates (accessed 31 October 2018).

Guion, P. 2015. 'DEA chief Michele Leonhart expected to resign over "sex parties" scandal', *The Independent* 21 April. Available at http://www.independent.co.uk/news/world/americas /dea-chief-michele-leonhart-expected-to-resign-over-sex-parties-scandal-10193508.html (accessed 27 July 2017).

Haines, R. 2004. *Charles Trevelyan and the Great Irish Famine*. Portland, OR: Four Courts Press.

Hajer, M. 2005a. 'Setting the Stage: A Dramaturgy of Policy Deliberation'. *Administration and Society* 36(6): 624–47.

Hajer, M. 2005b. 'Rebuilding Ground Zero: The Politics of Performance'. *Planning Theory and Practice* 6(4): 445–64.

Hajer, M. 2006. 'The Living Institutions of the EU: Analysing Governance as Performance'. *Perspectives on European Politics and Society* 7(1): 41–55.

Hall, P. A. and Taylor, C. R. 1996. 'Political Science and the Three New Institutionalisms'. *Political Studies* 44: 936–57.

Hargrove, E. C. 1994. *Prisoners of Myth: The Leadership of the Tennessee Valley Authority 1933–1990*. Princeton: Princeton University Press.

Harrison, D. 2010. 'Coalition pledges insulation scheme inquiry', *The Age* 16 July, 7. Consulted 13 December 2013 via *Factiva* database.

Hart, J. 1960. 'Sir Charles Trevelyan at the Treasury'. *The English Historical Review* 75: 92–110.

Hartwich, O. M. 2010. 'Ken Henry should get a new career—as a pollie', *The Sydney Morning Herald* 22 June. Available at http://www.smh.com.au/opinion/politics/ken-henry-should-get-a-newcareer–as-a-pollie-20100622-yv2z.html?comments=145 (accessed 6 September 2017).

Hastings, M. 2010. 'The runaway General', *Rolling Stone Magazine* 22 June. Available at http://www.rollingstone.com/politics/news/the-runaway-general-20100622 (accessed 31 October 2018).

Hay, C. 2010. 'Ideas and the Construction of Interests', in D. Beland and R. H. Cox (eds.), *Ideas and Politics in Social Science Research*. Oxford: Oxford University Press, 65–82.

Heintzman, R. 2014. *Renewal of the Federal Public Service: Toward a Charter of Public Service* (policy paper prepared for Canada 2020). Available at http://canada2020.ca/policy-papers/public-service-renewal/ (accessed 1 September 2017).

Hennessy, P. 1989. *Whitehall*. London: Free Press.

Henry, K. 2009. 'The Future of State Revenue'. Speech to Tax Commissioners' Conference, Sydney, 27 March. Available at http://taxreview.treasury.gov.au/content/Content.aspx?doc=html/speeches/04.htm (accessed 5 September 2017).

Henry, K. 2010. 'Fiscal Policy and the Current Environment'. Post-Budget address to the Australian Business Economists, 18 May. Available at http://archive.treasury.gov.au/documents/1813/PDF/Secretary_address_ABE.pdf (accessed 6 September 2017).

Heywood, J and Kerslake, B. 2013. 'Margaret Thatcher: Our kindly boss, by Britain's top civil servants', *The Daily Telegraph* 15 April. Available at http://www.telegraph.co.uk/news/politics/margaret-thatcher/9994375/Margaret-Thatcher-our-kindly-boss-by-Britains-top-civil-servants.html (accessed 31 August 2017).

Hicks, J. 2015. 'Bipartisan House statement expresses lost confidence in DEA chief', *Washington Post* 15 April. Consulted 27 July 2017 via *Factiva* database.

Hodge, M. 2016. *Called to Account: How Corporate Bad Behaviour and Government Waste Combine to Cost Us Millions*. London: Abacus.

Hondeghem, A. 2011. 'Changing Public Service Bargains for Top Officials'. *Public Policy and Administration* 26(2): 159–65.

Hood, C. 2010. *The Blame Game: Spin, Bureaucracy, and Self-Preservation in Government*. Princeton: Princeton University Press.

Hood, C. and Dixon, R. 2015. *A Government that Worked Better and Cost Less? Evaluating Three Decades of Reform and Change in UK Central Government*. Oxford: Oxford University Press.

Hood, C. and Lodge, M. 2006. *The Politics of Public Service Bargains: Reward, Competency, Loyalty—and Blame*. Oxford: Oxford University Press.

House of Commons 2013. *Department for Transport: Lessons from Cancelling the InterCity West Coast Franchise Competition*. Report by the Committee of Public Accounts. London: The Stationery Office Ltd.

Hustedt, T. and Salomonsen, H. H. 2014. 'Ensuring Political Responsiveness: Politicization Mechanisms in Ministerial Bureaucracies'. *International Review of Administrative Sciences* 80(4): 746–65.

IPAA 2016. *Twelve Speeches 2016: A Year of Speeches from Public Service Leaders*. Canberra: Institute of Public Administration Australia. Available at https://vs286790.blob.core.windows .net/docs/Twelve%20Speeches%202016.pdf (accessed 3 May 2018).

Jackson, M. D. 2011a. *EPA Social Media Policy*. EPA Classification No.: CIO 2184.0. 20 June 2011. Available at https://www.epa.gov/sites/production/files/2013–11/documents/social _media_policy.pdf (accessed 12 September 2017).

Jackson, M. D. 2011b. *Using Social Media to Communicate with the Public*. EPA Classification No.: CIO 2184.0-P02.1. 20 June 2011. Available at https://www.epa.gov/sites/production/files /2013–11/documents/comm_public.pdf (accessed 12 September 2017).

Jervis, R. 2010. 'BP spill shapes Allen's legacy: Incident commander leaves amid varied views', *USA Today* 27 September. Consulted 15 September 2017 via *Factiva* database.

Jivanda, T. 2014 'Somerset Levels Tory MP launches "brutal" attack on Environment Agency chief: "I will flush his head down the loo"', *The Independent* 7 February. Available at http:// www.independent.co.uk/news/uk/home-news/hes-a-coward-a-little-git-i-will-flush-his -head-down-the-loo-tory-mp-launches-brutal-attack-on-9115159.html (accessed 7 August 2017).

Johnson, B. 2017. 'My Vision for a bold, thriving Britain enabled by Brexit', *The Daily Telegraph* 15 September. Available at https://www.telegraph.co.uk/politics/2017/09/15/boris-johnson -vision-bold-thriving-britain-enabled-brexit/ (accessed 1 November 2018).

Jupe, R. 2013. 'New Development: Going off the Rails? Rail Franchising after the Cancellation of the West Coast Franchise Competition'. *Public Money and Management* 33(5): 337–41.

Kahneman, D. 2011. *Thinking, Fast and Slow*. New York: Farrar, Straus and Giroux.

Kakutani, M. 2018. 'James Comey has a story to tell: It's very persuasive', *New York Times* 12 April. Available at https://www.nytimes.com/2018/04/12/books/review/james-comey -a-higher-loyalty.html (accessed date 31 October 2018).

Kane, J. and Patapan, H. 2006. 'In Search of Prudence'. *Public Administration Review* 66(5): 711–24.

Kane, J. and Patapan, H. 2010. 'The Artless Art: Leadership and the Limits of Democratic Rhetoric'. *Australian Journal of Political Science* 45: 371–89.

Katz, J. E., Barris, M. and Jain, A. 2013. *The Social Media President: Barack Obama and the Politics of Digital Engagement*. Palgrave Macmillan.

Kavanaugh, A. L. et al. 2012. 'Social Media Use by Government: From the Routine to the Critical'. *Government Information Quarterly* 29: 480–91.

Kenny, M. 2013. 'Treasury pans Rudd claim on $10b flaw', *The Canberra Times* 30 August, 1.

Kernell, S. 2006. *Going Public: New Strategies of Presidential Leadership* (4th edn). Washington DC: CQ Press.

Kerslake, B. 2012. 'Why social media is a vital tool for the Civil Service', *The Guardian* 4 May. Available at http://www.theguardian.com/public-leaders-network/blog/2012/may/04/sir -bob-kerslake-social-media (accessed 31 October 2018).

Kingdon, J. W. 1984. *Agendas, Alternatives, and Public Policies*. Boston, MA: Little, Brown & Co.

Kirk, A. 2010. 'Senate urges royal commission into insulation scheme', *ABC News* 15 July. Consulted 13 December 2013 via *Factiva* database.

Kitson Clark, G. 1959. '"Statesmen in Disguise": Reflexions on the History of the Neutrality of the Civil Service'. *The Historical Journal* 2(1): 19–39.

Lazarus, D. 2017. 'So Trump wants the consumer watchdog sacked. Here's what's really going on', *LA Times* 4 August. Available at http://www.latimes.com/business/lazarus/la-fi-lazarus -lewandowski-cfpb-arbitration-20170804-story.html (accessed 4 August 2017).

Lewis, C. 2012. 'A Recent Scandal: The Home Insulation Program', in K. Dowding and C. Lewis (eds.), *Ministerial Careers and Accountability in the Australian Commonwealth Government*. Canberra: ANU E Press, 153–76.

Lewis, D. E. 2008. *The Politics of Presidential Appointments: Political Control and Bureaucratic Performance*. Princeton: Princeton University Press.

Lewis, E. 1980. *Public Entrepreneurship: Toward a Theory of Bureaucratic Political Power*. Bloomington and London: Indiana University Press.

Lindquist, E. and Rasmussen, K. 2012. 'Deputy Ministers and New Political Governance: From Neutral Competence to Promiscuous Partisans to a New Balance?', in H. Bakvis and M. Jarvis (eds.), *From New Public Management to New Political Governance*. Montreal and Kingston: McGill-Queen's University Press, 179–203.

Linzer, D. 2006. 'The money man in the terror fight—Levey helps lead Treasury efforts', *Washington Post* 5 July, A11. Available at http://www.washingtonpost.com/wp-dyn/content /article/2006/07/04/AR2006070400982_pf.html (accessed 2 September 2017).

Lord, K. M. 2006. *Perils and Promise of Global Transparency: Why the Information Revolution May Not Lead to Security, Democracy or Peace*. New York: SUNY Press.

Lowe, R. 2011. *The Official History of the British Civil Service: Reforming the Civil Service, Vol. 1: The Fulton Years*. London: Routledge.

Macpherson, N. 2014. 'Minute to the Chancellor of the Exchequer on the topic of "Scotland and a Currency Union"', 11 February. Available at https://www.gov.uk/government/uploads /system/uploads/attachment_data/file/279460/Sir_Nicholas_Macpherson_-_Scotland _and_a_currency_union.pdf (accessed 1 September 2017).

Margetts, H. 2008. 'Public Management Change and e-government: The Emergence of Digital-Era Governance', in A. Chadwick and P. N. Edwards (eds.), *The Routledge Handbook of Internet Politics* London: Routledge, 114–27.

Marland, A., Giasson, T. and Small, T. A. (eds.) 2015. *Political Communication in Canada: Meet the Press and Tweet the Rest*. Vancouver: University of British Columbia Press.

Martin, J. 2015. 'Situating Speech: A Rhetorical Approach to Political Strategy'. *Political Studies* 63: 25–42.

Mason, R. 2013a. 'Mandarin accused of failing to act in plebs row "conspiracy"', *The Daily Telegraph* 11 January, 10.

Mason, R. 2013b. 'Civil Service bosses accused of "prostituting" themselves by praising Margaret Thatcher', *The Daily Telegraph* 18 April. Available at http://www.telegraph.co.uk/news /politics/10003014/Civil-service-bosses-accused-of-prostituting-themselves-by-praising -Margaret-Thatcher.html (accessed 31 August 2017).

Matthews, F. and Flinders, M. 2015. 'The Watchdogs of "Washminster": Parliamentary Scrutiny of Executive Patronage in the UK'. *Commonwealth and Comparative Politics* 53(2): 153–76.

May, K. 2014. 'Privy Council Office defends top federal bureaucrat', *Ottawa Citizen* 16 June. Available at http://ottawacitizen.com/news/politics/privy-council-office-defends-top -federal-bureaucrat (accessed 1 September 2017).

McIlroy, T. 2017. 'New Public Service social media policy is "overreach": Union boss Nadine Flood', *The Sydney Morning Herald* 7 August. Available at https://www.smh.com.au/public -service/new-public-service-social-media-policy-is-overreach-union-boss-nadine-flood -20170807-gxqjyq.html (accessed 12 August 2018).

Medhurst, M. J. (ed.) 2006. *The Rhetorical Presidency of George H. W. Bush*. College Station: Texas A&M University Press.

Menzies, R. 1970. *The Measure of the Years*. Sydney: Cassell Australia.

Mergel, I. 2013. *Social Media in the Public Sector: A Guide to Participation, Collaboration, and Transparency in the Networked World*. San Francisco: Jossey-Bass.

Meyer, C. 2005. *DC Confidential*. London: Weidenfeld and Nicolson.

Moore, M. 1995. *Creating Public Value: Strategic Management in Government*. Cambridge, MA: Harvard University Press.

Moore, M. 2013. *Recognizing Public Value*. Cambridge, MA: Harvard University Press.

Morison, J. 2010. 'Gov 2.0: Towards a User Generated State?', *The Modern Law Review* 73(4): 551–77.

Mulgan, R. 2002. 'Public Accountability of Provider Agencies: The Case of the Australian "Centrelink"'. *International Review of Administrative Sciences* 68: 45–59.

Mulgan, R. 2008. 'The Accountability Priorities of Australian Parliamentarians'. *The Australian Journal of Public Administration* 67(4): 457–69.

Mulgan, R. 2012. 'Assessing Ministerial Responsibility in Australia', in K. Dowding and C. Lewis (eds.), *Ministerial Careers and Accountability in the Australian Commonwealth Government*. Canberra: ANU E Press, 177–93.

Mutz, D. C. 2015. *In-Your-Face Politics: The Consequences of Uncivil Media*. Princeton and Oxford: Princeton University Press.

Newton Dunn, T. 2013. 'Pleb botcher: Cabinet Secretary rapped over duff probe', *The Sun* 21 January, 2.

North, D. C. 2005. *Understanding the Process of Economic Change*. Princeton: Princeton University Press.

Norton-Taylor, R. 2001. 'Former MI5 chief blasts Secrets Act', *The Guardian* 8 September. Available at https://www.theguardian.com/uk/2001/sep/08/books.freedomofinformation (accessed 3 May 2018).

Odell, M. 2013. 'MPs pinpoint blame for West Coast rail debacle', *The Financial Times* 26 February, 4. Consulted 13 December 2013 via *Factiva* database.

Official Committee Hansard 2010a. Senate—Environment, Communications and the Arts References Committee. Canberra. 22 February. Available at www.aphref.aph.gov.au_hansard _senate_commttee_s12843 (accessed 10 June 2013).

Official Committee Hansard 2010b. Senate—Environment, Communications and the Arts References Committee. Canberra. 26 February. Available at https://www.aph.gov.au/Parliamentary _Business/Committees/Senate/Environment_and_Communications/Completed_inquiries /2008-10/eehp/hearings/index (accessed 1 November 2018).

Official Committee Hansard 2010c. Senate—Environment, Communications and the Arts References Committee, Canberra. 25 March. Available at www.aphref.aph.gov.au_hansard _senate_commttee_s12937 (accessed 10 June 2013).

Osborne, G. 2014. 'Speech by Chancellor of the Exchequer, George Osborne on the prospect of a currency union between an independent Scotland and the rest of the UK', Edinburgh, 13 February. Available at https://www.gov.uk/government/speeches/chancellor-on-the-prospect -of-a-currency-union-with-an-independent-scotland (accessed 1 September 2017).

Ospina, S. M. 2016. 'Collective Leadership and Context in Public Administration: Bridging Public Leadership Research and Leadership Studies'. *Public Administration Review* 77 (2): 275–87.

Page, E. 2010. 'Has the Whitehall Model Survived?' *International Review of Administrative Sciences* 76(3): 407–23.

Paris, C., Colineau, N., Nepal, S., Bista, S. K. and Beschorner, G. 2013. 'Ethical Considerations in an Online Community: The Balancing Act'. *Ethics and Information Technology* 15: 301–16.

Parkinson, M. 2014. 'Challenges and opportunities for Australia over the next decade'. Speech to the Association of Mining and Exploration Companies Convention, Perth, 2 July. Available at http://www.treasury.gov.au/PublicationsAndMedia/Speeches/2014/Challenges-and -opportunitiesfor-Australia-over-the-next-decade (accessed August 2014).

Parkinson, M. and Tune, D. 2013. 'Statement on costings by the Department of the Treasury and the Department of Finance and Deregulation' Media release, 29 August. Available at http:// parlinfo.aph.gov.au (accessed 2 November 2015).

PASC (Public Administration Select Committee) 2006. *Whitehall Confidential? The Publication of Political Memoirs*. Fifth Report of Session 2005–2006. London: The Stationery Office Ltd. Available at https://publications.parliament.uk/pa/cm200506/cmselect/cmpubadm/689 /689i.pdf (accessed 28 September 2017).

PASC (Public Administration Select Committee) 2008. *Mandarins Unpeeled? Memoirs and Commentary by Former Ministers and Civil Servants*. Fourteenth Report Session 2007–2008. London: The Stationery Office Ltd. Available at https://publications.parliament.uk/pa /cm200708/cmselect/cmpubadm/664/66403.htm (accessed 28 September 2017).

Patapan, H., Wanna, J. and Weller, P. (eds.) 2005. *Westminster Legacies: Democracy and Responsible Government in Asia and the Pacific*. Sydney: UNSW Press.

Peck, E., Freeman, T., Six, P. and Dickinson, H. 2009. Performing Leadership: Towards a New Research Agenda in Leadership Studies?' *Leadership* 5(1): 25–40.

Pelley, S. and Reid, C. 2015. 'A scandal involving US Drug Enforcement Agency seems to be getting worse by the day', *CBS Evening News* 14 April. Consulted 27 July 2107 via *Factiva* database.

Picketty, T. 2014. *Capital in the Twenty-First Century*. Cambridge, MA: Harvard University Press.

PM 2010. 'Ken Henry to Kevin Rudd: Hold your nerve', ABC Radio 18 May. Available at http:// www.abc.net.au/pm/content/2010/s2902970.htm (accessed 6 September 2017).

Rashbrooke, M. 2013. 'Are UK public managers doomed to fail in the Land of the Hobbit?', *The Guardian* 22 January. Available at https://www.theguardian.com/public-leaders-network /2013/jan/15/uk-public-managers-new-zealand (accessed date 31 October 2018).

Rhodes, R.A.W. 2011. *Everyday Life in British Government*. Oxford: Oxford University Press.

Rhodes, R.A.W. 2014. 'Administrative Leadership', in R.A.W. Rhodes and P. 't Hart (eds.), *The Oxford Handbook of Political Leadership*, ch. 7.

Rhodes, R.A.W and Wanna, J. 2007. 'The Limits to Public Value, or Rescuing Responsible Government from the Platonic Guardians'. *Australian Journal of Public Administration* 66(4): 406–21.

Rhodes, R.A.W and Wanna, J. 2009. 'Bringing the Politics Back In: Public Value in Westminster Parliamentary Government'. *Public Administration* 87(2): 161–83.

Rhodes, R.A.W. and Weller, P. 2001. *The Changing World of Top Officials: Mandarin or Servant?* London: Open University Press.

Rhodes, R.A.W., Wanna, J. and Weller, P. 2009. *Comparing Westminster*. Oxford: Oxford University Press.

Richards, D. and Smith, M. 2015. 'In Defence of British Politics against the British Political Tradition'. *The Political Quarterly* 86(1): 41–51.

Richards, D. and Smith, M. 2016. 'The Westminster Model and the "Indivisibility of the Political and Administrative Elite": A Convenient Myth Whose Time Is Up?' *Governance* 29(4): 499–516.

Ridley, J. 1970. *Lord Palmerston*. London: Constable.

Roberts, A. 2006. *Blacked Out: Government Secrecy in the Information Age*. Cambridge: Cambridge University Press.

Rodrigues, U. M. and Niemann, M. 2017. 'Social Media as a Platform for Incessant Political Communication: A Case Study of Modi's "Clean India" Campaign'. *International Journal of Communication* 11: 3431–53.

Rohr, J. A. 1986. *To Run a Constitution: The Legitimacy of the Administrative State*. Lawrence, KS: University Press of Kansas.

Rohr, J. A. 1995. *Founding Republics in France and America*. Lawrence, KS: University Press of Kansas.

Rohr, J. A. 2002. *Civil Servants and their Constitutions*. Lawrence, KS: University Press of Kansas.

Rolfe, M. 2008. 'New Wine into Old Bottles: Ethical Appeals and Democratic Discourse'. *Australian Journal of Political Science* 43: 513–29.

Rudd, K., Bowen, C. and Wong, P. 2013. 'Transcript of Prime Minister Kevin Rudd press conference'. Commonwealth Parliamentary Offices, Melbourne, 29 August. Available at http://parlinfo.aph.gov.au (accessed 2 November 2015).

Salter, J. A. 1961. *Memoirs of a Public Servant*. London: Faber and Faber.

Savoie, D. 2003. *Breaking the Bargain: Public Servants, Ministers, and Parliament*. Toronto: University of Toronto Press.

Savoie, D. 2008. *Court Government and the Collapse of Accountability in Canada and the United Kingdom*. Toronto: University of Toronto Press.

Schillemans, T. 2012. *Mediatization of Public Services: How Organizations Adapt to News Media*. Frankfurt: Peter Lang.

Schmidt, V. A. 2010. 'Taking Ideas and Discourse Seriously: Explaining Change through Discursive Institutionalism as the Fourth "New Institutionalism"'. *European Political Science Review* 2: 1–25.

Schudson, M. 2015. *The Rise of the Right to Know*. Cambridge, MA: Harvard University Press.

Scotsman 2014. 'Scotland "will have range of" currency options', *The Scotsman* 14 February. Available at http://www.scotsman.com/news/politics/top-stories/scotland-will-have-range-of-currency-options-1-3306336 (accessed 1 September 2017).

Seidman, L. W. 1993. *Full Faith and Credit: The Great S&L Debacle and Other Washington Sagas*. New York: Times Books.

Selznick, P. 1957. *Leadership in Administration: A Sociological Interpretation*. New York: Harper & Row.

Selznick, P. 1966. *TVA and the Grass Roots: A Study in the Sociology of Formal Organization*. New York: Harper & Row.

Shergold, P. 2014. 'Mandarins', in G. Davis and R.A.W. Rhodes (eds.), *The Craft of Governing: The Contribution of Patrick Weller to Australian Political Science*. Crows Nest, NSW: Allen & Unwin, 75–96.

Sherman, J. 2012. 'Taxpayer hit for £6m more in rail bid fiasco', *The Times* 14 December. Consulted 13 December 2013 via *Factiva* database.

Skowronek, S. 2008. *Presidential Leadership in Political Time: Reprise and Reappraisal*. Lawrence, KS: University Press of Kansas.

Smith, C. 2014. 'Don't blame the Environment Agency for floods, blame the spending rules', *The Guardian* 9 February. Available at https://www.theguardian.com/environment/2014/feb/09/flooding-chris-smith-speaks-out (accessed 1 November 2018).

Stark, A. 2018. *Public Inquiries, Policy Learning, and the Threat of Future Crises*. Oxford: Oxford University Press.

Stone, D. 2012. *Policy Paradox: The Art of Political Decision Making*. New York: W.W. Norton & Co.

Strassel, K. 2017. 'Scott Pruitt's back-to-basics agenda for the EPA', *The Wall Street Journal* 18 February, online version. Consulted 26 February 2017 via *Factiva* database.

Stuckey, M. E. 2010. 'Rethinking the Rhetorical Presidency and Presidential Rhetoric'. *Review of Communication* 10: 38–52.

Suleiman, E. N. 1974. *Politics, Power and Bureaucracy in France: The Administrative Elite*. Princeton: Princeton University Press.

Sulitzeanu-Kenan, R. 2010. 'Reflection in the Shadow of Blame: When do Politicians Appoint Commissions of Inquiry?' *British Journal of Political Science* 40(3): 613–34.

Swan, W. and Rudd, K. 2010. 'Stronger. Fairer. Simpler. A tax plan for our future'. Joint media release, 2 May. Available at http://ministers.treasury.gov.au/DisplayDocs.aspx?doc=pressreleases/2010/028.htm&pageID=003&min=wms&Year=&DocType (accessed 5 September 2017).

Syal, R. 2013. 'Pro-Margaret Thatcher article by two senior civil servants angers MPs', *The Guardian* 18 April. Available at https://www.theguardian.com/politics/2013/apr/18/pro-thatcher-artcile-civil-servants-row (accessed 1 November 2018).

't Hart, P. 1993. 'Symbols, Rituals and Power: The Lost Dimensions of Crisis Management'. *Journal of Contingencies and Crisis Management* 1(1): 36–50.

't Hart, P. 2014. *Understanding Public Leadership*. London: Palgrave Macmillan.

't Hart, P. and Wille, A. 2006. 'Ministers and Top Officials in the Dutch Core Executive: Living Together, Growing Apart?' *Public Administration* 84(1): 121–46.

Talbot, C. 2009. 'Public Value—The Next "Big Thing" in Public Management?' *International Journal of Public Administration* 32(3–4): 167–70.

Theakston, K. 1999. *Leadership in Whitehall*. Basingstoke: Palgrave Macmillan.

Thomas, N. 2012. 'West Coast Rail fiasco bill could grow, admits DfT', *The Daily Telegraph* 13 December. Available at https://www.telegraph.co.uk/finance/newsbysector/transport/9742649/West-Coast-Rail-fiasco-bill-could-grow-admits-DfT.html (accessed 1 November 2018).

Thompson, E. 1980. 'The "Washminster" Mutation'. *Politics* (precursor to *The Australian Journal of Political Science*) 15(2): 32–40.

Topham, G. 2013. 'Transport: More rail contracts may be bungled, MPs warn', *The Guardian* 26 February, 24. Consulted 13 December 2013 via *Factiva* database.

Toye, R. 2011. 'The Rhetorical Premiership: A New Perspective on Prime Ministerial Power since 1945'. *Parliamentary History* 30: 175–92.

Toye, R. 2014. 'The Rhetorical Culture of the House of Commons after 1918'. *History: The Journal of the Historical Association* 99(335): 270–98.

Treasury Board of Canada Secretariat 2013. *Policy on Acceptable Network and Device Use*. Ottawa. Available at http://www.tbs-sct.gc.ca/pol/doc-eng.aspx?section=text&id=27122 (accessed 21 January 2014).

Treasury Board of Canada Secretariat 2016. *Policy on Communications and Federal Identity*. Ottawa. Available at http://www.tbs-sct.gc.ca/pol/doc-eng.aspx?id=30683 (accessed 12 September 2017).

Trevelyan, C. E. 1848. *The Irish Crisis*. London: Longman, Brown, Green & Longmans.

Trevelyan, L. 2012. *A Very British Family: The Trevelyans and their World*. London: I.B. Tauris.

Tulis, J. 1987. *The Rhetorical Presidency*. Princeton: Princeton University Press.

Uhr, J. and Walter, R. (eds.) 2014. *Studies in Australian political rhetoric*. Canberra: ANU Press.

Uhr, J. and Walter, R. 2015. 'The Rhetorical Standards of Public Reason in Australia'. *Australian Journal of Politics and History* 61: 248–62.

US Government 2016. *Policy and Supporting Positions*. Committee on Homeland Security and Governmental Affairs, United States Senate. Washington DC: U.S. Government Publishing Office.

Van Wart, M. 2003. 'Public-Sector Leadership Theory: An Assessment'. *Public Administration Review* 63(2): 214–28.

Van Wart, M. 2013. 'Administrative Leadership Theory: A Reassessment after 10 Years'. *Public Administration* 91(3): 521–43.

Van Wart, M., Hondeghem, A. and Schwella, E. (eds.) 2015. *Leadership and Culture: Comparative Models of Top Civil Servant Training*. Basingstoke: Palgrave Macmillan.

Vincent, D. 1999. *The Culture of Secrecy: Britain 1832–1998*. Oxford: Oxford University Press.

Walters, S. 2014. 'I won't be printing 'Save Chris Smith' T-shirts, says Pickles as he calls for flood boss to apologise', *The Mail on Sunday* 8 February. Available at http://www.dailymail.co.uk/news/article-2554901/I-wont-printing-Save-Chris-Smith-T-shirts-says-Pickles-calls-flood-boss-apologise.html (accessed 8 August 2017).

Wanna, J., Vincent, S. and Podger, A. 2012. *With the Benefit of Hindsight: Valedictory Reflections from Departmental Secretaries, 2004–11*. Canberra: ANU E Press.

Watt, H. 2011. 'Naked civil servant who mocked Eric Pickles is stripped of job', *The Daily Telegraph* 4 July. Available at https://www.telegraph.co.uk/news/politics/8614026/Naked-civil -servant-who-mocked-Eric-Pickles-is-stripped-of-job.html (accessed 31 October 2018).

Watt, N. 2013. 'Mitchell may be victim of "gigantic conspiracy": Cabinet Secretary tells of review into "Plebgate" row: MPs astonished at limited scope of his investigation', *The Guardian* 11 January, 7.

Weaver, K. 1986. 'The Politics of Blame Avoidance'. *Journal of Public Policy* 6(4): 371–98.

Webb, J. 2018. 'America's pompous, prissy protector', *The Times* 21 April, 11.

Weber, M. 1968. *Economy and Society, Volume Two*, ed. G. Roth, and C. Wittich. New York: Bedminster Press.

Weller, P. 2001. *Australia's Mandarins: The Frank and the Fearless?* Crows Nest, NSW: Allen & Unwin.

White House 2010. 'Transcript from press briefing on ongoing response to oil spill', 1 May. Consulted 15 September 2017 via *Factiva* database.

Whitehead, J. 2009a. '2009 Job Summit'. Address to the 2009 Job Summit, 27 February, Manukau, Auckland. Available at http://www.treasury.govt.nz/publications/media-speeches /speeches/jobsummit/jobsumm09-spch.pdf (accessed 23 December 2010).

Whitehead, J. 2009b. 'Positioning New Zealand for a post-recession world'. New Zealand Institute of Directors Breakfast Function, 3 June, Wellington. Available at http://treasury.govt .nz/publications/media-speeches/speeches/postrecession/sp-postrecession-03jun09.pdf (accessed 23 December 2010).

Whitehead, J. 2009c. 'The New Zealand economy: Outlook and policy challenges'. Summary of address to the Institute of Directors' 2009 Company Chairman's Workshop, 25 September, Queenstown. Available at http://www.treasury.govt.nz/publications/mediaspeeches/ (accessed 22 December 2010).

Whitehead, J. 2009d. 'New Zealand's Long-term Fiscal Statement: Challenges and choices'. Speech launching New Zealand's Long-term Fiscal Statement, 29 October, Wellington. Available at http://www.treasury.govt.nz/publications/media-speeches/speeches/pdfs/sp -longterm-29oct09.pdf (accessed 22 December 2010).

Widmaier, W. 2016. *Economic Ideas in Political Time: The Rise and Fall of Economic Orders from the Progressive Era to the Global Financial Crisis*. Cambridge: Cambridge University Press.

Wildavsky, A. 1979. *Speaking Truth to Power: The Art and Craft of Policy Analysis*. Boston, MA: Little, Brown.

Williamson, D. 2013. 'Rail fiasco: MP calls for heads: Report slams collapse of franchise deal', *Liverpool Echo* 26 February, 4. Consulted 13 December 2013 via *Factiva* database.

Wilson, R. 2003. 'Portrait of Profession Re-visited'. *Public Administration* 81(2): 365–78.

Wintour, P. 2012. 'Pleb row: Emails sent by officer posing as witness "were not considered reliable"', *The Guardian* 19 December. Available at http://www.theguardian.com/politics/2012 /dec/19/pleb-row-emails-police-witness/print (accessed 31 October 2018).

Wintour, P. 2014. 'Eric Pickles apologises over floods and blames Environment Agency advice', *The Guardian* 9 February. Available at https://www.theguardian.com/environment/2014/feb /09/eric-pickles-apologises-floods-environment-agency-somerset (accessed 8 August 2017).

Woodham-Smith, C. 1962. *The Great Hunger: Ireland 1845–1849*. London: Hamish Hamilton.

Woodman, P. 2012. 'Franchise fiasco bill "could grow"', Press Association National Newswire, 13 December. Consulted 13 December 2013 via *Factiva* database.

Wright, P. 1987. *Spycatcher: the Candid Autobiography of a Senior Intelligence Officer*. Sydney: Heinemann Australia.

Wright, R. 2008. 'Stuart Levey's war', *New York Times Magazine* 31 October. Available at http://www.nytimes.com/2008/11/02/magazine/02IRAN-t.html (accessed 2 September 2017).

Wright, S. 2006. 'Government-run Online Discussion Fora: Moderation, Censorship and the Shadow of Control'. *British Journal of Politics and International Relations* 8(4): 550–68.

Wright, S. and Probyn, A. 2013. 'Treasury backlash against $10b hole', *The West Australian* 30 August, 6.

Wright, S. and Street, J. 2007. 'Democracy, Deliberation and Design: The Case of Online Discussion Forums', *New Media and Society*, 9(5): 849–69.

Young, H. 2013. 'Margaret Thatcher left a dark legacy that has still not disappeared'. *The Guardian* 8 April. Available at https://www.theguardian.com/politics/2013/apr/08/margaret-thatcher-hugo-young (accessed 31 August 2017).

Young, S. 2007. 'Political and Parliamentary Speech in Australia'. *Parliamentary Affairs* 60: 234–52.

INDEX

A NOTE ON THE TYPE

This book has been composed in Adobe Text and Gotham.
Adobe Text, designed by Robert Slimbach for Adobe,
bridges the gap between fifteenth- and sixteenth-century
calligraphic and eighteenth-century Modern styles.
Gotham, inspired by New York street signs, was designed
by Tobias Frere-Jones for Hoefler & Co.